BLACK FATHERS

AN INVISIBLE PRESENCE IN AMERICA

SECOND EDITION

BLACK FATHERS

AN INVISIBLE PRESENCE IN AMERICA

SECOND EDITION

EDITED BY

MICHAEL E. CONNOR
ALLIANT INTERNATIONAL UNIVERSITY

JOSEPH L. WHITE
UNIVERSITY OF CALIFORNIA, IRVINE

Routledge
Taylor & Francis Group
New York   London

Routledge
Taylor & Francis Group
711 Third Avenue
New York, NY 10017

Routledge
Taylor & Francis Group
2 Park Square, Milton Park
Abingdon, Oxon, OX14 4RN

International Standard Book Number: 978-0-415-88366-5 (Hardback) 978-0-415-88367-2 (Paperback)

Visit the Taylor & Francis Web site at
http://www.taylorandfrancis.com

and the Psychology Press Web site at
http://www.psypress.com

Dedication

This book is dedicated to my professor, mentor, colleague, and friend, Dr. Joseph L. White, who has been in my life since 1965. Dr. Joe, I appreciate you taking me under your wing when I was a young man with a head full of dark hair. I am also appreciative of the ongoing and consistent love, support, guidance, nurturing, and direction you have been providing me since that time. I am thankful you are a part of my family.

I recognize the importance of having African descended men in my life over these many years to direct, acknowledge, and reinforce me and my activities. With this small tribute, I want to honor and to thank you.

"keep the faith"

Michael E. Connor, Ph.D.

Contents

Preface

Some years ago, a friend and colleague who was on the program committee of a national conference called to invite me to participate in a panel discussion regarding whether fathers were needed in families. I was initially confused about the topic and inquired as to context for the session. He shared that at a previous meeting a couple of researchers offered the thesis that dads are rather superfluous to families and perhaps families did better without them (i.e., they do not offer anything that mothers cannot provide). Because the presentation had created/generated interest, support, and concern, the organization decided to offer it again at subsequent annual meetings. After some brief interaction, I accepted the invitation and thanked him for the call.

Although I had accepted the invitation, I was confused and concerned that anyone would question the need for paternal involvement/ engagement. As the conference approached, I remained confused about the topic but was prepared to share my thoughts and experiences. At the conference, I discussed my work with low-income men along with the results of my workshops with professional men across racial groups. My work suggested the need for *more* not *less* paternal engagement.

Two presenters suggested that some children do fine when dads are not present, but their comments seemed to focus on what the mother(s) wanted and her ability to care for her children. Thus, their arguments flowed from an adult vantage point, where there was satisfaction. But, what about children and their needs/desires? Do they want their fathers present? Who in female-headed households models appropriate behaviors for males? Who demonstrates how men who care about women treat them? Who shows males how to become responsible men and fathers? And, why do some women believe they can *father* children? Do fathers believe that they can *mother* children?

In the first edition of *Black Fathers: An Invisible Presence in America,* African descended men shared the important roles fathers played in their lives. These men spoke of the need for father engagement and they wrote about the impact of biological, social/communal, and step fathering. Some of these men had suffered the impact of misguided social policies that did not encourage or support their fathers' involvement. The need for and value of consistent and ongoing father engagement were major themes.

In this second edition, we continue the discussion of Black father issues and expand the theory and research base. As in the first volume, the contributors believe it is important that fathers are involved and engaged with their children (sons and daughters) and they note problems associated with fathers' absence. Although no attempt was made to cover all types of fathers (that is beyond the scope of the book), we did request contributions from nonfathers (fathers-to-be?) who were reared in father-present homes, from "new" fathers who are present in their children's lives, from long-term fathers, from social/communal fathers, from fathers in the academe, from community activist fathers, from women who discuss fathers, and from retired men who are fathers. We expanded the conversation to include a historical context for some of the issues confronting African descended fathers, the impact of significant health issues on Black fathers, the need for therapeutic interventions to aid in the healing of fathers, the impact of an Afrikan-centered fathering approach, and the need for research that considers systemic problems confronting African American fathers. Additionally, each chapter ends with a conclusion and reflective questions appropriate for group discussion.

The book is divided into three sections. Section I is titled *Impact of father engagement* and begins with a historical overview of African descended fathers in an attempt to provide a context by which to view these men, their strengths and shortcomings, over the years (Connor, Chapter 1). Achebe Hoskins (Chapter 2) shares his compelling story as a father and communal/social father working with the underserved youth in Oakland, California. Valata Jenkins-Monroe (Chapter 3) discusses her father, who was not present during her early years but chose to enter her life during her adolescence. Gary Cunningham (Chapter 4) expands the discussion and writes about not knowing his father until he was in his middle years. He discusses the importance of mentors. Rashika Rentie (Chapter 5) then shares her research on father–daughter relationships, including the impact of the father's absence on daughters. She also discusses the nature of kinships in African American families. Jelani Mandara, Carolyn Murray, and Toya Joyner (Chapter 6) add to the discussion regarding father absence/presence on the development of gender identity in adolescent males and females. William Allen (Chapter 7) finishes Section I with a description of his work serving adolescents in the foster care system. He notes many of these males will likely become fathers and discusses the need for direction and training to aid them as they grow and develop.

In Section II, titled *Father stories,* African American men discuss their fathers or becoming a father. Bedford Palmer (Chapter 8) shares the importance of being reared in a two-parent home and lessons his father taught him as he transitioned to manhood. Ivory Toldson (Chapter 9) writes of communal fathering and the importance of social fathers. He celebrates the birth of his daughter and discusses the interconnectedness of men across generations. Kevin Cokley (Chapter 10), also a "new" dad, shares the impact of his son and the importance of rearing his child in an equalitarian home. Phillip Rosier (Chapter 11) writes about the struggles Black men face with role definitions; that is, he asks the question "Who am I?" He believes the question can be answered by understanding one's sense of purpose. This purpose focuses on actions, deeds, and contributions to others and to the community. He concludes with a discussion on the roles of fathers/social fathers in providing young men with a sense of purpose. Larry Tucker (Chapter 12) discusses how men are involved in the lives of children. He explores historical backgrounds, cultural implications, barriers to relationships, and myths.

Section III, titled *Thoughts and reflections*, begins with Gerald Green's (Chapter 13) reflections on adoptions (both his and his son's), a loving and supportive mate, and physical health issues. He has lived with cancer since 1995 and recognizes the need for Black men to attend to their health. William Allen, Phillip Rosier, and Larry Tucker (Chapter 14) cover the need for appropriate and sensitive strategies and resources to improve the effectiveness of therapeutic interventions when working with Black men. Hurumia Ahadi/Lionel Mandy (Chapter 15) proposes an Afrikan perspective that is centered in the traditions and cultures of Afrika in learning to become a father. He notes one must be a man before one can be a father. Michael Connor (Chapter 16) finishes the volume with an overview of an intervention model geared toward aiding males to move into their manhood/fatherhood. The chapter concludes with suggestions for future research and study.

Dr. White and I are appreciative of the reviewers of the volume, A. J. Franklin (Boston College), Frances Goldscheider (Brown University), Daryl Rowe (Pepperdine University), Catherine Tamis-LeMonda (New York University), and Robert Williams (Washington University). We thank them for their time, effort, direction, and support.

Finally, since publication of the first edition of *Black Fathers*, much has changed in the United States and much has remained the same. It had never occurred to me (like most African descended folks my age) that a Black man would occupy the White House in my lifetime. I am proud of him and I am proud that the country elected him. For the first time in my adult life, I (naively) felt that America would actually move toward its innate greatness and make the effort to attempt to realize its enormous potential. Sadly, the history of racial struggle and progress, followed by resistance, again repeats itself. A group of Euro-Americans rose up against the President, taking to the airways and highways to remind us that the country has changed little at its core. So, once again, the resilience of African Americans will be challenged. The challenge is not new; we will move through another cycle of struggle, progress, and resistance, and keep on keeping on. And the reality remains: A Black man (and his family) is in the White House! In this man, I see the genius I see in so many of the young people I encounter daily; I see hope for the country's future; I see resolve and commitment to "do better"; I see the swagger in his confident stride which I see in so many of the youth I am privileged to serve; I see intelligence combined with a thoughtful articulate presence; I see a loving competent father and husband; I see a man who attempts to encourage those around him to work together; and I see a man who embodies that which is good and decent in my fellow humans. For this, I am apprecia-tive of President Barack Obama and say, "God bless you!"

Michael E. Connor, Ph.D.
Father of daughters, Malia and Kanoelani
Grandfather of OniMasai and Nanea

section one

Impact of father engagement

chapter one

African descended fathers
Historical considerations

Michael E. Connor
Alliant International University
San Francisco, California

As noted in the first edition of this book, too often both the professional and commercial literature presents African descended fathers as deadbeat, deficient, lacking, uninvolved, uncaring, and absent (Connor & White, 2006). Certainly, these notions are accurate and appropriate for *some* African American fathers, but they do not tell a complete or accurate story in that African American fathers who are and have been involved/engaged with their children and families (and perhaps other children in their communities) are completely ignored. Additionally, these stereotypes minimize or ignore the circumstances and contexts in which African American fathers make their decisions. Thus, we offered numerous opportunities in which present and engaged fathers shared their stories. These men had a history of being present, involved, engaged, and important in the lives of their sons and daughters, stepchildren, and extended family members, or they shared information regarding their own involved fathers.

This chapter discusses the impact of some of the historical circumstances in which Black fathers made parenting decisions (or, in some cases, had the decision made for them). The actions, conditions, responses, decisions, and behaviors of Black fathers all take place in a social, historical, political, and environmental context. And, as noted above, this context is seldom discussed, provided, or considered when researching, studying, teaching, or developing social policy designed to impact the Black community. As in the African tradition, to understand where one is going, it is important to understand where one has been; that is, it is important to frame one's presence in relationship to one's past.

As pertains to effective fathers/fathering, the norms used to determine successful fathering tend to reflect a Eurocentric, middle-class bias emphasizing income and financial provision. By this definition, more privileged men (having benefited from higher education and solid employment opportunities) are perceived to be "good" fathers (whether or not they spend much time with their children), whereas those with minimal education, skills, and income are perceived as deficient (even if they spend significant time with their children).* Societal factors that mitigate against receiving a quality education and thus a solid vocational background are ignored (as are the advantages and privileges afforded some in obtaining a quality education), and the amount of time spent with children seems not to be an important variable. In this chapter a brief overview of the history of African descended men as fathers in the United States is offered. Fathering constraints during the periods of Maafa (the Holocaust of Enslavement),[†] Reconstruction/the Jim Crow era, civil rights–desegregation, the decay of urban communities, and the resultant gang activity and War on Drugs are considered. In this manner, it is hoped to provide a context pertaining to the plight, situation, options, and positions of Black men over the years. Any serious discussion pertaining to meaningful resolution must be in the context of these problems.

Maafa/enslavement

The first Africans arrived on the shores of South Carolina in 1526 in Spanish slave ships (Rasbury, 2010). They soon revolted and fled, seeking refuge with Native Americans. Shortly thereafter this early Spanish colony dispersed. Blacks arrived in *English America* in August 1619, and the first Black child was born in the Virginia colony in 1624.

Some years later, in 1641, slavery was introduced in the Massachusetts colony. The Christian men and women who captured Africans, transported them to America, and developed, enforced, and profited from enslavement were motivated by money, position, power, privilege, and racism. But all was not smooth. The first legal protest against slavery took place in 1644 and the first serious slave conspiracy in 1663. Slave revolts date back to 1708, and they took place routinely across the colonies (Bennett, 1984). Thus,

---

* Interestingly, educated business and professional men who tend to spend little time with their offspring provide us with the idea that it's not the amount of time that is important, but rather what is being done with the time spent—that is, the quality versus quantity time argument. It is peculiar that an opposite argument is used in justifying the amount of time put into work—that is, unless one puts in a lot of time on the job, one is not considered competent or successful. The process raises the question of how competent anyone is at something one does 10 to 15 minutes a day. Although it is true that high incomes allow one to buy things for one's children, does material provision alone constitute competent parenting in any society that claims to value children?

† Karenga (2002) uses the term Maafa to refer to the "Holocaust of Enslavement." It denotes a direct, purposeful, focused action on the part of Europeans and European Americans, rather than the more benign term slavery, which tends to place the onus of the condition and the resultant problems on the victims rather than the perpetrators.

although African men arrived in the New World prior to the onset of the peculiar institution, it was the onset and promulgation of enslavement that shapes and contributes to the position and status of Black men, women, and families today (as well as the status and position of White America).

It is under the watch of these Christian folks that the original absentee/ deadbeat fathers came to have a devastating impact on African descended fathers and their families. Although laws and statutes regarding pater- nal responsibilities were in place during these colonial times, they did not extend to White men who fathered Black babies. For example, two of the fundamental attributes of "good" dads were that they acknowledged paternity and that they supported the children they fathered (Dayton, 1991). White men who failed to assume the responsibilities of paternity were only considered sinners and criminals if their natal partners were White. These women could subsequently name them as the father of their child(ren), obtain a warrant, and force them into court to be held account- able. Although White fathers were legally responsible for the debts of their children (Pleck, 2004), this responsibility did not extend to their chil- dren with non-White mothers: Enslaved Africans had no rights beyond what their masters deemed reasonable. Thus, the original deadbeat dads (i.e., slave masters) have yet to pay their due.

Additionally, profit-motivated slave owners mated and bred African men and women in an attempt to develop stronger, more durable "stock" that could perform more work (much as farmers have done with farm ani- mals for generations). To justify these inhumane actions, Africans were designated as less than human. Other than preparing them to work, there was little expectation that they desired, or were capable of, taking care of their offspring.

As part of the dehumanization of the enslaved Africans, slave owners advanced several myths, including the seemingly irrational notion that African slaves were well taken care of, that they did not mind their posi- tion, and that they were "happy-go-lucky," as evidenced by their singing in the fields while working hard all day. The harsh reality is that being treated as property and being frequently separated from their family and tribesmen caused serious trauma to African men, women, and children. These traumatic experiences were a major cause of sporadic slave revolts. Because of the constant threat of severe punishment and death, African fathers often had little control over themselves, much less their partners or children.

In spite of these harsh conditions, there is good evidence to suggest that many African descended men in the 17th century were actively and directly involved in family life. Genovese (1978), for example, notes that enslaved men were willing to risk punishment in order to keep families together. He indicates that some slave owners were cognizant of this and often argued against separation of Black families because slaves worked better when kept together. He also indicates in studying runaway slaves that the importance of family life was second only to the resentment of punishment as reasons for running away. Gutman (1976) writes that large numbers of slave couples lived in long marriages, and most lived in double-headed households. Thus, whereas the owners may not have recognized marriages, enslaved people did.

It is impossible to know how many African children were born as a result of (forced) breeding programs and/or by the impregnation (interracial rape) by slave owners at the time of the Emancipation. It is also difficult to determine the impact on the psyche of the Black men and Black fathers to have been so emasculated. But, in the more than 220 years of enslavement (10 to 11 generations), certainly there were major, long-term impacts on African family life. These may have included procreation in the absence of parental bonds or sufficient plans for childrearing, having to care for and raise the children of others (i.e., slave owners) over one's own children, reenactment of public beatings and humiliations within one's own family, and in general, becoming dependent on White oppressors for one's survival.

Reconstruction–Jim Crow era

The period following the "end of slavery" (1863–1877) reflected an attempt to rebuild the social and economic institutions of the South in a manner that, to an extent, included newly "freed" Africans. The efforts were met with resistance and violent opposition toward the newly freed men by the Ku Klux Klan and other White supremacist organizations. With the Compromise of 1877, the U.S. military was withdrawn from the South and gains previously made quickly dissipated. Interestingly, Harris (1976) found that during the years following the Civil War, two-parent households were dominant in the African American community, in spite of the mounting intolerance and hostilities. Black fathers and mothers were attempting to hold their families together under extreme adversarial conditions.

This period predates the major migration of African descended people from the Deep South to what would become the industrialized North. The migration that occurred was primarily from the "border states" to the Northeast and New England states, and cities like Boston and New York. After a few years primarily employed in domestic work such as cooks, maids, and servants, many African Americans returned to the South. Much of this was the result of unanticipated problems they faced as supposedly "freed" people. These included the difficulty men encountered finding work and considerable hostilities from recent immigrants arriving from Europe, who were often competing for the same jobs and limited housing (Johnson & Campbell, 1981).

The conquered South was resentful, and with the removal of military support under the Johnson presidency, Blacks were quickly returned to a form of enslavement with Jim Crow laws and practices in place. As relates to Black fathers, the inability to obtain an education, the lack of work, the social controls, and the related ongoing White hostilities continued to take a major toll. Racism was expressed harshly, directly, and with little fear of punishment. Some 5,000 African American citizens (primarily males) were lynched between 1860 and 1890 (they were first castrated, then shot or burned, and then hanged, often in a festive, picnic-style atmosphere). There is no evidence that a single White or group of Whites was ever charged or prosecuted for these horrific crimes. Yet, in this way the societal imperative to control, oppress, and, if necessary, emasculate African males continued.

The "Kansas Exodus" of 1879 was a planned and organized migration of freed people to the Kansas Territory to seek a better way of life. Blacks migrated in large numbers for social, political, and economic gains. Some traveled with their families, others by themselves. But the areas they left and the places they arrived had an uneven ratio of men to women. Some of the Black settlers bought farms or successfully homesteaded, but most were ill-prepared for the harsh Kansas winters. They were also unprepared for the hostilities of Whites, who passed laws that made it difficult for Blacks to own land, or to remain in certain communities after dark (so-called sundowner laws), and that generally limited the political powers of Blacks to govern themselves.

During the early 1900s, African American men, women, and children came north in large numbers seeking a better way of life. This was the Great Migration, which led to the urbanization and industrialization of masses of Blacks. Data suggest that single men, women, families, and married men without their families participated in the movement. Some families were forever torn apart as a result of this movement. Promises and dreams of an independent life off the farm and in the city were enticing. Unfortunately, the dreams became nightmares as only Black women were permitted (domestic) work, while there was nothing for the masses of Black men (Genovese, 1978). Housing and education continued to be problems, and Blacks were (re)settled in large numbers in racially segregated parts of the cities.

The years following World War I were harsh ones for African Americans. Systematic exclusion from all facets of life was pervasive. "Jim Crow" was alive, well, and thriving. Political, economic, educational, and social advances were slow in coming and painfully gained, and African Americans continued to be subject to mob violence: Between 1880 and

1951, 3,437 African Americans were lynched in America, south *and* north. The country that fought a great war to "make the world safe for democracy" made few and feeble attempts to include African Americans or other people of color in any democratic processes.

By the 1930s, the country was in the midst of a Great Depression. Unemployment of White Americans was at an all-time high (24.9%), and examples abound regarding the devastating impact of this unemployment on White families. Many families broke up as men became despondent and left their families, and newspapers reported rampant homelessness, hunger, and a general lack of hope that led the most desperate to suicide or suicidal attempts. Although American society came to understand the potentially catastrophic impact of widespread poverty on White families, there was little appreciation of how these forces were affecting Black families at the same time. For example, during the 1930s the unemployment rate for Black males in the North was 38.9% and 23.2% for Black females (McMahon, 2009). White America evidenced little understanding, tolerance, compassion, or concern of this on Black fathers' ability to provide for their families.[*]

By the early 1940s, the country was moving toward a second great war to make the world "safe for democracy." During the early years of the war, there was less north-to-south migration of Blacks because of the lack of employment possibilities in northern cities and the hostilities encountered. As World War II intensified and White males were increasingly leaving jobs to fight overseas, the demand for Black laborers increased. By 1944, increased hiring triggered historic migrations of Blacks from the mostly rural South to the more industrialized Northeast, Midwest, and Northwest in search of employment opportunities. Black males were usually primary players in these migrations, and this sometimes created uneven sex ratios either in the communities from which they came or those into which they moved. Such displacements not only affected whole communities but often had disruptive effects on individual families and family members within them.

Additionally, when family units migrated, an entirely new set of social problems evolved. In a racially segregated America, there was a shortage of housing (single-family homes) for these newly arriving families. To "solve" the problem, existing single-family houses were converted to tenements, resulting in exorbitant housing costs (and high profits for the absentee owners), overcrowding, and public health problems. (Housing projects were designed and developed to solve these problems!)

---

[*] More recently, before the current economic crisis, the unemployment rate for Black males ages 25 to 54 was 21%. Two years into the recession, the rate was 31% (Perlo, 2010).

Prostitution, homicide, drug addiction, juvenile delinquency, and violence ensued (Johnson & Campbell, 1981).

Civil rights–desegregation

The 1950s were a time of heightened tension between the races. As Whites were afforded aid and opportunity in a growing, thriving post-war America, the lack of jobs, poor housing, inadequate educational opportunities, and the lack of political strength continued to frustrate the masses of Blacks. Inferior segregated schools, housing covenants resulting in "de facto" segregation, continued enforcement of Jim Crow laws/practices, and the lack of employment opportunities continued to take a toll on Black America. However, Black family life and family support were initially solid in Black communities throughout the United States. In 1950, 91% of African American homes were dual-headed, and though that percentage had decreased to 67.7% by 1970, 54.2% were still headed by two parents as late as 1980 (Glick, 1997). However, the cumulative effects of poverty, racism, White privilege, and the resultant segregation had exacted an enormous toll.

Clearly, the historical attempts to disrupt Black families and communities have had devastating psychological, sociocultural, and economic effects on African Americans. These especially affected Black males whose traditional roles centered on providing for and protecting their families (McAdoo, 1993). Billingsley (1970) wrote that the majority of Black families were headed by men, most of whom were married to their original wives and who were employed full-time but were unable to pull themselves from poverty. Misguided social policies exacerbated the problems Black males encountered in fulfilling these roles. For example, the growing number of low-income, single Black mothers who sought relief through Aid to Families with Dependent Children (AFDC) learned they could lose these "benefits" if a male resided in the home. When this included the father of her child(ren) (who may not have been able to find work or who was underemployed), it increased the likelihood of family disintegration.

Pinkney (1969) wrote that in 1965, 72% of all Black families were composed of husband and wife. He notes, "The economic and social conditions under which Black Americans have lived have led to a disorganized family life … characterized by instability" (pp. 94–95). According to his figures, about one fourth (28%) of U.S. Black families at that time were "disorganized," and this one fourth is presented as being representative. Moynihan (1965, 1968), in analyzing and comparing Blacks and Whites primarily from the 1960 census data on items such as illegitimacy, unemployment, father-absent homes, and welfare dependency, concluded that the problems facing the Black community were primarily due to family disorganization. Moynihan failed to consider the impact of racism and White privilege in his analysis. He also ignored the psychological impact of the elimination of the national African American male leadership of the time, including Medgar Evers, Malcolm X, and Martin Luther King, Jr. The late 1960s saw the rise and subsequent elimination of the Black Panther Party for Self Defense. The author believes that this systematic decimation of Black male leadership contributed to the development, growth, and proliferation of urban gangs, which provided disenfranchised Black youth with opportunities for involvement, leadership, and a sense of family and "community," first in south-central Los Angeles and then across the nation.

Finally, the civil rights movement of 1950s and 1960s, which attempted to outlaw racial discrimination and gain suffrage through acts of non-violent protest and civil disobedience, ushered in the rather short era of affirmative action. In an attempt to "level the playing field" as it relates to education and jobs, Blacks and others who had not been afforded favorable circumstances in which to compete were now offered "equal opportunities." The goal was to end the programs once the "field was leveled." The first affirmative action policy was enforced in 1965, but by 1978, many in the White community had organized protests decrying any remedial efforts that potentially disadvantaged Whites, and eventually, these effectively curtailed the policy. Thus, the damage sustained by Blacks and other people of color over 360 years was deemed by a majority of Americans to have been eradicated in a short 13 years!

Urban deterioration/war on drugs

As noted earlier, the elimination of Black male leadership left a void felt most keenly in low-income urban communities, but it also destabilized Black families and communities across the country. Young men banded together to create a sense of family for protection, survival, fellowship, support, acceptance, and companionship. The documentary film, *Crips and Bloods—Made in America* (Davis, 2008), provides insights into the growth and influence of urban gangs in the late 1960s through the 1980s in south-central Los Angeles. The film discusses the impact of the lack of a viable family, including the lack of an involved father, plays on youth who gravitate to gangs. It chronicles the introduction of drugs (especially crack cocaine) and the flood of automatic weapons into low-income, inner-city, Black communities and thus sets the stage for the urban war zones that continue to plague cities across the nation. Where adult males/fathers have been eliminated, gangs may function as surrogate families/fathers.

Unfortunately, without viable, mature, functioning adult males to provide guidance and direction, youth flounder as they seek to find appropriate father images to emulate.

With meager resources, the lack of vocational training, minimal employment skills, and inadequate educations, some youth turn to street crime as a means to make money. These activities, in turn, contribute to the decline of the quality life in urban areas of the cities and ensure that marginally functioning Black youth will become marginally functioning Black adults.

Civil rights attorney Michelle Alexander (2010) argues that although the Jim Crow statutes and laws of the 19th century are no longer enforced and vestiges of those racist practices have largely disappeared from contemporary society, they have been replaced with a new form of Jim Crowism under the guise of the "War on Drugs."

Alexander (2010) writes, "In each generation, new tactics have been used for achieving the same goals—goals shared by the Founding Fathers. Denying African American citizenship was deemed essential to the formation of the original union" (p. 1). She notes, "An extraordinary percentage of black men in the United States are legally barred from voting. … They are also subject to legalized discrimination in employment, housing, education, public benefits and jury service" (pp. 1–2). According to Alexander, the American racial caste system has not ended but rather has been redesigned under the auspices of the so-called War on Drugs, developed in 1982 during the Reagan administration, *before* crack cocaine became a negative force/problem in urban centers; men are jailed for possessing small amounts of drugs for their personal use rather than for sale or distribution. Alexander notes that drug abuse is a *public health* issue rather than a criminal one and that more Whites use drugs than Blacks (a fact not reflected in arrest, conviction, and incarceration rates). She writes that it is an "odd coincidence that an illegal drug crisis suddenly appeared in the black community after—not before—a drug war had been declared" (p. 6).

Thus, the social controls imposed on Black males during the earlier caste system are now evident via mass incarceration and its aftermath—"one in three young African American men is currently under the control of the criminal justice system—in prison, in jail, on probation, or on parole" (Alexander, 2010, p. 9). Those labeled criminals are controlled both in and out of prison, in that once released, the former prisoners are subject to discrimination and social exclusion. With a felony conviction, they are forever trapped in a second-class status and subject to discrimination, devoid of the ability to vote, excluded from any jury duty, excluded from holding jobs or taking advantage of educational opportunities, destined to reside in public housing, and subject to ongoing and continuous control by the system. Thus, Alexander concludes, the racial caste system, which began with the enslavement of Black people, continues to this day with the War on Drugs.*

Comment

Given the historical trauma and continuing societal barriers they face, it is not surprising that some Black fathers have inappropriate notions about children, childrearing, and responsible relationships with the mothers of their children. In many ways, they are continuing the legacy of enslavement. These males tend to seek self-serving physical gratification with no conscious regard or concept as to sexual (adult) responsibility. They have the notion that contraception is their partner's responsibility and once they "make a baby" they must "step up to the plate" and be accountable. They do not seem to grasp what is involved with responsible child engagement, what it costs to rear a child, the sacrifices, energy, activity, nurturing, and love required to be a father. Thus, in many ways, they function as the "breeders" of earlier times.

However, most of the males with whom I interact seem resistant to this enslavement mentality. Although they may not have planned having children, or anticipated the committed work involved in rearing them, they understand and accept responsibility for their children. Thus, it is inspiring when they demonstrate their effectiveness as loving fathers. As was noted in the first edition of this book, Black fathers, who are meaningfully involved with their children, tend to be ignored. However, it is they who hold the solutions and answers to problems that plague the community. In my work, I often hear from young fathers, who do not reside with their children, complain that the mothers of their kids are "turning my kids against me." I suggest that although the primary caregiver (usually the mother) might make it difficult for the other caregiver to foster a reasonable relationship with the children, the primary caregiver cannot turn the kid(s) against their father. Only fathers can do that, based on how they act and interact. To illustrate, consider the following situations.

---

* According to Alexander, the "War on Drugs" was declared when drug usage was at a low and was followed by legislation that ensured long-term incarceration of nonviolent offenders (i.e., the "three strikes law," which ensured significant time for petty offenses). Because so-called street crime is much easier to detect and prosecute than white-collar crime, Black and Brown males are disproportionately targeted, arrested, charged, and ultimately convicted. Approximately 30% of those arrested are Black or Brown males, and many of these men are fathers. Thus, a large number of children are now "visiting" their fathers' homes (jail). The future impact of youth seeing their fathers warehoused in such a manner will likely be devastating.

Madu

Madu is a 36-year-old, single male who has a 12-year-old daughter with whom he had little contact during her first 8 years. He chose not to marry the mother of his child and on the night of her birth, after visiting her in the hospital, went to a current girlfriend's house to "celebrate." Because he chose not to work, he was unable to support his child and did not help with child care in any meaningful manner—additionally, he seemed to have no idea as to how or what it took to support his child. He apparently believed that loving her would suffice. The child's mother returned to work shortly after giving birth, getting up early to catch a train to take the child to Madu (he resided with his parents), and then returning to the city to work. After work, she caught the train back to Madu's parents, retrieved the child, and made the trip home where she would bathe, feed, and care for her baby before going to bed. This was her schedule for the first year of the child's life. Her living quarters were a small, cold, dark, basement apartment, warmed by one small space heater, and the child was prone to upper respiratory problems.

It is not clear why Madu did not make the effort to meet her halfway, to provide child care at her home, to seek employment himself, or why his parents did not intervene to help him become more responsible. Upon being made aware of the living conditions and the lack of paternal support, her parents invited her and the baby to return to the house where she was reared (some 200 miles away), where she and her baby would each have a room, adequate heat, and food, and her mother would quit working in order to provide child care so that the child's mother could continue to work. She chose to do this, and over the next three years the child thrived.

Interestingly, Madu had little or no contact with the mother or his baby during the duration of their stay with the maternal grandparents. He seemed unaware of the sacrifices the maternal grandparents made for his child and thus did not consider thanking them for taking in his child. Court action was commenced to establish visitation and child support. When he failed to appear, a default judgment was rendered; however, no child support was paid. At the age of 4, when the child left the grandparents' home, she was healthy, happy, and articulate, could read at the first-grade level, possessed appropriate physical and social skills, and had been exposed to involved caring males in the way of social fathers.

Although moving within 20 miles of Madu's parents and establishing monthly contacts with them so that the paternal grandparents would know their grandchild, there was little effort by Madu to form a relationship with his child. Rather, he commenced a campaign of heated discussions with whomever would listen as to how he was being barred from contact with his child. Eventually, he spent some time with his daughter when she visited his parents (she was now 9 years old). However, much of his interactions with her centered on talking negatively to her about her mother and maternal grandparents, with whom she continued to have a loving and caring relationship. After a short period of time, the child began to decline visits with her father, indicating she did not appreciate him "badmouthing" the people who had reared her when he was not providing. Now, at the age of 12, the child has declined all but the most meager visits with her father. She seems depressed, unhappy, angry, and sometimes "lost." Unfortunately (and predictably), Madu's daughter intends to inform the court that she wants even further reduced time with him. The future is not good as relates to any meaningful father–daughter relationship as she states she looks forward to the time she does not have to see him.

Howard

Howard is a 59-year-old never-married male with two adult children (ages 26 and 32) from a previous long-term relationship. Although he chose not to marry the mother of his two children, he did choose to maintain a relationship with them and their mother. The mother enjoys a long-term successful marriage with a man who seems to enjoy his stepfather role. When asked if he provided for his children, Howard looked incredulous and replied, "Of course, they are my children." The notion that he would support them financially, emotionally, and socially was a given. He shared that his father, uncles, grandfather, and extended male kin would have seen him as less than a man if he did not provide—it was a given for which there was no option.

He went on to say that his children spent summers with him and his side of the family; he understood the concept of child support and paid on a consistent, regular basis; and he has always maintained a positive relationship with them (both are college graduates and are enjoying professional careers; neither is currently married). Further, while he acknowledged there were some rough times initially with the children's mother, he was open to input and suggestions and worked diligently to learn, grow, and participate as a father. Using a child-focused approach, he was able to place his shortsighted, selfish immature notions (his words) aside and attend to the needs of his children. As soon as he and the children's mother learned to focus on what was best for their offspring and put their need to fight aside, they rather easily worked out differences around the children's needs.

Observing Howard interact with his son and daughter over the years, their loving, respectful relationship is obvious. They openly express themselves to one another (i.e., their love, respect, concerns, needs, future goals, relationships, professional lives, etc.). The parents are also respectful of one another and, reflecting about their children, both are appreciative that they chose to stop bickering and learned to focus on their children's needs.

Lawrence

Lawrence is a 49-year-old divorced father of two adult daughters (now 27 and 24). Both he and the children's mother remarried; she is currently divorced for the second time. Both children are college graduates; one was married for a short time, and the other is currently engaged. Lawrence sought help when his children were 11 and 8. He was distraught after his wife had informed him that she was bored in the relationship and wanted a divorce. She noted that all he did was work, talk about the kids, and spend time with his side of the family. She indicated that although he was a solid provider and father, she wanted more out of life. She asked him to leave the house so the kids would have some consistency and to continue to support them. She assured him that he would have access to, and visitation with, his daughters.

Lawrence left the house, renting a room from some friends. He faithfully paid child support and contributed to his children's college fund. Things went smoothly for the first seven months when, for some unknown reason, the mother began withholding the children from visiting with their father or speaking with him on the phone. He was quite distraught, discussed discontinuing the payment of child support, returning to court to fight her, and enlisting the sheriff's office to accompany him to forcefully obtain the children for his visits. Although he certainly could have taken these actions, he also recognized they may not be best for the children. He was asked if he could be patient, focus on the long term, and follow some directives, the goal of which was to ultimately have a meaningful relationship with his children. He indicated he would try and was advised to get a notebook for each of his daughters and start to write thoughts, comments, and reactions to each of them. He was to date the entries, keep them brief, and write nothing about their mother.*

Thus, he recorded thoughts about missing the children and not being present, about saying good night and good morning to them, about missing or not being included in their special days and events, about not being included at school events, about showing up for his visitations and the

---

* Consider: One parent "badmouthing" the other to the children has negative outcomes for the "badmouthed," only if what is being said is true. If not, the "badmouthing" can come back at some point to haunt that parent. If what she is saying to the kids is accurate, he needs to change; if it is not accurate, then he should be himself and when the children are old enough, they will figure it out on their own and take whatever action they see fit.

children not being present (home), and so forth.* Additionally, he was asked to continue sending birthday, holiday, and special event cards, gifts, and messages. When they were returned, he was to keep them in one of two containers maintained for each child. And he was advised to continue contributing to his children's college fund.

There was minimal contact for some years, until Lawrence accidentally encountered his older child at a local shopping mall. She approached him in an angry manner indicating he had lied about her college funds and there was no money in either child's accounts. Shocked, he did not know what to say and merely asked that she stop by his home over the next couple of days allowing him time to try and figure out what had happened to the money and what they might do to resolve the problem.

As soon as he got home, he made some calls and soon determined all the money had indeed been withdrawn from both accounts by his ex-wife. Several days later, his daughter stopped by, still angry. Rather than listening to her complaints and negative comments, he gave her the box of items he had saved over the years. He asked that she go through the items when she calmed down and make plans to come back to talk. She did take the box, but was rude and disrespectful as she departed.

Apparently after calming down, she went through some of the items and was shocked at what she found. Her mother had been saying negative things about her father for some time, indicating he was no good, did not care about the kids, and was making no effort to be in their lives. Now, the evidence before her suggested this was neither accurate nor truthful. She angrily confronted her mother about having been deceived about her father and withholding her from him. She indicated she wanted to live with him and attempt to develop a relationship. Her mother also acknowledged that she had taken and spent the college money.

Immediately thereafter, she apologized to her father and asked to move in with him so they could come to know one another. In a relatively short period of time, they developed a loving, caring relationship, which continues to this day. And, after moving in with her father, she was able to attend college, with his help. While she maintains a relationship with her mother, she remains concerned as to why her mother created a wedge between the daughters and their father, and as such is no longer fully trusting of her mother. Her younger sister also has a relationship with the father but is not as close to him. The daughters do well together.

---

* In my work, I have found that some men discontinue attempts to see their children because of the personal pain and agony they experience in attempting to navigate a hostile family court system, maternal gatekeeping activities, inequitable social service procedures, and their personal frames of reference. "Men don't express hurt and pain; men don't cry"— thus, these men seem to accept being perceived as absent fathers when in fact they are staying away to minimize their pain and anguish. They are wounded fathers.

Conclusion

Given the history of how African descended males have fared in the United States, what is interesting regarding these three cases is not that Madu has little understanding of what being a man or a father entails; rather, it is fascinating and noteworthy that given the history of Black fathers in the United States, both Lawrence and Howard chose to place their children's needs over their own and were able to act accordingly. Both have maintained consistent and positive relationships with their children, and both of them are happy and satisfied with the relationships. Both indicate that it was often difficult, but they recognize that life in America for Black men has always been difficult. It is likely that Madu's situation would be different if he stopped fighting his daughter's mother, listened to his child, apologized to and thanked those who have had a consistent hand in her rearing, and commenced being a positive force in her life.

Certainly, African and African American males have been subjected to consistent, unwarranted, hostile abuse during the years in the United States. One of the three men presented here made choices that demonstrated a lack of awareness of the impact of his actions on others, including children, mates/mothers, and the community. However, two of them put their children's needs first, and this allowed them to made appropriate adjustments, adjustments that recognized and considered the needs of their children. These fathers are to be acknowledged, commended, and reinforced—they have answers to some of the problems plaguing the community. Additionally, as energy is expended in support of those fathers making poor decisions, it is important not to ignore fathers who are responsible, attentive, and responsible to their children. Any serious remediation attempts must include their solutions. Paraphrasing my colleague and friend, Dr. Thomas Parham (2002) in a keynote address delivered to college students at Cal State, Long Beach, "Mental liberation is needed in any effort to liberate one's community." When African descended men know who they are, their true history, their worth, and their abilities, they take care of themselves, their children, and their communities, just as Lawrence and Howard have done and continue to do.

Reflective questions

1. Most funding agencies support social programming at 3- to 5-year cycles. How realistic is it to anticipate this approach will have any meaningful impact on problems that have been several hundred years in the making?
2. The United States presents itself as being a "child-friendly" society. Do you agree or disagree? Discuss your answer in the context of the

historical mistreatment of Black males and their efforts to be good fathers.

3. Given the history, how do you explain/or account for African descended fathers who are involved and engaged with their children and families?

4. What can Madu learn from Lawrence and Howard to develop a meaningful relationship with his daughter?

References

Alexander, M. (2010). *The new Jim Crow.* New York: New Press.

Bennett, L. (1984). *Before the Mayflower* (5th ed.). New York: Penguin Books.

Billingsley, A. (1970). Black families and White social science. *Journal of Social Issues, 26*(3), 127–142.

Connor, M., & White, J. (2006). *Black fathers: An invisible presence in America.* Mahwah, NJ: Erlbaum.

Davis, B., Halsted, D. (Producers), & Peralta, S. (Producer/Writer/Director). (2008). *Crips and Bloods: Made in America* [Motion picture]. (Available from Bullfrog Films, Oley, PA)

Dayton, C. (1991, January). Taking the trade: Abortion and gender relations in an 18th century New England village. *William and Mary Quarterly, 48,* 19–49.

Genovese, E. D. (1978). *The Myth of the Absent Family.* In R. Staples (Ed.), *The Black family: Essays and studies* (pp. 35–40). Belmont, CA: Wadsworth.

Glick, P. C. (1997). A demographic picture of Black families. In H. P. McAdoo (Ed.), *Black families* (3rd ed.) (pp. 118–138). Beverly Hills, CA: Sage.

Gutman, H. (1976). *The Black family in slavery and freedom, 1750-1925.* New York: Pantheon Books.

Harris, W. (1976). Work and family in Black America, 1880. *Journal of Social History, 9*(3), 319–330.

Johnson, D. M., & Campbell, R. V. (1981). *Black migration in America.* Durham, NC: Duke University Press.

Karenga, M. (2002). *Introduction to Black studies* (3rd ed.). Los Angeles: University of Sankore Press.

McAdoo, J. (1993). The roles of African American fathers: An ecological perspective. *Families in Society, 74,* 28–35.

McMahon, K. A. (2009, January 16). *Invisible women of the Great Depression.* Retrieved from http://ezinearticles.com/?The-Invisible-Women-of-the-Great-Depression&id=1888970

Moynihan, D. P. (1965). *The Negro family: The case for national action.* Washington, DC: U.S. Department of Labor.

Moynihan, D. P. (1968). *Family and nation.* New York: Harcourt Brace Jovanovich.

Parham, T. (2002). *Mental liberation.* Keynote address, Student-sponsored Teaching Students of Color Conference, California State University, Long Beach.

Perlo, A. (2010, February). *African Americans and the jobs crisis.* (April 22, 2010) http://politicalaffairs.net/african-americans-and-the-jobs-crisis/

Pinkney, A. (1969). *Black Americans*. Englewood Cliffs, NJ: Prentice-Hall.
Pleck, E. (2004). Two dimensions of fatherhood: A history of the good dad–bad dad complex. In M. Lamb (Ed.), *The role of father in child development*. (pp. 32–57). Hoboken, NJ: Wiley.
Rasbury, A. (2010, Winter/Spring). Charleston unbound. *American Legacy*.

chapter two

Black fatherhood through my eyes

Achebe Hoskins
Reentry Specialist
The Mentoring Center
Oakland, California

The men and fathers in my life

I grew up with men in my life. Some were more productive than others, some were more nurturing and attentive than others, but they were there. Fathers, stepfathers, grandfathers, great-grandfathers, uncles, great-uncles, play uncles, grown cousins, and some men whose relationship to the family is still a mystery. But these men played an active role in rearing us. They showed up.

I was the fourth born into a family of eleven children: seven boys and four girls. Unfortunately my parents divorced, resulting in the children being reared by our grandparents, a bittersweet experience that shaped our lives. The foundation for my core values, principles, work ethic, and spirituality originated at my grandparents' house, on a steep hill in an active, "everybody knows everybody" community in San Francisco, California. We, the grandchildren, had no idea or interest in what our grandparents had lived through and experienced as firsthand accounts from their parents. They were born and reared in the Deep South in the early 1900s, during a time of great economic depression and intense racial segregation. Those grandparents on whose laps I sat as a child were but one generation removed from enslavement. Their parents (two of whom I met as a child) were primarily responsible for actively attempting to undo what hundreds of years of slavery had done to destroy African tradition and culture: Slavery had ripped apart the African family, rendering the African male ineffective, irrelevant, and almost invisible. This had a disastrous effect on Black men, who, in spite of all the barriers, still successfully built communities, raised families, and carried themselves as responsible, effective fathers.

My father

When I look at the men in my family album, I see men who worked the fields as hired hands, contractors to supply hands, sharecroppers, as well as men who were land and property owners. We have men who worked in businesses and a few who owned businesses. As I flip the delicate pages of the old album, I see the pictures of men like my father, who joined the military, and went to war in an attempt to show their patriotism and gain pride and dignity through the uniform. Although my father was physically strong, smart, and industrious, he, like most Black men in the navy at that time, was not allowed to rise above the rank of chief cook. I know that the effects of this discrimination was the impetus for him to push us young men to be creative, productive, and knowledgeable.

I was introduced to a wonderful story depicting the struggle of Black men in the navy during World War II, which reflected my father's and probably many other fathers' stories. A similar story was made into a movie called *Men of Honor*, the true story of Master Chief Carl Bashier. As it was for Master Chief Bashier, the navy uniform did not shield my father from the racism in the military, nor did it open the doors of the segregated bars and restaurants in his native Mississippi. The uniform did, however, catch the eye of a beautiful young nursing student named Rosa Lee (my mother). They went on to be married for 20 years. I keep a picture (taken in the 1940s) of the young couple on my laptop. It is a reminder of my dad's husband and fatherhood journey. It is also the foundation for all I understand about fatherhood and fathering. I will share these experiences in this chapter.

Fathers teaching responsibility

A number of areas stand out as crucial in the understanding of fatherhood and the activities associated with successful fathering. I begin with the notion of teaching responsibility. Being around men in my early life and listening to their stories, discipline and rewards constituted their way of teaching. For me, this represented a valuable period of learning, which led to my belief that (manhood/fatherhood) teaching should begin long before a young man becomes a father. I also believe that men must be aware and purposeful in understanding that anytime and every time children are in our presence, teachable moments are offered.

Elders and the group

Recently I facilitated a group of 20 young men between the ages of 15 and 17. Two are fathers, 18 are not, and none had his own father or any positive males in his life. When I asked how they felt about their fathers not being present, some shrugged their shoulders and said, "It means nothing; you can't miss what you never had." A few others shared some rather ugly stories about their fathers, stepfathers, and men that had been in their lives at one time or another. Clearly they were carrying pain and anger relative to these missing paternal figures. I asked the guys, "With what you are feeling right now, if you were a father, would you put a child through the kind of pain you are feeling?" All the guys said "No." "Why?" I asked. "Cause I would take care of my business," one young man replied. I posed another question: "What do you think is the most important aspect of fatherhood?" I asked the young men to write their answers down so each would give only his own response and not just agree with what the person next to him had said. All but one gave the same answer, "Be *responsible*." I then said, "If all of you really believe that *responsibility* is the most important aspect of fatherhood, when do you think a person should be *responsible*—before the sex or after the birth?" I saw this as an opportunity for a teachable moment, but nobody answered. As they thought about their answers, I asked, "Is it *responsible* to use protection?" They all replied, yes, that *responsibility* should start before the sex. I inquired, "If you are not being *responsible* before there is a child, will you probably struggle with *responsibility* after the child is born?" Most disagreed. One young man stated, "Just cause a person slipped up [unintended ejaculation] don't mean he ain't gonna be responsible and handle his business." I agreed with him. This group is about critical thinking and the fact of the matter is that in our community most pregnancies are unplanned; that is, a lot of children are born in our community based on a "slip up." In the past, an unplanned pregnancy did not mean that the child was going to be fatherless. And, it does not necessarily mean that today. However, it does suggest that it is not enough for men to know the word *responsibility*; they must be prepared to associate the word with appropriate behaviors in order to get the outcome the community so desperately needs in assisting to uplift the next generation.

Next, a scenario was presented to the young men wherein they were in a situation about to have sex: You and your potential sexual partner are fully aroused. You recognize that neither you nor your partner has protection. Do you

(A) get up, go to the store, and get protection,
(B) fool around, but not have intercourse, or
(C) forget the whole thing?

Those that spoke up said, "I ain't gonna even lie; I'd do it without the protection." I then asked, "Are you saying that you would not be *responsible*? That you would risk pregnancy, STDs, even risk catching HIV/ AIDS?" Silence fell over the room. "I never really thought about it like that," replied one youth.

The discussion then moved to exploring some of the reasons why their fathers were not present in their lives and what that feels like. Most admitted that not having their fathers around was painful beyond description. "Man I can't even tell ya," one said. Another stated, "I don't even wanna talk about it; let's just move on." A follow-up question was then presented: "Would you want another child to experience that kind of pain?" All replied "No." Then they began to realize the point. One of the young men blurted out, "Oh I get what you sayin'. You sayin' that if we don't want to be responsible for no other kid's pain, then we should be *responsible* and *strap up* before we get busy." "Now you got it fellas: Fatherhood *responsibilities* start before you are a father. What's on your mind gives rise to your thoughts, your thoughts can give rise to your actions, and actions have outcomes and consequences." As a responsible man you must think about the actions that lead to fatherhood, particularly if you are not ready to share your life with the child, support the mom, nurture, rear, and teach your child and give your child your name.

Black fathers and names

I believe that the process of naming a child or children is an unforgettable event and an important factor in understanding some of the roles and responsibilities of Black fathers. This naming process speaks to the parents' understanding of their relationship to our past and our hopes for the future through our children. As Hilliard (1986, p. vi-vii) notes,

> When African people name the children, it is based upon a complex set of ideas about the world and the role of human beings in it. This way of thinking about children is quite different from the Western idea that a child comes into the world as a "blank tablet," or that it "has no personality until it is six months old." Children are the reward of life. They are the fruits of creation. They deserve a place, a sense of belonging, a sense of purpose.

Today, many Black parents may be aware of their African roots and may even name their children African or African-sounding names. Names, be they Native American, African, European, or Asian, invoke an image and a message (once the name is translated and understood). It is the hope of many parents that the child will live up to the legacy of their name. Therefore, the parent may give the child a name such as "walks with pride" or "hope of the people." If the name is a traditional family name, that of an ancestor or a past relative, the goal may be to pass on the spirit, history, and legacy of that relative to the next generation.

One of the most important factors in the traditional process is that the name is tied to family or an individual's core values, principles, goals, and aspirations. It can be a tremendous advantage and responsibility for a father to say to his young son, even before the child is able to speak clearly, "I named you Sekou (leader of your people) after my uncle."

It is my experience that when positive family traditions, including nurturing, careful rearing, and loving attention, are paid to that child, there is a greater chance the child's behavior will be much more predictable, manageable, and positive. It is these core values and principles that can determine the health and well-being of an individual, a family, and the community at large.

Madhubuti (1991, p. 187) writes,

> Stable families and communities are absolutely necessary if we are to have productive and loving individuals. ... Families are the foundation for community. Like a family, a functional community provides security, caring, wealth, resources, cultural institutions, education, employment, a spiritual force, shelter, and a challenging atmosphere. Families and community shape the individual into a productive or non-productive person. Without family, without community, individuals left to "everything is everything."

What happens when the naming is left to those whose values and principles are not in the best interest of the community? In Oakland, there is a very long street that was formally named Grove and later renamed in honor of Dr. Martin Luther King, Jr. As crack cocaine began to show up in the community in the late 1980s, certain elements living on Martin Luther King Street and the surrounding area renamed the area "ghost town." Thus, the street no longer invoked images of the civil rights struggle or the pride of having a prominent African American man who made the ultimate sacrifice in giving his life in the service of his people. What happens when individuals begin to name/rename themselves and their children in the most destructive manner? Names like "Killa," "Murderin' Mobster," or "Shorty the Pimp" become the individual's identity and, in some cases, their reputation. "Now you got the name, what you gon' do?" The name can begin to dictate and reinforce behaviors.

In some communities, the destructive traditions become the prominent behavior. Without counterbalancing positive activities or community traditions, the destructive behaviors may suck in the best young minds in the community and all those who are attempting to do the right things. Even though the positive young minds attempt to live the positive core values and principles of their families, they have an extremely difficult and sometimes dangerous time growing up in some communities. This is an area where Black fathers play a crucial role in the lives of Black children. Every child needs to be and feel safe, secure, and protected.

I have lived for years in what could be considered the roughest areas in our city. One of my sons was born with sickle cell anemia and has always been a measure smaller than other boys his age. Years ago while he was attending the public high school in the area, he was victimized by several bullies. His mother and I were estranged but still very much in partnership in the rearing of our children. Our son did not tell either of us that he was being bullied. Years later when he did speak of his plight at that school, I asked, "Why did you not tell me? Did you think that I would not come to your aid?" He replied that he wanted to handle it himself. My son had observed me for years take on crack houses and other community issues, work with the most challenged kids on the block, and deal with guys who are incarcerated. Knowing that I probably knew people on that school campus, he did not want me to be involved in his issue. He wanted to handle it himself. And he did. Knowing that he had backup was enough for him to handle the problem and graduate with dignity from the high school.

Social fathers on the block

The role of social fathers in the community is essential for the overall health of the community. Being active is as important as being visible. The inventiveness, creativity, and skill sets which Black fathers possess and use can make a difference in the lives of the young folks for years, maybe generations to come.

When I first moved to my block, there was not a lot of negative activity even though we were but one block from a drug "hot spot." However, within one year the foot traffic moved from main street to my block, into a house across the street. Having three kids at home, three others over on the weekend, and any number of nieces and nephews at any given time, I recognized that I was going to have to be proactive.

Slowly but deliberately as the block changed, I realized the first challenge was to understand what I was seeing, then to develop a strategy to actively meet the issues directly. The person who was responsible for selling the illegal product had casually moved in with his grandparents, and what started with his having friends dropping in turned into consistent traffic. Things began to escalate, with kids parking cars in front of my house at all hours, playing music at full volume, and having loud conversations over the music. I responded by putting my speakers out on my porch and playing speeches from Malcolm X. Because I was a soundman for several performing groups, I had significant volume. They eventually got the message and moved on. Unfortunately, so did the dealer's grandparents. Those humble elderly residents who had lived on that corner for over 20 years could no longer take the traffic, the noise, and probably the reality that they had unknowingly invited into their home the person who was responsible for some community destruction. One day they just packed up and left the house to the dealers.

The community responded by organizing a home alert group, electing a block captain, and constantly reporting the illegal activity in that house. My mailbox, on the corner in front of the house, soon became a popular spot to gather, sit on top of, use as a drum, and just "kick it." I'm a percussionist so I didn't mind the impromptu drumming sessions. Unfortunately, folks began urinating in the bushes next to my front steps. It was time to put my dog Blackie out to guard the front perimeter. He was eventually attacked by a pit bull, but he survived and continued to hold down the front yard for as long as we lived on that corner. At every juncture in our struggle on the block, our presence as Black men was crucial.

Soon the dealer began to attract some of the younger boys. I responded by organizing a group we called the "Boys On The Block." BOTB consisted of 10 to 12 boys. My focus was to keep them busy with positive activities. At that time, I was center director at a local YMCA. The center served as a recreational haven and a base of operations away from the block. We kept the boys busy, sponsoring overnights, forming a radio-controlled car racing club, and raising money to rent a large motor home once a year in which we traveled to several theme parks in the area.

On one of our motor home trips, we went to a go-cart racing park. Because we were short on money, each youngster had the opportunity to drive but one time. While they were appreciative to have the opportunity to drive even once, it did not diminish the disappointment once their turn was done, as they stood on the side and watched other kids driving over and over. As we were leaving, the guys had their heads down and walked to the gate slowly dragging their feet. I stopped them, sat them down, and started giving them a pep talk about staying positive and good things will come. I suggested that next year we would raise twice the money so we can do more. Unbeknownst to me, a man was standing behind me listening to my speech to the boys. He was a man I had met months ago at a conference (the Young Black Males at Grave Risk Conference), sponsored by the then-presiding juvenile court judge. "Are all these boys yours?" he asked "Today they are," I replied. He pulled out a wad of money, peeled off a number of bills, and said, "Let those boys drive some more." The boys were elated, I was relieved, and our benefactor must have looked like a hero in the eyes of his sons. He was most definitely our hero that day.

The community fought for over two years to shut down and board up the crack house. During those two years we got permits to hold several block parties where the residents came out to enjoy food, performances, good music, and most importantly to celebrate community control of the block. The last block party was a special celebration because of our victory, and our children, especially the boys, observing Black men fighting to bring a better quality of life to the community.

Fathers and cultural relevance

Culture is defined in many ways. I offer this definition. Culture: a refined understanding or appreciation of the customs, arts, social institutions, achievements, attitudes, and behavior characteristics of a particular nation, people, or other social group.

As a child in the 1950s, I was fascinated with Greek mythology. I knew many Greek gods and their stories. My fascination spread to France with the Three Musketeers and then to Mexico with Zorro. On to the Wild West with the Lone Ranger and Tonto, and even to "darkest" Africa, but only for Tarzan, Jane, and Boy.

I didn't know it then, but I was inexplicably, almost hypnotically drawn to certain aspects of culture from people different from myself. The images produced by these cultures always appeared to be strong, smart, sometimes funny, always domineering and in control. The images to which I was exposed that reflected me, my father, and grandfather were those of enslaved, conquered, or scared Africans, waiting to be rescued by Tarzan or Jane. Or, the tap-dancing Black men serving drinks to Shirley Temple and her family, or Black folks whose eyes would pop out with fear as they interacted with the Three Stooges. My grandfather would get angry and say, "Keep watching them stooges and you will grow up to be a stooge." Then he would snatch the power cord out of the wall and send us outside. He knew what these images could do to a young mind deprived of positive, uplifting images.

When I was 5 or 6 years old, my grandmother enrolled me and three of my siblings in several classes. We had tap dance, acrobatics, and, for some reason, a limbo class. The limbo did not interest me, but the drum took me on a journey that changed my life. I found myself listening for anything that had a bongo or conga drum in it. My favorite records were those that had outstanding percussion, like Harry Belafonte's "Banana Boat" song, "Day-o, day-o, daylight come and me wan' go home," the Temptations' "Beauty's Only Skin Deep," and others. I began to make a cultural connection through the drum. This led to learning African dance and ultimately the South African gumboot dance (performed by men and boys). The gumboot dance was a gateway to my understanding of history of the people of South Africa, Apartheid, the plight of Nelson Mandela; activity, and knowledge and history sparked by learning one cultural instrument, the drum.

The introduction of African American History in high school, coupled with my love and knowledge of the drum, seemed to bring it all together. My head exploded with the knowledge of events and accomplishments of people who looked like me. Day by day my confidence and self-esteem grew as I joined the BSU (Black Student Union) and formed our own drama club to write and perform plays about our community and the people in it.

The key to our ability to get things done on that campus, where we were the minority, was Mr. McClanahan. He was an auxiliary policeman and metal shop/mechanical drawing teacher, one of two Black male teachers on our campus. Both men served as more than mentors.

By this time my parents had split up, I had left my grandmother's house, and I had no adult male presence in my life. These two Black men, as social fathers, provided my brother and me the guidance, direction, and skills we needed to navigate during that period of growth, including an awareness of our African/African American cultural consciousness. This was a huge leap in our understanding of our place and time in the world.

Today as I work with the predominately African American young men at one of California's juvenile corrections facility, I always introduce a challenging African art form. When the young men get it, I see the same gleam in their eyes that Mr. Mc must have seen in mine: the glow that says, with pride, I am part of something great.

The cultural expression of rap and hip hop

A lesson garnered from these experiences is that one of my strongest and most effective tools is the ability to facilitate opportunities for these young men to express themselves culturally. This cultural expression cuts through emotional and traumatic layers and touches a special place in them. I recognize that rap and hip hop are such powerful forces worldwide because they give youth the power to express themselves from the heart while fostering dreams of wealth, power, fame, and respect.

However, like other powerful apparatuses used without proper guidance and instruction, rap and hip hop began to speak directly to young rebellious spirits in a new and powerful way. It became so prevalent on the airways, and so marketable by corporate America, that many began to refer to it as Black culture, representing deviance.

> The false point of origin for the belief that poor black people have a debased and dysfunctional culture that emerged from civil rights efforts and programs (and that black women's family leadership was a key reason for such dysfunction) hides the fact that the very same argument not only was a cornerstone of the means by which African-Americans were deemed suitable for enslavement but also formed the basis for maintaining slavery. Myths of black cultural dysfunction have served as a key explanation for racial inequality throughout most of the twentieth century. (Rose, 2008, p. 64)

In our discussions with young folks who are into hip hop, we suggest that rap is a cultural expression, an art form, unique no doubt, but no less derived from the many art forms that preceded it. This is often a tug of war. Some of the young folks indicate that they want to feel like they are part of something that their generation created. Youth tend to have strong needs for a recognized identity, and those devoid of role models are left to their own devices relative to creating or choosing that identity. The choices are not always those that will work in their best interest. The cultural expression of rap and hip hop may offer youth the identity they seek, but without the historical framework or guidance, it is like a runaway train with a whole generation of our youth on board.

As we work with them to develop mutual understanding of what culture is, what it is not, and what it does, we suggest that African American culture should represent an understanding of our social order, religions, spirituality, core values, principles, politics, laws, financial status, educational institutions, patriotism, norms, customs, traditions, artistic expressions, and the production of goods and services. The young folks who take part in these discussions usually come away with a different view and understanding of the phenomena of culture.

I recently posed a question to a group of youth in a youth juvenile detention facility with whom I will be working for a minimum 6 months.

Let's say we are all going to the same kinds of
schools; we are listening to the same music genre;
all watching the same kinds of videos and TV
shows; we all idolize and patronize the same celeb-
rities; and we all hang out with people who believe
the same things and have the same habits. Lastly,
we are all in jail, on parole, on probation, or on electric monitoring. If we wanted to change our lives for
the better and ensure our sons and daughters' lives
were better, what in our culture should we change?

The group went through the aspects of culture previously discussed
and decided that to change their life circumstances, they would have to
change in several areas, including cultural expression. There was much
heated discussion about how cultural expression can influence the community and thus create a dominant peer group. They felt that they could
not stop anybody from saying what they wanted to say, but they would not
support it or let it influence them like they had in the past.

I then shared a story I had recently read about a horrific and tragic
accident that took place on the Red River bank in Shreveport, Louisiana.
A group of 20 young people were out for a day of swimming and barbe-
cue when 7 teenagers walked down the beach area into about 3 feet of
water. One of the youth fell into a sink hole and the others, one by one,
were pulled in. None could swim. Each was trying to save the other, and
eventually all drowned in the 18 to 20 feet of water. Only one person had
a life jacket, and only one child was saved.

When we hear of such tragedies, we most certainly empathize with
those who have suffered such a catastrophic loss. During the interaction
we discussed how heroic it was for one to attempt to save another. The
idea that we are responsible for each other is something that has always
been part of our culture. While growing up, if we went anywhere, the
older one was always responsible for the younger one. A key factor is that
those to whom the responsibility is given must be prepared to handle
potential problems. If we went on the bus, you were supplied with enough
bus fare; if it was a long trip, you always took enough food and drink; if
we went swimming, somebody had to know how to swim.

The lesson in that tragic story for our young men is, when you are
about to walk into an unfamiliar area, it's best to get guidance. We see it
happen to our young men in music, sports, business, and relationships.
One stands a much better chance if tethered to a lifeline. Black fathers
and elders are that lifeline. We must be present to keep our youth afloat as

they attempt to navigate unfamiliar waters. One of our tasks is to guide our youth away from danger and toward knowledge, success, safety, and positive cultural traditions.

For the young men in our critical thinking sessions, understanding the meaning of culture was an important step. Understanding the need for culture and how it fits into our daily lives was an even bigger step. Finally, recognizing how aspects of culture help shape our identity and our reflective behaviors is a huge leap in their understanding. Our cultural analysis helped this group of youth understand that cultural expression such as rap, spoken word, and street art are tied to a much larger cultural phenomenon that represents a brief snapshot of who we are as Black people at this particular time in our history. It also speaks volumes about Black fathers and our ability to give guidance to our sons and daughters.

Black fathers and anger

The absence of Black fathers in the lives of our children is a deep open wound that grows and festers, sapping vital energy and creating an emotional imbalance in many Black children. A child attempting to balance his or her range of emotions faces a monumental task, even with guidance and a supportive family structure. Without guidance and support, many of our children call on the one emotion that appears to give them what they need in the moment: anger.

Several years ago while working at the Mentoring Center, I received an interesting message from a local middle school about a mile from our center. The caller was the school nurse, who was assigned to the urban school site by the county health department. The nurse stated it was an emergency call and that the school needed someone to come to conduct "rage management" sessions for a group of boys. As an anger management facilitator, I was intrigued with the request.

Although my caseload was packed, I decided to follow up anyway. The nurse was elated that I returned the call. It turns out that she had made a number of calls before contacting our center. Although I informed her that I was not in a position to fulfill her request, she felt that there was too much at stake for me not to engage. She said that she was not the kind of person to take no for an answer when it comes to serving these boys. "This we have in common," I replied and set up a time to visit the campus to discuss how we might collaborate.

I entered the school and was directed by a security officer to the office. The office was a large counter occupied on one side by a secretary busily going from one task to another: first answering the phone, then giving a student a pass and sending him to class, reminding him to make no stops along the way. She then made an announcement over the intercom about a special assembly, while pointing out the location of forms for a substitute teacher. On my side of the counter, there were two boys who had apparently just had an altercation. Both were blaming the other for starting it. One was threatening to get the other after school; the second boy was saying, "We can do it right now." The busy secretary suddenly appeared from behind the counter to give a stern warning. "You two better sit here and close your mouths, or I will call your parents right now." She then asked if she could help me, just as the nurse entered. Never missing a beat, she admonished the boys, introduced herself to me, and escorted me and the boys to her office.

Her office was made up of three sections. One was the reception area, which already had two individuals waiting to be seen. The second was an area with a cot to allow kids to lie down. The third was her office, where she took the boys after asking me to wait as she dealt with them. A few minutes later she came out, sat the boys down, and invited me into her office.

We formally introduced ourselves and went into some detail about what we do professionally. She explained why she felt it was important to raise the alarm by requesting rage management. "These boys are beyond angry and mad. They are enraged."

After hearing a few stories, I volunteered to help find someone who could make a commitment to come by weekly. After several attempts at trying to find someone to help, I committed to stop by over the next 10 months.

It took a week to develop a mission statement and strategy; we located a suitable space, and I met the principal and staff who would be involved. Because some parents had been litigious in their efforts to address issues on the campus, understandably the principal was initially cautious and less than enthusiastic.

We were given a small room for the first group session/lunch. I proceeded to set up a video projector to which I connected to my laptop, finishing just in time to receive a group of 10 racially diverse boys assigned to anger (rage) management. It didn't take long to understand why these particular individuals were chosen. As they came in, I observed several other boys in the halls teasing them by saying, "Ah ha, you gotta go to the retarded group." Within 5 minutes of entering the room, a dispute ensued over who was sitting in which chair. I quickly learned that my attempts to solve the issue by speaking to them had no effect whatsoever. These two boys were triggered and could not hear me or anything else, including the eight other boys who were agitating the two potential combatants. I launched myself between the two boys, took both their chairs, and ordered them to opposite corners of the small room. One boy protested, exclaiming his right to the chair. The other was so mad that he could not speak as tears streamed down his face. I then took the lens cover off the projector and began showing an animated clip that portrayed a man who was extremely mad and was accidentally breaking his belongings because of his anger. This made him madder and caused him to break more of his things.

The movie distracted the boys and one of them said, "Dang, if he keep gettin' mad, he gonna tear up all his stuff." This was a teachable moment. The boys were able to see themselves through the cartoon. This was our first lesson.

I set out to accomplish a number of goals with the boys. First, I wanted to know who these boys were and allow them to know me as "Baba" (the first infusion of culture). I wanted to know what were the particular circumstances and challenges they faced which might be the primary cause of their anger. I also wanted to give them a few tools that would help them to understand anger and possibly reduce the time it took for them to cool down once they were triggered. Lastly, I wanted to teach them a cultural expression that would allow them to stand out among their peers in a positive way.

I quickly learned each boy's story, life circumstances, and living environment. It was not long before I recognized that each boy had these wonderfully creative personalities that were present whenever the child was not angry. I knew then that I would accomplish my goals with this group, and I allowed them to rename it to make it their own.

As the weeks passed, I was able to build rapport and teach the boys a number of concepts and strategies for controlling anger through games and role playing. They recognized that the more they controlled themselves, the less trouble they got into and the better things were for them. I was able to get tickets to an Oakland As baseball game and promised them to anyone who had no infractions for a month. Eight of the ten boys were able to use the anger control strategies to win tickets for the game. We attended the game and strengthened the bonds between and among ourselves.

Each of the meetings that followed was intense and sometimes contentious. It was as though they were under consistent pressure in their lives. Occasionally the group would get a visit from parents or caregivers who dropped in to observe the person assigned to deal with their son's anger. Sometimes the conversations would be calm and civil; on other occasions the parent visits would be a test of my people skills. The most challenging visits were those of mothers who were currently or recently in conflict with the child's father. I became the face and representative father of their sons. I am happy to say that every confrontation had a positive outcome.

During October, I announced that I would not return to the school in January after the winter break. I told the boys that I had one last thing that

I wanted them to learn and do. I wanted them to perform at the winter assembly during the last day of school. All of the boys reluctantly agreed but wondered what they would perform. I pulled up some footage of the gumboot dance. "That is our performance. I know you don't know how to do that dance yet, but in three months you will. Who is in?" All agreed to participate.

For the next 2 months, we mixed anger management concepts with physical movements of dance and a South African traditional song. We set up a video camera to capture the boys' progress. Their excitement and enthusiasm were off the charts. They seemed to forget what had originally brought them to the group. The boys were working in harmony and unity.

In November, just before the Thanksgiving holiday, I was informed that my job was having a retreat that I was required to attend. The retreat would be held on the same day of the assembly at the school. I told the boys that they would have to perform without my being present. Although they were disappointed, they appeared to be up for the challenge. Every meeting/practice was focused and serious. We discussed what they would wear, who would be invited, how they would enter the auditorium, and how they would exit. This represented the first and only appearance as a group in front of the entire school, including classmates, teachers, administrators, parents, and community volunteers.

I saw this as a test of their transformation and recognized it could be a very bad idea. I remember telling myself that given the pressure of being on stage in front of all those people, one loud giggle from these K–6 graders could send my former enraged group of boys into a retaliatory rant that could require the presence of school security. It could represent an opportunity for them to self-destruct, and there would be nothing I could do about it. They were on their own.

On the day of their performance, I stopped by the school before joining my colleagues at the retreat. I brought each boy a black T-shirt from The Mentoring Center. On the front of each shirt, in big red letters, was the slogan, "Go Smart." On the back was two hands enclosing a pyramid. At the top of the pyramid was the question, "Who Am I?" At the bottom, "How Do I See Myself?" and the bottom right read, "What Is My Life's Purpose?"

The boys were elated to receive the shirts, which provided them a uniform and cohesiveness. One of the (gumboot dance) fathers volunteered to come to the school in my stead, allowing for the boys to have adult supervision and to stay out of class until the assembly started.

I went to the company retreat, which focused on transformative mentoring. As important as the subject matter was, my mind was several miles away, back at the school with the boys. I announced that I would be leaving at lunch to go see how things had gone, and I could hardly wait for the lunch break.

When I arrived at the school, the assembly had started, but the boys had yet to perform. They were as glad to see me as I was to see them. The captain pulled everybody into a room off from the auditorium, and to my surprise he had everybody join hands and offered a short prayer. I cannot describe my feelings while holding hands with the boys in this circle. My mind flashed back to the first anger management meeting and how far they had come. "Please God, let us do good today in the assembly, and thank you for letting Baba be with us." I was filled with emotion and pride.

When the time came for the boys to take the stage, they were more nervous than they had ever been in their young lives. They had practiced the moves on the stage for weeks; each move was choreographed and committed to memory; they performed each jump and slap of the boot perfectly and in time with the other dancers; and the audience was spell-bound. They received an outstanding ovation, and as they left the stage, the looks on their faces were of disbelief. "We did it! We did it!" They had done it!

That was my last meeting with the boys before they graduated to middle school. I left my card and encouraged them to maintain contact over the winter break and into the new year. Recently, I saw one of them at a neighborhood grocery store. He was almost as tall as me. I asked if he remembered the group. He smiled and said, "Shosholoza" (the South African chant). We shook hands, bumped shoulders, and went our ways.

In summing up this experience, in 10 months the boys went from rage to control, from conflict to cooperation. They were able to experience a Baba/mentor in an educational group setting with a cultural foundation. Their anger/rage issues were addressed through a series of positive lenses and strategies. At the end, they were exhibiting vastly improved social behavior and were able to spend more time in the classroom than out. One aspect that I found to be particularly valuable for them was having a consistent father image that focused on making them feel wanted, needed, and valued. It is clear that Black families need fathers including social fathers and serious mentors. Although there are many barriers facing Black fathers, we must accept the challenge of working with boys to bring them to healthy manhood. This includes helping them to realize that fatherhood responsibility includes the decision of not having a child until you can truly be responsible. Additionally, Black fathers must work with young fathers to teach them ways of rearing children to be healthy and successful, including ways of dealing with the mothers of their children in a prosocial and positive manner. To meet these challenges, we, as Black fathers, must continue to master ourselves in order to help prepare the next generation to understand and master themselves. The work is ongoing.

Conclusion

As noted at the beginning of the chapter, adult African American men (Babas) are needed to be present in the lives of boys to effect growth from boyhood to manhood (and then to fatherhood, ideally). And, as with the Black men in my life, they must *show up* to model appropriate behaviors, to teach responsibility, to demonstrate work behavior, and to "give back." When adult men are engaged and present, they can attend to the numerous teachable moments that youth present throughout the many daily interactions. These are critical opportunities during which life lessons can be shared and critical thinking skills can be learned. In this manner, young African American males can learn to make responsible decisions.

Additionally, Babas must know their own families and their own roots in order to impart the value of this information to youth. Knowledgeable adults can then aid the youth in finding themselves, their histories, and their importance to the community. In so doing, youth can discover their cultural roots and learn the value and utility of cultural rituals and customs, including the importance of naming. They can also learn to express themselves culturally through music (including rap and hip hop), dance, and social interactions.

It is critical to understand that young people feel and express hurt when fathers are not present. They are lost, angry, disappointed, confused, and often enraged—but they can respond positively to engaged, competent men functioning as social dads. Thus, men in the community must consider committing time, energy, and effort to come to the aid of our youth.

Each time that I am blessed with the opportunity to stand before a group of young folks or meet with some of them one-on-one, I am compelled to ask myself several important questions:

Can I impact this youngster's life in a deep, meaningful, and positive way?

Can I relay the crucial life lessons given to me by my father and other men in my life?

How will these young folks impact the community if they do not understand responsibility, culture, racism, or their roles within this society?

How can I help my young audience to be mindful of the consequences of out-of-control emotions, particularly their anger?

Are we, as fathers and elders, fully prepared to uphold the tradition of training the next generation to be strong, conscious, competent, creative men and fathers?

I believe the task of uplifting our communities lies in our hands. Like my grandfather, Ernest Neal, used to say, "Takin' care of business is better than beggin' for pardon." For our children's sake, let's take care of business.

Reflective questions

1. What role does culture play in the rearing of children? What specifically can Black fathers do?
2. What is the pain experienced by not having a father in one's life?
3. Discuss the African process of naming a child. What is the potential impact on the child?

References

Hilliard, A. G., III. (1986). Foreword. In N. Damali (Ed.), *Golden names for an African people*. Atlanta, GA: Black Wood Press.

Madhubuti, H. (1991). *Black men: Obsolete, single, dangerous? The Afrikan American family in transition*. Chicago: Third World Press.

Mentoring Center. (2010). *Mentoring Center Curriculum: An overview and information*. Oakland, CA.

Rose, T. (2008). *The hip hop wars*. New York: Basic Books.

chapter three

Daddy's baby girl
The overlooked story of reappearing fathers

Valata Jenkins-Monroe
Alliant International University
San Francisco, California

The African American father absence literature is often dominated by stereotypical assumptions and assumed negative outcomes for Black children raised in fatherless homes (Blankenhorn, 1995; McLanahan & Booth, 1991; Spencer, 1990). Clichéd descriptions of these children range from lower academic achievements and cognitive abilities to repressed socialization skills, while more negative assumptions have focused on long-term affective disorders, poor relationships, and a pattern of unavailability. The literature on the sons of these fathers has attracted the most attention and has highlighted themes of early juvenile delinquency, gang affiliation, truant behavior, and substance abuse, often leading to later adult criminal involvement (Dishion, Capaldi, & Yoerger, 1999; Gorman-Smith, Tolan, & Henry, 1999). More recent studies have focused on the impact father absence has on daughters' psychological and social development and have looked specifically at sex-role socialization, depression, and eating disorders (Nielsen, 2008).

Slowly, the acceptance of the changing family structure for many families—in particular, families of majority and higher social economic status—has helped to facilitate more studies integrating a methodological approach that is designed to look at resiliency and include more strength-based considerations (McAdoo, 1988, 1993; Zinn & Eitzen, 2005). More so, the demands for cultural inclusion and context have supported moving away from seeing the African American family from a deficit or pathological model to viewing their strengths (McAdoo, 1993). Shifting to examining and understanding the role the extended family may play in fatherless homes begins to unravel the more positive stories often ignored, and such a move begins to validate the maternal influence and role, that are time and again, only highlighted from a more at fault position.

Still, the literature is most lacking and meager in examining "absent" fathers that "reappear" and assume a primary parenting role in their child's life. There are some data to support that African American fathers are not as invisible or absent from the lives of their children as typically portrayed (Connor & White, 2006). Also, there is literature that explores fathers' absence due to illness, employment, imprisonment, deployment, and litigious separations and divorces. There is not as much discussion and exploration, however, when fathers' whereabouts are unknown during critical stages of their child's development, and the possible impact of reentry in their child's lives during other vital stages of growth.

The particular course and experience of having an "absent–present" father in my emergent ethnic and cultural identity as an African American girl, adolescent, and young woman is the subject of this chapter. Sharing my early developmental tasks, transitions, and possible gaps during my father's absence, while contrasting my developmental goals and responsibilities during the years of my father's presence, will provide a context for understanding our father–daughter relationship. The unique bond we developed and shared will be contrasted by my initial, early questions that lingered and subsequently haltered areas of my development. This period was followed by the confrontation and learning how to communicate and listen effectively to each other.

Who is my dad?/Where is my dad?

I didn't think about not having a dad in my home so much until the two questions were periodically posed by classmates: "Who is your dad?" and "Where is your dad?" Uncomfortable and embarrassed by the questions, I quickly learned to claim my dad as "dead"! My response halted the pending series of questions and silenced my peers. I was left, however, with a sense of guilt and feeling of being responsible for my dad's absence, in some way. The conflict between my strong spiritual and religious upbringing and morality about lying to my peers seemed to enhance my anxieties and uncertainty about my identity. I reason, after all, during my first nine years, I had no memories or recollections of a dad, as he had not been in my life since less than the age of 1 year. My uncle and older brother were my available father figures when needed; however, I relied and depended on the reassurance and comfort of my mother, aunts, and grandmother.

Described as quiet, shy, and somewhat of a "mother's baby girl," although I had three younger siblings, I would not openly acknowledge I missed having a dad. And yet, during my frequent, recluse reading and quiet moments, I often created a "dad" figure, which actively participated in my adventures and praised me for my accomplishments. I was good at pretending and role playing, and would secretly share my "report cards" and awards with my imaginary dad. My need to practice, pretend, and connect in some way with my absent father has been consistently documented as a critical developmental task in identity development (Hughes, 1995) and a constructive way in rehearsing relationships. On the other hand, periodically, I searched for photos as evidence that I once had a dad although I remember the rare occasion I was scolded by my mother for destroying a photo of my dad. Could I also have been angry with my dad for leaving me?

I was consistently praised for my academic achievements and pursuits and became more and more independent and determined to be the best. It was difficult for me to ask for help, as I interpreted that as not being "good or smart enough." I was particularly close with women teachers but hesitant of male teachers. I lived for school and all of the books that were available to me—until the third grade. For the first time, I had a male teacher and no longer looked forward to going to school. Somewhat perplexed about what was wrong with me, the principal suggested moving me to a different classroom. Reportedly, I immediately resumed back to myself, and the interpretation for the change in my behavior was believed to be related to class peers' teasing me, although there was no evidence of that. I was described as having strong peer relationships and viewed as a leader.

Although my similar reticence of boys and males was not viewed as a concern, years later, my mother shared my sensitivity to male voices as a baby and my inability to easily be consoled by close male relatives. She also shared her primary concern that her later decision to agree to a change in custody to my father was related to my uneasiness around men (with the exception of my brother and uncle). As I grew older, I simply learned to avoid interacting with boys and men, as I was primarily in a large extended family of women. I wasn't fully conscious of my disinclination toward male figures, although I distinctly recall the tension in my stomach and the uneasiness experienced in casual encounters with the opposite gender.

Although the initial absence of my father was before the age of 1 year, it is also conceivable that the possible lack of emotional availability from my father began at the time of my conception (Piaget, 1968). Could I have experienced the expression of anger between my parents in some way? (Cummings, 1989; Hawley, 1998). The anticipation and ambivalence of my birth, another baby or third child, within 6 months of my parents' second child, presented a strain in their relationship, as well as financial woes that seemed insurmountable for him. My father's initial decision to abandon the family to pursue employment opportunities was never part of my early understanding of his absence. As I developed, and both of my parents' lives took different courses, I lived in a fatherless world, certain I was not good enough, yet determined to prove that I was, until my dad reappeared when I was almost 10 years old.

Culturally competent models as overarching and alternative theoretical frameworks

With a growing interest in absent fathers, many researchers have attempted to identify variables that can help to explain the development and possible consequences on a child's development from more of a shortfall model. For example, specific aspects of girls' developmental penalty for missing fathers have included sex-role socialization difficulties, depression, eating disorders, substance abuse, sexual promiscuity, and low self-esteem. Not seeing the diversity and community resources within shortfall models has been the focus of Sue's (1998, 2005) cultural competence differential approach. The goal of Sue's approach includes cultural knowledge, distinguishing between generalization and individualization, and culturally specific expertise.

Culturally competent models allow for a comprehensive knowledge base of the absent dad and fatherless child that includes a historical understanding of the African diaspora. That is, the chronological root of being considered less than a man, racist practices and socialization of African men, along with a history of trauma, cannot largely be ignored, nor should it be the only explanation for choices that are sometimes selected by fathers (Gutman, 1976; Staples, 1986). It follows that the missing father cannot be viewed simply from models that are rooted in linear and cause–effect approaches. Instead, approaches that emphasize the importance of a developmental perspective that includes more cultural specific tasks and internal psychological processes impacted by a legacy of trauma, discrimination, and racism may begin to help us understand the absent–present fathers and abandoned daughters.

Attachment theory has largely been offered to explain that the fundamental development need and task for all human beings is to form emotional bonds (Bowlby, 1982). According to Bowlby, a primary function of attachment bonds is to ensure the natural survival of all human beings—to protect, comfort, support, and assist one another (Bowlby, 1988). Several studies have generalized the model to explain that disruptions in development occur when specific parenting styles emerge (Ainsworth, Blehar, Waters, & Wall, 1978); and, some generalizations are made that cross-cultural developmental demands have similar patterns.

What has been limiting by the attachment theory, however, are possible differences in cultural needs and tasks; requiring more restructuring and allowance for differential experiences in socioeconomic conditions, worldview ethos, family relationships, morality, spirituality and religion, and the critical role racial identity plays in the lives and relationships of African Americans. For example, the study of Black racial identity and self-esteem has helped to flush the essential aspects surrounding the development of self (GoPaul-McNicol, 1988; Harris, 1995; Tajfel, 1981). And yet, what continues to be a focus for several studies are the "penalties" in African American children with absent fathers; thus, lacking and limiting discussions on the culture's resiliency, strengths, and resources that have a valuable role in mediating father's absence and father's reentry.

To what level and extent does having a strong black racial identity and self-esteem become a protective factor for daughters in fatherless homes and in homes where fathers are present? What theoretical framework is offered to explain critical stages of development when there is a shift in the fundamental structure of the family? And, finally, what, if any, developmental stages and tasks are renegotiated when fathers reenter their daughter's course of development and a relationship is established?

Daddy's home

Almost 50 years ago to the date, I can vividly recall my father's homecoming and reappearance. With only 2 days before Easter, anticipation of the resurrection of Jesus, my Easter Sunday speech, and the Easter egg hunt monopolized my thoughts. The excitement of my younger sisters running to meet me with news about the "stranger" who bore gifts and awaited my arrival initially was difficult to comprehend, although, I distinctly heard, "Your daddy is here!" I didn't think about it; I simply ran as hard as I could, away from the direction of my sisters, around the corner, and into the safe arms of my grandmother. My grandmother helped me to dry my tears, allowed me to hold on to her tightly, and then told me to get into her car, as she was driving me home to meet my father. She continued to talk and share her joy and excitement about the Good Friday services we had just attended, while reminding me of God's forgiveness and God's plan.

Seeing my father with open stretched arms, a warm smile, and greeting me with "there's Daddy's baby girl," surprisingly, I didn't need very much coaxing or persuasion to greet my father. I was familiar with being called Mu Dear's baby girl, although technically, having three younger sisters, the reference was not accurate. That day was the first time, however, I was referred to as "Daddy's baby girl" and it felt perfect! I couldn't believe the immediate facial recognition and familiarity that checked out. That was, I had the same eye color, similar nose shape, and round face and could see myself in my father. The pastel Easter dresses and Easter candy were ideal gifts for sealing Daddy's homecoming.

Following the end of the school year and the start of the summer vacation, my older brother and sister and I were packed up and put on the Greyhound bus to visit my father and his new wife in upstate New York. My initial excitement about the lunch bag of fried chicken and pound cake, and mapping the historical landmarks we would see, gave way to the nervous stomach and anxieties about being away from my mom, grandmother, younger sisters, and host of relatives—the only relatives I had ever known. The few letters that were exchanged between my father and me in preparation for the visit did not reassure me that I would survive the bus trip, and more importantly, I didn't want to go!

Arriving in Buffalo, New York, I was convinced that I was definitely dreaming up all of this, as my world instantly began to change. There were a host of paternal relatives who welcomed us, and I immediately accepted and became attached to my stepmother and stepbrother, more easily than I did to my father. Consumed by all of the newness and exposure to opportunities that we were not previously afforded, the summer weeks quickly passed by, and I became more excited about the end of the vacation and returning back home.

Learning to trust

I'm not sure if it was the purchase of new beds, the school immunization updates, the new school supplies, or the transfer of school records, when it became obvious that we would not be returning "home." My protests were manifested by sleepless nights and cries in the dark. My stepmother and mother attempted to console me and tried to focus my attention on the "opportunities" that were now available to me. There was an attempt to manage my anxieties through a range of activities, including church choir, dance, school plays, charm school, and even speech therapy to help correct my more southern pronunciations. Daddy's baby girl, however, was deeply saddened and inconsolable, as my father's "homecoming" meant the loss of my mother and family.

With all of the attention given to keeping me busy and distracted, there was no formal recognition of the depth of my sadness, as my behavior seemed to suggest the opposite. I continued to excel in academics, was well-liked by my teachers, and had very good relationships with peers. I was viewed as the polite southern little girl with manners, who addressed adults as "Ma'am" and "Sir." Outwardly, I did not resist opportunities that were presented to me, as I also reasoned that I did not want to disappoint my mother, and felt guilty about my new environment and resources that my younger sisters did not have access to. I promised to be the "good girl" and relied on the flood of letters exchanged with my mother and grandmother. The letters always began and ended with a Bible scripture that I was encouraged to memorize.

Father–daughter relationship begins

I had little knowledge that my father was aware of the depth of my sadness, as I thought I hid it fairly well. Daily, he required me to assist or help him in the kitchen as he took pride and assumed primary responsibility for the preparation of our meals. During periods of my father's AWOL status, he shared with me that he was a short-order cook and chef in hotels and restaurants, throughout the Southern-Eastern Coast. Throughout the years, his story began to be uncovered, and I learned he was a chef in the army. He also spent a lot of time cooking with both his father and grandfather, who primarily raised him, as he lost his mother when he was a toddler. After his grandfather passed, there was less stability for him, and he found himself moving from one relative to the next, cooking for them in lieu of room and board.

In the kitchen, Daddy was almost a perfectionist and required the chopping of vegetables to be precise. He was an organic and naturalist cook before his time, as he preferred the use of fresh herbs and naturally grown vegetables. As we chopped together, he encouraged me to rely on my taste buds to determine what was needed or should be added to a dish. He was fascinated by what he stated was a natural cooking talent and ability for me, and we began to collaborate on newer versions of more traditional dishes. Daddy did not bake and valued my baking additions to the menu. He consistently praised and complimented me; all the while, our relationship began to unfold.

Continuing in the kitchen, and as an added practice for my charm school program, Daddy and I set the table and rehearsed the proper order of silverware and glassware. He taught me how to fold napkins into multiple designs and took pride in the presentation of the meal for the day. As precise as his cooking, Daddy was also particular about the cleaning of the kitchen. He seemed to enjoy cleaning the "eyes" of the stove and shelves in the refrigerator, as he demonstrated the art of cleaning.

As we either cooked or cleaned together, Daddy expressed interest in my readings and was fascinated by my ability to read for hours and be consumed by the characters in the story. He encouraged me to read excerpts from several books and often inquired about the various meanings of words. Daddy shared having missed a lot of school during his elementary years and how he struggled to learn to read at a later age.

Somewhat surprisingly, he shared being teased about his speech and his desire for me to not experience such teasing; this was the reason for the speech classes. He also shared his fascination in listening to my "long Easter speech" that I shared with him when we first met, and his subsequent desire for me to give speeches like those of Martin Luther King. He began to reward me by buying me a book periodically for my accomplishments, and weekly walked me to and from the library to check out and return books. We stayed away, however, from conversations and topics from the past, until the 10-year-old blossomed into the precocious teenager!

Confronting daddy: Our talk

Coinciding with adolescence and what our relationship could now handle, I was able to confront my daddy about his whereabouts the first nine years of my life. The timing wasn't too late or too soon but timely in the level of questioning I began at around the time of my menarche. Although I'm sure I wanted to be able to "confront" Daddy the first time I met him, how equipped was any 9-year-old to take on such a topic? Recall, I was also the polite, mannerable southern little girl, who was more concerned with pleasing others and being the good girl. I didn't plan to have our talk and during this developmental period, I had convinced myself I didn't even like cooking with him anymore; after all, "I wasn't the maid." My "mouth" is likely how it all began; that is, as most confrontations often start, the topic was rather benign.

Daddy seems to tolerate more verbal bantering with me than with my older sister, and it appeared I was given more latitude for being the daughter with "good grades." By the end of the brief exchange, however, Daddy told me, "You do what I say because I'm your daddy." It didn't take long before I was in an emotional spin and blurted out, "I didn't have a daddy for 9 years and don't need a daddy now!"

I'm not sure what actually saved me or why I'm not describing how I picked myself up off the floor ... but that's not what happened. My daddy did reach for me to gently hold me, as he began to cry. His story is a story that I thought was unique to him but now understand is a story of far too many African American men. Although the details are individualized, his journey parallels a history of marginalization, abandonment, minimal education, discrimination, racial identity, and his definition of masculinity.

Specifically, to answer my question, "Where were you?" Daddy first said he was "selfish" and was trying to find himself. At the age of 21 years old, he was the father of three children and didn't know how to be a father. He described working in temporary jobs, up and down the East Coast, until he was able to secure a "solid factory job, with benefits." He also shared feeling badly that he wasn't "providing for his children," and he didn't know how to "make good." Years later, he described feeling more prideful, competent, and "having something" to now give to his children.

"Our talk" ended for that day, when my daddy stated, "But, Baby Girl, I came back and I'm not going anywhere!" Our talk was only the beginning of many difficult conversations during my adolescence. And, I'm sure, from time to time, we both confronted each other about various topics. The ease and willingness, however, for my daddy to "go there" with his adolescent daughter, and not back away from these engaging but complicated conversations, largely contributed to my sense of self and confidence in relationships.

Daddy's advice

Throughout my adolescent years, Daddy didn't hold back on his opinions and advice. And, while he had a way of presenting his "perspective," he also had expectations that you would abide or follow his advice. My father was a young father of an adolescent daughter, just in his mid to late 30s, when I was told I was "beginning to feel myself." You see, when my daddy came back into my life, so it seemed went my early, young girl's reluctance and hesitation about the opposite sex. I was now being told by "boys" I was cute and was "feeling and acting as if I was cute." Daddy, however, made it clear that he knew the "intentions" of all boys, as he had stories about his own prowling, just a few years ago. He also made it clear that I was destined to attend a university, and boys and their "intentions" would simply distract and detour me. Initially, his perspective included the ideal age for dating was 16, but as I got closer to age 16, he thought it was probably a better idea to have "group dates" rather than one-on-one dates with a boy. Then immediately following my junior high school graduation and entry into the ninth grade, my daddy took me on my "first date."

I suspect my stepmother planned and organized my date with my daddy, although, I can't be certain. The date was during the fall/autumn season, just before the Harvest Feast and Halloween. I went to the beauty shop and had my hair "done"—washed, pressed, and curled. Daddy "arrived" to pick me up for an early dinner at 5 p.m. and brought me my favorite candy bar, "Mr. Goodbar," and a small autumn bouquet. He opened the car door for me and complimented me on how "nice" I looked and made note of my curls. We ate at one of his favorite steak restaurants in Niagara Falls, Canada, and our date ended with a visit to Niagara Falls—so much for my curls!

At the time, it didn't dawn on me that Daddy was giving me the "sex talk" and the "drug talk" while we toured Niagara Falls and while explicitly stating that I should never lower my expectations from the date we were having. "Boys will treat you the way you allow them to treat you" was the beginning motto that continues to ring in my head today. He also told me I was his "second" prettiest and cutest daughter—no longer was I being called "Daddy's baby girl." The main advice that evening, though, was that I was "smart"—smart enough to "always keep my legs crossed like a lady."

Lessons I learned from my father

If asked about lessons I learned from Daddy during my adolescent years, "my driving lessons" immediately come to mind. Obtaining my driving license was somewhat of my 16-year-old rite of passage and on the surface appears to be a mundane activity and desire of an adolescent. For my father, however, the "lessons" were opportunities for him to share his relationships with his father and grandfather, who informally taught him how to drive, at age 12. Even more so, my daddy shared stories about his own carelessness and recklessness while driving during his years of absence, resulting in his permanent physical disability (my dad walked with a limp). Although his many lectures for me were to be a "responsible driver," the theme of being a "responsible and productive" individual permeated the life lessons I learned beyond adolescence.

I sometimes interpreted the subject matter of "responsibility" as a way my daddy shifted his own responsibility to me. When asked or perhaps even expecting the new dress or new pair of shoes, my father made it clear that those were my "wants and desires" and not what was "needed." The countless stories I endured, and felt compelled to listen to, began to weave my understanding of his upbringing that included limited access to basic "fundamentals." Consistently, my daddy reminded me that he provided what was essential and the "extras or optional desires" required me to work for them. I don't remember a time that I didn't work for those most wanted items—from babysitting before junior high school to securing a job at the A&P grocery store as a checker at age 16. After all, although I was allowed to drive my father's car, I was expected to pay for half of my insurance, and the gas!

Perhaps even more powerful than the lessons on being responsible, although somewhat related, is Daddy's "race matter" lessons. Daddy was an active "union representative" in the plant where he was employed during all of my adolescent years. At the dinner table, he shared the latest union negotiations, and the significance and the role the union played in "helping to even out the playing field." My daddy was a strong supporter and active cardholding NAACP member, who closely followed and discussed the civil rights movement while making it clear that his expectations of me were twofold: "Always stand up for yourself" and "know you're somebody"!

Yes, sometimes I thought my father was too harsh and whispered he did not give me adequate credit for being as responsible as I was. One example that initially strained our relationship and put some distance between us was when I requested my father to "cosign" for my first, brand-new Volkswagen car. By that time, a sophomore, I was attending a university over 3,000 miles from home. As a full-time student with a GPA of 3.5, I worked two part-time jobs and had saved more than half of the purchase price for a brand-new Volkswagen Beetle. Given my young age, the dealership required a cosigner, which I assumed would not be a problem. My daddy often wrote encouraging letters to me and consistently complimented me for my tenacity and hard work. So, I was devastated when he told me he would not cosign for a "foreign car." He "lectured" against using credit and presented the "resale value" case, while suggesting the "used-car option"—all nonconvincing arguments for a 20-year-old. At that time, it only silenced me and pulled for my "determination," although my dad would likely say, my more "stubborn stance."

Years later and today, I would like to remember my apology conversation with Daddy, for not understanding what the "new car lesson" was all about. I don't think it ever happened, although I hope I demonstrated I got it! At some point, he spouted out that sometimes lessons are learned the hard way and through trials, and the best lesson is learning through your mistakes.

Conclusion

I didn't plan for this chapter to be a tribute to my daddy for reappearing in my life, but how can it not be, when the story is often overlooked or untold? Far too often, discussions about absent fathers have focused on the potential impact and challenges in their child's growth. The literature, however, has been sparse in examining the possible alterations or repairs in development, for both father and child, when fathers reappear and engage in their child's lives. Though Daddy had his "homegoing" almost 4 years ago, his presence in my life is daily pronounced in my multiple identities as a wife, mother, friend, sister, and professional.

Early on, the absence of Daddy was a part of my pretend world, as either he was dead or a part of my play. In either case, it was a way for me to validate my sense of self and value to the world. The nurturing, consistency, and continuity within my maternal models provided the basis for my identity; however, I experienced some apprehension and distrust of the opposite gender. On one hand, my close-knit environment evolved around my spiritual and religious upbringing and was a protective factor in my development. On the other hand, my interpretation of my religious beliefs may have contributed to my guilt and later difficulty in expressing anger more directly. Although my cognitive development was considered advanced and my social-emotional development appeared on track, some would argue my early sex-role socialization was injured by the absence of a father.

Although the focus of this chapter is not on maternal influences in my development, it is important to highlight their weight in my father's reentry into my life and in facilitating our father–daughter relationship. Recall, it was my grandmother who comforted me and wiped my tears while driving me home to meet my father. Later, both my grandmother and mother provided spiritual messages through the art of letter writing. And, whereas my mother fully understood my strong attachment to her, she also seemed to have the wisdom to recognize the potential role my father could play in my life. There were no formal court mandates or recommendations from psychological reports to direct or influence my mother's decision—only, what I was later told by my mother, her strong spiritual practices. Lastly, my stepmother clearly modeled and supported my father on how to parent. From encouraging my father to take me on my first date, to helping to soften him around my dating, to teaching him how to do the waltz for my first cotillion, amazing African American women strongly facilitated my father's reentry.

The timing of my father's reentry clearly altered the course of my development. From experiencing uneasiness, worry, and anxieties around the opposite gender, I gained the confidence to confront my father, while valuing and respecting our unique relationship. His initial patience and willingness to express his vulnerability largely contributed to my sense of safety and provided a trusting foundation for our relationship. More importantly, Daddy's desire to change his own course of development— that is, to be teachable while acknowledging his own limitations and to love and nurture while being emotionally open and available to me— validated his parenting capabilities. The benefit for me was in helping to shepherd me into an emotionally sound, competent, and successful daughter!

The overlooked story of a reappearing father, however, is told from the experiences and position of Daddy's baby daughter. So, how different, and in what ways, is the story told from Daddy's eldest daughter? What are the experiences of Daddy's only son and eldest child, who may have assumed a major fathering role during Daddy's absence? Even more, what's the impact for the siblings within a family with different dads when only one reappears or engages? Are there critical stages and tasks that are most impacted when reentry occurs during infancy versus preschool, school age versus preadolescence, and early adolescence versus late adolescence? To what extent does early bonding and attachment have on later rebonding? What are the possible ways maternal influence hinders or facilitates father's reentry? And, what are possible protective factors for the child for reentry fathers? Lastly, exploring the stories of African American father's messages around masculinity and the experiences of loss and racial trauma might begin to reframe our understanding of absent–present fathers.

Reflective questions

1. What is the impact of father absence on a daughter's development?
2. Can the possession of a solid African American self-identity mitigate the impact of father absence in daughters? Sons?
3. What is the impact of absent fathers (re)entering their children's lives? What issues should be considered?
4. Discuss the need to talk with one's children. Why do some parents find the task so difficult?

References

Ainsworth, M., Blehar, M., Waters, E., & Wall, S. (1978). *Patterns of attachment: A psychological study of the strange situation.* Hillsdale, NJ: Erlbaum.

Blankenhorn, D. (1995). *Fatherless America.* New York: Basic Books.

Bowlby, J. (1982). *Attachment and loss: Vol 1. Attachment* (2nd ed.). New York: Basic Books.

Bowlby, J. (1988). The role of attachment in personality development. In *A secure base* (pp. 119–136). New York: Basic Books.

Connor, M., & White, J. (2006). *Black fathers: An invisible presence in America.* Mahwah, NJ: Erlbaum.

Cummings, M. E. (1989). Children's responses to different forms of expression of anger between adults. *Child Development, 6,* 1392–1404.

Dishion, T. J., Capaldi, D. M., & Yoerger, K. (1999). Middle childhood antecedents to progressions in male adolescent substance use: An ecological analysis of risk and protection. *Journal of Adolescent Research, 14,* 175–205.

GoPaul-McNicol, S. (1988). Racial identification and racial preference of Black preschool children in New York and Trinidad. *Journal of Black Psychology, 14,* 65–68.

Gorman-Smith, D., Tolan, P. H., & Henry, D. (1999). The relation of community and family to risk among urban poor adolescents. In P. Cohen, L. Robins, & C. Slomkowski (Eds.), *Where and when: Influence of historical time and place on aspects of psychopathology* (pp. 349–367). Hillsdale, NJ: Erlbaum.

Gutman, H. (1976). *The Black family in slavery and freedom, 1750–1925.* New York: Pantheon Books.

Harris, H. W. (1995). Introduction: A conceptual overview of race, ethnicity, and identity. In H. W. Harris, H. C. Blue, & E. E. H. Griffith (Eds.), *Racial and ethnic identity: Psychological development and creative expression* (pp. 1–14). New York: Routledge.

Hawley, T. (1998). *Starting smart: How early experiences affect brain development*. Washington, DC: Zero to Three National Center for Infants, Toddlers, and Families.

Hughes, F. P. (1995). *Children, play, and development*. Boston: Allyn & Bacon.

McAdoo, J. L. (1988). Changing perspectives on the role of the Black father. In P. Bronstein & C. P. Cowan (Eds.), *Fatherhood today: Men's changing role in the family* (pp. 79–92). New York: John Wiley

McAdoo, H. (1993). Ethnic families: Strengths that are found in diversity. In H. McAdoo (Ed.), *Family diversity: Strength in diversity*. Newbury Park, CA: Sage.

McLanahan, S., & Booth, K. (1991). Mother only families. In A. Booth (Ed.), *Contemporary families: Looking forward, looking back*. Minneapolis, MN: National Council on Family Relations.

Nielson, L. (2008*). Between fathers and daughters: Enriching and rebuilding your adult relationship*. Nashville, TN: Cumberland House.

Piaget, J. (1968). *On the development of memory and identity*. Worcester, MA: Clark University Press.

Spencer, M. B. (1990), Parental values transmission: Implications for the development of African American children. In H. E. Cheatham & J. B. Steward (Eds.), *Black families: Interdisciplinary perspectives* (pp. 111–130). New Brunswick, NJ: Transaction.

Staples, R. (1986). *The Black family: Essays and studies*. Belmont, CA: Wadsworth.

Sue, S. (1998). In search of cultural competence in psychotherapy and counseling. *American Psychologist, 53* (4), 440–444.

Tajfel, H. (1981). *Human groups and social categories: Studies in social psychology*. New York: Cambridge University Press.

Zinn, M. B., & Eitzen, D. S. (2005). *Diversity in families* (7th ed.). Boston: Allyn & Bacon.

chapter four

Toward an African American agenda

Restoring the African American family and community

Gary L. Cunningham
Northwest Area Foundation
St. Paul, Minnesota

A visit from an old friend

In the summer of 2007, I had just begun my new job as the Vice President of Programs and Chief Program Officer for the Northwest Area Foundation. I had spent the summer working with the board of directors on developing a new strategic plan for the foundation that would focus on poverty alleviation and sustainable prosperity in rural, reservation, and urban areas of our eight-state region.* Around that time, I was paid a visit by an old friend and mentor, Dr. Joseph White. Dr. White and I had worked together from 1999 through 2005 to create the African American Men Project, which focused on the lives young African American men living in Hennepin County, Minnesota, specifically those living in the poorest communities in Minneapolis. Dr. White, at my request, came to talk about the lessons we had learned from this project and to think about what the next steps would be in rebuilding and repairing the breach within the urban African American community.

I met Dr. White in 1999, when a group from the University of Minnesota sponsored him for a book tour. Dr. White had just finished writing his

---

* The Northwest Area Foundation is dedicated to supporting efforts by the people, organizations, and communities in Minnesota, Iowa, North Dakota, South Dakota, Montana, Idaho, Oregon, and Washington to reduce poverty and achieve sustainable prosperity. These states were served by the Great Northern Railway, founded by James J. Hill. In 1934, Hill's son, Louis W. Hill, established the foundation.

landmark work, *Black Man Emerging: Facing the Past and Seizing a Future in America* (1999). The university folks had heard that I was beginning to work on the African American Men Project and asked if I was interested in cosponsoring the event. I had never heard about Dr. White, so I got a copy of his book and spent the weekend reading it.

I had surveyed a significant portion of the literature on the plight of African American men, and most of it painted a very negative picture. This was the first book that acknowledged the issues that Black men face, while painting a hopeful and realistic framework that "carved out a positive template of the Black male identity" (White & Cones, 1999, p. 4). I was very moved by the book, and the foundation for the African American Men Project was laid. I agreed to cosponsor the event and would be able to meet with Dr. White as a part of his visit.

As I think back to my first meeting with Dr. White, I remember a small-framed, caramel-colored man with large glasses, white hair, and an open gait. He had an almost undetectable swagger with a cool bump in his step, reminiscent of the brothers hanging on the corner that I grew up with. Not your typical psychology professor was one of my first thoughts.

Dr. White spoke on the "Seven Major Strengths of African Americans": improvisation, resilience, connectedness to others, spirituality, emotional vitality, gallows humor, and a healthy suspicion of White folks. His presentation was intellectually rigorous, entertaining, and deeply connected to the authentic experiences of his audience. Little did I know that Dr. White and I shared some deeper historical connections.

After his presentation, Dr. White talked about growing up in Minneapolis in the early 1930s and 1940s in the Seven Corners area. My family, like many African Americans at the time, also lived in the same segregated area of town. In our first conversation, off the top of his head, he named my mother and several of my uncles; there was no question we had a deeply rooted connection. Later, when I talked to my mother, she said, "You mean little Joe White? We all lived in the same building." It was remarkable. Here was a African American man from Minneapolis who started the University of California Educational Opportunity Program, which has helped over 300,000 students graduate and move on to professional careers; who was responsible for establishing one of the first Black Studies programs in the United States, at San Francisco State University; and who, in 1970, changed the field of psychology with his article in *Ebony* titled, "Toward a Black Psychology."

After our first meeting, I hired Dr. White as senior advisor to the African American Men Project. As he is always fond of joking, "Gary, you are keeping me out of assisted living." Dr. White's advice and counsel were instrumental in the many successes of this important project.

As Dr. White and I sat in the summer sun at a café in downtown Minneapolis in 2007, we conducted a postmortem of our work with the African American Men Project. Although the project continues to this day, it never quite reached the level of change that we had envisioned in those glorious and heady early years.

Who am I?

> My inquisitor was asking me to explain my exis-
> tence. Why was I successful, law abiding and literate,
> when others of my kind fill the jails, morgues, and
> homeless shelters? ... The only answer is life itself.
> (Staples, 1994, p. 256)

I was born on the west bank of the Mississippi River in Minneapolis, Minnesota, in 1957, in a hospital where I now sit on the board of trustees. My birth certificate says that I was born a Negro. The man listed as my father on my birth certificate was not my biological father. He and my mother were separated at the time, but not divorced, so I became Gary Leonard Cunningham. In many ways our nuclear family was no different from many of the families in the African American community at that time. My four siblings and I had different fathers, although that never seemed to matter much to us. We were very close in our formative years. My mother's parents, two generations out of slavery, moved from Muskogee, Oklahoma, to Minneapolis in 1946, as part of the Second Great Migration of African Americans. More than 5 million African Americans from the South migrated to northern industrial cities from 1941 to 1971.

My grandparents, like most African Americans of their generation, came to Minnesota to escape Jim Crow laws, the Klan, and sharecropping. They migrated like the Swedish, Norwegians, Germans, and Jews before them in order to make a better life for themselves and their children. My grandfather was a shift worker at Munsingwear clothing factory for over 20 years until his retirement and death soon thereafter in 1971. He supplemented his regular income developing a real estate business catering primarily to African Americans in the Twin Cities. My grandmother worked part-time as a maid and cook for wealthy White families. Together, they raised a family of six children on less than $9,000 a year in the 1960s. They owned their own home and car. Each of their children was required to take music lessons, to do well in school, and to be involved in the local church.

In 1985, while working on my first research project on the role of people of color and women in real estate occupations in Minnesota, I discovered that my grandfather was one of the state's first Black licensed realtors. In a subsequent study on people of color and women in construction occupations in Minnesota, I discovered that my great uncle was one of the first African American carpenters admitted into Carpenters Union 1644 in Minneapolis. This was not something that either of these two men talked about, let alone bragged about, at the time. However, these revelations were important to me as a young man. Realizing that some of the men in my family were trailblazers had a powerful influence on my own life. What I didn't realize at the time was that my grandfather was one of the positive male role models in my life as a boy growing up. He would take us boys to baseball and football games and family picnics. He would also provide discipline and guidance when we needed it. He provided for his family, and I never once saw him raise a hand against my grandmother.

Although I didn't live with my grandparents, the environment at my grandparents' house provided a stability that was elusive and fleeting at home. I remember being envious of my Uncle Charles who was 2 years older than I. He knew who his father was and had a relationship with him. He also had stability and normalcy, something I longed for as a young boy. Psychologist Joseph White refers to this phenomenon as "father hunger" (Schulte, 1990).

The male role models we see as young children establish patterns for our future lives and relationships. Most of the Black men I knew until I was about 13 years old were hustlers, pimps, and drug addicts. Being successful from their point of view was having a nice car, lots of women, very nice clothes, and a nice house. In some ways, these material trappings of well-being are no different from many that White middle-class people want to obtain. But people on the streets want to obtain the material goods and earthly pleasures by any means necessary. One has to ask the question, "Was it choice or necessity that some of these men became predators within their communities?" I would argue that it is the confluence of culture, policy, and economics that create the circumstances and the conditions for the perpetuation of intergenerational poverty: the lack of opportunity coupled with personal choice.

In his groundbreaking book, *Code of the Street: Decency, Violence, and the Moral Life of the Inner City* (2000), Elijah Anderson deciphers a complex code of rules that govern African American life in inner-city communities, and how these cultural norms give rise to frustrated ambitions and perpetuate the cycle of intergenerational poverty. Through his ethnographic study, Anderson acknowledges the impact of discrimination and institutional racism in shaping the culture of street life. He also convincingly demonstrates that street culture plays a significant role in the perpetuation of drugs, violence, and out-of-wedlock births. The struggle between raising a "decent family" and being part of the street culture is something many African American families grapple with.

Childhood memories

> Are black fathers necessary? You know, I'm old and I'm tired, and there are just some things I just don't want to debate anymore. One of them is whether African-American children need fathers. Another is whether marriage matters. You bet it does. Are fathers necessary? Damn straight we are. (Raspberry, 1998, p. 4)

One of my vivid early childhood memories is of my mother looking out the window of our small house in one of the poorest neighborhoods in Minneapolis. Outside, in the dead of winter, White men were standing around a backhoe digging up the street to turn off our gas main. That night my mother and her five children spent the coldest night of the year in the main room upstairs (which doubled as a bedroom I shared with my brother) under heavy blankets in front of a small electric space heater. In 1967, there was no cold-weather rule prohibiting poor families' gas from being shut off in winter. If you couldn't pay your gas bill, your heat was shut off. No questions asked, no consideration of your situation, and no regard for children in the home. Our water pipes would freeze and eventually we would be evicted. We would move to another poor area of town, and the pattern would begin again. Maybe next time the electricity would be shut off or we wouldn't be able to pay the rent.

We were always living on the edge, clinging to the bottom of the safety net. The welfare check never provided enough to support our family. We survived with some help from my grandparents and other relatives, with rummage sales for clothes and furniture, with food stamps and free and reduced lunches at school.

Growing up on welfare meant that we could expect a social worker to visit our home every month to make sure that there were no adult men living in the house. The social worker would walk through our house looking in closets and in drawers; nothing was off limits from her prying eyes. She would then ask my mother and us kids questions to deduce if an adult man was, or had been, present and living in our house.

From 1935 to 1996, the national welfare policy, implemented through the Aid to Families with Dependent Children (AFDC) program, disqualified two-parent families from living together and receiving welfare benefits (the "no adult men in the home" rule). For decades to come, this policy would have devastating, long-term, and unintended consequences for low-income African American families. In 1963, African Americans had one of the highest marriage rates in the country: 70%. Today, African American marriage rates are the lowest in the country: Approximately 43% of Black men and 42% of Black women in America have never been married. Between 1970 and 2001, the overall marriage rate in the United States declined by 17%; for Blacks, it fell by 34%. African American women are the least likely in our society to marry (Jones, 2006).

Harvard sociologist William Julius Wilson (1996) frames this issue as the lack of marriageable African American males (p. 96). In many urban communities, the industrial jobs dried up in the late 1960s and early 1970s. The dream of a northern promised land for African Americans would soon give way to the fact that America was moving from a producer to a consumer nation. The Rust Belt was beginning, and the service economy was in ascendance.

With little hope of employment, many low-income African American men were further marginalized, becoming invisible within their families and communities. At the same time, a fledgling educated African American middle class emerged, due in part to hard-fought civil rights legislation and to the riots that exploded across the low-income African American communities from 1968 through the early 1970s. This group began moving out of low-income Black communities and into more affluent urban areas. The formation of a new African American underclass and a new African American middle class were emerging simultaneously out of a once united, yet segregated, community.

A state of emergency

> Deutsh (1967) and Ward (1982) in contemplating the education of disadvantaged children imply that "disadvantaged" is not a homogeneous group. That is, within each group are great variations. This view is significant because it communicates that some black men as adolescents learn to be high achievers in an environment more challenging than most children face. Consequently, it reminds us that black mainstream is not a tangle of pathology. Rather it demonstrates a source for strength and resilience that is deeply rooted and viable against incredible odds. (Griffin, 2000, p. 5)

Education is one of the key passports to social and class mobility for a majority of African Americans. In his classic work, *A Theory of Justice*, the late philosopher and Harvard professor, John Rawls (1971, p. 101), eloquently elucidated why education is a critical component of social mobility: "The value of education should not be assessed solely in terms of economic efficiency and social welfare. Equally if not more important is the role of education in enabling a person to enjoy in the culture of his society and take part in its affairs, and in this way to provide for each individual a secure sense of his own worth."

My experience as a child growing up poor was one of continuous housing instability and school mobility; I attended four elementary schools, three middle schools, and two high schools in Minneapolis.

Patterns of housing segregation, housing instability, and school mobility are still prevalent today for many poor inner-city homeless or semi-homeless children. These factors have a significant impact on students' academic achievement and exacerbate the achievement gap. But mobility and housing instability are not the only issues impacting student achievement. Child readiness, teacher preparation, the curriculum, parent involvement, discipline, and reading and writing proficiency are salient issues for African American students in urban communities.

Even with my chaotic home life, I did well in school in my early years. I was always interested in learning and had a few great teachers who really took an interest in me and my education.

When I was 12 years old, the transition from boyhood to manhood was a very confusing time for me, as it is for most young men. I was having an identity crisis. In the nomenclature of psychology, "[C]risis refers to a period of emotional and mental stress that can lead to significant alterations in worldview in a limited time. For example, a crisis may lead to changes in group or peer associations, political beliefs, or engagement in risk-taking behaviors" (Spencer, et al. 2006, p. 636). The challenges of an identity crisis are opportunities to grow, and opportunity to demonstrate resilience.

As a young Black boy, things that I felt in my life regarding racial pride and social justice were incongruent with the images painted for me in the media, especially on TV. I would watch movies like *Tarzan*, *It's a Wonderful Life*, or *Holiday Inn* and see people who looked like me represented as savages, servants, or worse. Questions about who I was and what I wanted to be or what I thought I could be in this society were continuously present.

During adolescence, I began to understand that race mattered in the world. I began to understand that "racism is omnipresent, though often subtle: it is channeled through multiple levels of context. … It is inclusive not only of discriminatory behavior, but also of structural power relationships, political ideologies, and institutionalized practices, all of which can be normative, albeit unacknowledged, components of society. There are various and salient ways racism impacts lives, not only by disadvantaging people of color, but also by privileging White people" (Spencer et al., 2006, p. 643).

When I was 13, I ran away from home and lived on the street for a few months. This was one of the best things that had happened to me up until then. Soon after, I moved in with my Uncle Moe and his family. That environment gave me the stability I craved and the homeschooling I needed.

In the mid-1970s, on the heels of the civil rights and Black Power movements, there was a great deal of support for education within the African American community. Many African Americans were beginning to fill prominent roles in education in Minneapolis, including Richard Green, the first African American Superintendent of the Minneapolis Public Schools; Harry Davis, the first African American Chair of the Minneapolis School Board; and a host of dedicated administrators such as Bill McMoore, Marvin Trammel, Mel West, Joyce Jackson, and others. These trailblazers were critically important for many African American students in Minneapolis, including me. They pointed, by example, at what was possible and they opened the doors to educational opportunity for many of us at that time.

Under their leadership, I was able to participate in many opportunities that expanded my worldview, including the Urban Journalism Workshop, the National Close Up program, and the Central High School debate team. I was an editorial writer for the high school newspaper. These experiences were invaluable to my growth and development.

The cultural and community expectation was that you could and would achieve academically. This civic-centered focus on education served as a protective factor against the stereotypical threat many young African American adolescents face in today's academic settings.*

Much has changed in the intervening years. A number of factors have converged, creating a cumulative impact on the social and human capital development within low-income, urban African Americans communities. Some of these factors include the flight of middle-class African Americans and Whites from low-income urban areas, which, in turn, has significantly increased the concentration of poverty; the loss of a once vibrant family structure in low-income African American communities, exacerbated by the legacy of national welfare policy; the dislocation of economic opportunity afforded to the early generation through manufacturing jobs; and continued patterns of structural discrimination in

---

* *Stereotype threat* refers to being at risk of confirming, as self-characteristic, a negative stereotype about one's group. This term was first used by Steele and Aronson (1995), who showed in several experiments that Black college freshmen and sophomores performed more poorly on standardized tests than White students when their race was emphasized. When race was not emphasized, however, Black students performed better and equivalently with White students. The results showed that performance in academic contexts can be harmed by the awareness that one's behavior might be viewed through the lens of racial stereotypes.

housing, access to credit, and employment opportunities. As so aptly stated in the 9-11 Commission report, "a large, steadily increasing population of young men" has been created, "without any reasonable expectation of suitable or steady employment—a sure prescription for social turbulence" (9-11 Commission Report, 2007, p. 54).

Some have argued that the logical choice for many disadvantaged, young African Americans with bleak futures and very few economic opportunities is to turn to activity marked by violence and the lure of more lucrative payoffs (Phillips, 1997). Some statistics bear this out:

Among men, Blacks (28.5%) are about 6 times more likely than Whites (4.4%) to be imprisoned during their lifetime. Among women, 3.6% of Blacks and 0.5% of Whites will enter prison at least once.

Homicide is now one of the leading causes of death for African American men. More often than not, the perpetrator is also African American. In fact, the data on all violent crimes (e.g., rape, homicide, assault) demonstrate that violent crimes are primarily intraracial: Both victim and offender are of the same race.

For every 1% increase in the level of Black male unemployment, the homicide rate increases by 1.28 per 100,000 (Western, 2006).

Over twice as many African American men are in prison (1 million) than in college (less than 500,000). In contrast, with only 600,000 White men in prison and 3.5 million in college, there are 5.8 times as many White men in college as in prison.

Nearly one in three (32%) Black males, age 20 to 29, is under some form of criminal justice supervision on any given day—in prison or jail, on probation or parole.

If there is a case to be made for a state of emergency, this is it!

The African American community must muster the political will to restructure its civic and cultural institutions. African Americans must begin to rebuild their fragmented leadership structures and begin to build a new civic infrastructure. The consequences for failure are clear.

Leadership matters

When we teach, write about, and mode the exercise of leadership, we inevitably support or challenge people's conceptions of themselves, their roles, and most importantly their ideas about how social systems make progress on problems. Leadership is a normative concept because implicit in people's

> notions of leadership are images of a social contract. Imagine the differences in behavior when people operate with the idea that "leadership means influencing the community to follow the leader's vision" versus "leadership means influencing the community to face its problems." (Heifetz, 1994)

The call to action in the final report of the African American Men Project asks African Americans to put aside our individual and personal differences and to work toward collective, transformational solutions. It is in this way that we can build the coalitions and alliances necessary to create a better future for all people in our community. There is a need for common agendas among African American leaders and within the African American community as a whole. Without them, it will be impossible to forge concerted and courageous solutions. The issue of low-income African Americans living in ghettoized, concentrated poverty will not be addressed using old thinking or old ways of doing business.

Historically, the African American community, through much sacrifice, has played a vital role in helping this country live up to its highest democratic values and principles. We are at another critical juncture, as we grapple with a deep recession. We should each ask ourselves, Did Dr. King die so that half of us would make it and half of us perish? (Gates & West, 1996, p. xvii) (Leadership, particularly African American leadership, is at the heart of this question.)

According to Simon J. Buckingham (2003),

> wicked problems cannot be easily defined so that all stakeholders agree on the problem to solve; require complex judgments about the level of abstraction at which to define the problem; have no clear stopping rules; have better or worse solutions, not right or wrong ones; have no objective measure of success; require iteration—every attempt to build a solution changes the problem; often have strong moral, political or professional dimensions, particularly for failure. (Buckingham, 2003, p. 12).

In the African American community, systemic intergenerational poverty has persisted despite a plethora of nonprofit organizations and social services, and decades of programmatic responses. There are no easy answers. People of goodwill have been working for many years to address some of these "wicked" problems within inner-city America. Not only do the problems persist but they have become deeper and more embedded.

Further complicating the leadership question in the African American community is who is considered a leader. Many individuals hold positional power or might appear on the list of *Ebony* magazine's 100 Most Influential Blacks. Although counted as African American leaders, many do not exercise leadership in, or for, the African American community. In the past, it was assumed that if you were an elected Black official, your base of support came primarily from the African American community. Today, as we have moved from the era of civil rights to the age of Obama, we can no longer make this assumption. In their seminal work, *Bibliography of African-American Leadership,* Walters and Johnson (2000) state, "There is no era in which black leaders or their organizations did not play a central role in the advancement of the black community, although as indicated in our study, it is also clear that the because whites have access to the monopoly of power, they had exercised far more leadership of the black community than blacks themselves" (p. xxi).

In cities across the country, I have witnessed fragmentation and polarization within local African American communities and their leadership. Some of these differences are due to differences in philosophy and approach; some are exacerbated by competition for limited resources. Part of the fragmentation is also based on egos and power relationships of old guard leaders versus new, emerging leaders. The fragmentation and polarization are continued impediments to advancing a united agenda to improve the conditions of low-income African American people.

These issues have become so explosive that, in many situations, African Americans with different philosophical approaches are physically intimidated, harassed, and castigated by individuals who have no legitimate constituencies in the African American community, other than they happen to be African American. It then becomes impossible to hold a civil dialogue or seek common ground. Many of these individuals spend their time treating other African American people as enemies, but have very limited track records of making a difference for the community of which they purport to be a part. Unless bridges can be built to move from transactional, zero-sum relationships to transformational solutions, many low-income African Americans will remain in a prisoner's dilemma, trapped in the cycle of intergenerational poverty.*

The role of religious leaders is a critical component of leadership within the Black community, both historically and currently. This is true

---

* The prisoner's dilemma is a fundamental problem in game theory that demonstrates why two people might not cooperate even if it is in both their best interests to do so.

whether one focuses on African American leadership that developed out of slavery, the civil rights movement, the Black power movement, or the present-day issues of racial profiling and disparities.

Today, African Americans now hold prominent positions in nonprofit organizations, government, arts, business, education, and philanthropy. Combining the historic leadership of the clergy with the emerging leaders in government, business, and the nonprofit sector could create a potent force in building bridges toward a common agenda within the African American community.

In a powerful and prescient essay, "The Future of the Race," Henry Louis Gates, Jr., and Cornel West (1996) identify areas where common agreement among African American leaders may be forged. They write:

> Not to demand that each member of the black community accept individual responsibility for her or his behavior—whether that behavior assumes the form of black-on-black homicide, violations by gang members against the sanctity of the church, unprotected sexual activity, gangster rap lyrics, misogyny and homophobia—is to function merely as an ethnic cheerleaders selling woof tickets from the campus or the suburbs, rather than saying the difficult things that may be unpopular with our fellows. Being a leader does not necessarily mean being loved; loving one's community means daring to risk estrangement and alienation from that very community, in the short run, in order to break the cycle of poverty, despair, and hopelessness that we are in, over the long run. For what is at stake is nothing less than the survival of our country, and the African-American people. (p. xvi)

This is the call for leadership in the African American community—to find leaders from all our sources of strength who are able and willing to lead on community issues among all people, with a message of responsibility and civility, whether popular or not.

The second half of the story

> The hero is introduced in his ordinary world, where he receives the call to adventure. He is reluctant at first but is encouraged by the wise old man

or woman to cross the first threshold, where he encounters tests and helpers. He reaches the innermost cave, where he endures the supreme ordeal. He seizes the sword or the treasure and is pursued on the road back to his world. He is resurrected and transformed by his experience. He returns to his ordinary world with a treasure, boon, or elixir to benefit his world. (Campbell, 2010)

The quest to know where I came from and the people I was connected to began one summer afternoon when I got a call from a great-uncle in his late 80s on my mother's side of the family. Uncle Otis said he wanted to stop by my house, that he had something to give to me. It was highly unusual for Uncle Otis to ask to stop by out of the blue. I was surprised and didn't know what to expect.

When he pulled up to the curb a short time later (he was still driving at age 89), he carried a long scroll of paper and what looked like some very old photographs. We hugged, and without sitting down, my Uncle Otis started talking about our family history. It felt like a prepared speech, each word of the narrative rehearsed and memorized in the tradition of an oral history. He then presented me with the scroll he held as if he were performing a ceremony of grave seriousness and importance. My Uncle Otis was letting me know, in no uncertain terms, that he was passing down sacred family heirlooms to my trust and care for the next generation.

He told me that the photographs were of my great-grandmother and grandfather (on my mother's side). He then gave me a list of all of my relatives, with addresses and phone numbers, from around the country. I unrolled the scroll onto my dining room table. There before me was a very finely crafted, hand-drawn family tree that depicted my great-grandparents, grandparents, and their siblings, all the way down to me and my own siblings. It was as if the torch had been passed of some unidentified responsibility.

Several days later, as I looked at my family tree, it dawned on me that nothing connected me with my father's side of the family. That place on the family tree where my father was supposed to be was empty, unknown, and even scary. It was on that day that I began my quest to find my father.

I never knew my father. Whenever I would ask my mother about him, both as a child and as an adult, she would close up and refuse to talk. My grandmother would tell stories about my father when I was young. I could tell that she liked him. From her I learned his first name, where he worked in Minneapolis, and some of his accomplishments.

These clues, buried in my memory, proved helpful in my journey to find my father. Through them, I learned that he lived in Minneapolis until 1972 and that he had another family. I later learned through a friend of a friend of my father's that he had moved to Jackson, Mississippi, three decades ago. I thought he was probably dead. He was born in 1922 and few African American men live to be 80.

After many false trails and dead ends, I found what I thought were his current phone number and address. I wrote him a letter and introduced myself. I told him what I knew about him and asked if he was indeed my father.

A week later he called me. "Yes," he said, "I believe I'm your dad. I had an affair with your mother for about a year back in the 1950s. But when we broke up, I didn't know she was pregnant. We never ran into each other after we split, and she never told me a kid was involved."

I said to this man, whose first name was Robert, "I'd like to come and see you." At first he hesitated, because he had a wife and 10 other kids, all of whom he'd surely have to tell about me. But after we talked for an hour or so, he agreed to meet.

Two months later, I drove to Jackson, Mississippi, and he and his wife, Lillian, came to my hotel. At first, Robert and I sat there for a long time, looking at each other. Both of us thought we didn't look much alike. "Your nose seems big. What size shoe do you wear?" Still, it wasn't long before the three of us were exchanging stories, filling one another in, and laughing together. We found ourselves revisiting our separate pasts through one another. We talked for 7 hours, finally calling it a night at 3 a.m.

Before I left Jackson, Robert and I took a DNA test to determine beyond a reasonable doubt, that I was in fact his son. The results took several days to arrive, and I had already returned to Minneapolis when Robert called and said, "Looks like you're in the family."

Meeting my dad and Lillian provided some wonderful closure for me. I now knew, quite literally, who I was. Yet I felt another door opening at the same time. It was a quest fulfilled—my own personal version of Joseph Campbell's monomyth, the hero's journey of separation, initiation, and return that culminates in personal transformation and ends back home with family.

A few days after I learned the test results, I got a call from my new sister, Delia. "I'm so happy to have a new brother," she said. She was coming up to Minneapolis for a wedding and wanted to meet me. We agreed to have lunch at the Mall of America.

When I arrived at the restaurant, it was nothing less than a grand homecoming. Unbeknownst to me, my new sister had invited several other local relatives—even my new niece and nephew. Our lunch became a celebration, welcoming me to the family.

I discovered that the neighborhood man I saw every morning when I walked my dog was my brother too. He lived only four blocks away.

By now I've met or talked with most of my new siblings, and everyone has been enthusiastic, delighted to meet me, and as welcoming as a sister or brother can be. And every one of them has told me, "Gary, we're so glad to get to know you. We want you to be part of us."

At age 47, I was restored to my family.

For over 40 years, I had been isolated from half of my biological family. Its blood was in me well before my birth, and I belonged to it from the day I was born. Yet neither I nor my relatives knew this. Each of us knew only half the story—the official, public half—about our own family. It was a big relief—and a bigger blessing—to finally meet my lost family members, to discover all that we had in common, and to be welcomed into the group that, paradoxically, I had been a part of all my life.

Many young African American men live with a similar paradox. They seem isolated from their communities and from mainstream culture, hanging out on the street corner while much of the rest of the world hurries past and disapproves. Yet what appears to be isolation is, in fact, a form of collective blindness. Neighbors see these men as problems. City and county governments see them as users of our social service and criminal justice systems. And many of these men see themselves as outside the mainstream of American life.

But all of this is simply the result of knowing only half the story—the half that focuses on failure instead of success and on delivering government services instead of building personal power and responsibility.

Connecting the dots

About a year after finding my father, he invited my son and me to a family reunion in Jackson, Mississippi. This reunion was not only powerful—I met my father's family for the first time—it was also transformational. It was there, for the first time, that I really understood what it meant to be a descendent of slaves.

Slavery for life was legal within the United States from 1654 until 1865. Twelve million Africans were shipped to the Americas from the 16th to the 19th centuries. Of these, an estimated 645,000 were brought to the United States. The slave population in the United States had grown to 4 million by the 1860 census.

Slavery was a brutal system throughout the United States, and it was particularly brutal in Mississippi, where my father's people are from. According to David J. Libby (2004), in his book, *Slavery and Frontier Mississippi, 1720–1835*, "Some Mississippi slaves resisted this grim oppression and rebelled by flight, work slowdowns, arson, and conspiracies. In

1835 a slave conspiracy in Madison County provoked such draconian response among local slave holders that planters throughout the state redoubled the iron locks on the system. Race relations in the state remained radicalized for many generations to follow" (p. 208).

Being raised in Minnesota, I would hear my grandparents talk about slavery. I had read a quite a few books and taken courses on the "peculiar institution." I had also watched *Roots* on TV with millions of other Americans in the 1980s. But I really had only an abstract view of slavery. It was somehow remote and distant from me. Slavery was part of my history, surely, but not a part of who I was in my day-to-day existence.

That was all about to change as we gathered on the bus that hot summer day in Jackson, to be transported back in space and time to the small town of Bolton. As we drove the short way down the highway toward Bolton, the cotton fields stretched on as far as the eye could see. I thought of the struggles and the back-breaking toil of human beings picking cotton. I thought about the generations of African Americans who were owned as property by other human beings and had no rights and no opportunity to make choices about their lives.

Bolton, like many other small southern towns, was a sleepy village of mostly African Americans. They were friendly and polite and made you feel welcome. We stopped at a little church called Chapel Hill and piled out of the bus—over 100 of us, of all ages and generations. Once we were settled in the pews, my father walked up to the front of the altar and led us in prayer. He then began to recite a few great stories from the Bible. My father is known for being a great storyteller and is invited to local churches throughout Mississippi to do so. It was a real treat.

After he finished storytelling, he provided a historical reference about what Bolton and the church we were sitting in represented to our family. He said that while it was a relatively new church, it sat on the foundation of his childhood church, when he was a child and a sharecropper on this land. He talked about his father, Daniel, a local minister, sharecropper, community leader, and street lawyer for many of the African American residents of Bolton and surrounding communities. He talked about my great-grandfather, Papa (pronounced Pa-pay), who was a slave on the same land. He was known throughout the community as a good man. Sometime later, I asked my father what that meant. He said, "Papa was somebody that was known to help out the community in times of need, someone who would go out of his way for others and someone who would fight against injustice in the face of overwhelming odds." My heart swelled with pride and emotion.

After we finished in the church, we walked around back to a small cemetery where my ancestors are buried. Only a few had tombstones; most were marked by a tree or a rock. My dad or another relative would point to a spot and let us know who was buried there. My son and I wept along with all of my new relatives. Standing with the sun beating down on the cotton fields, in the cemetery where my people were slaves, I was finally able to connect the dots and understand the power and the sacrifice my ancestors made so that I could be here today. I also understood on that day the significant debt that I owed to be worthy of this legacy.

I am the fourth generation of my family out of slavery. That history and that suffering is a part of who I am. It is not something I want to forget, nor is it something I need to forget and just move on, as some would suggest. It is something that drives me to ensure that all people—regardless of race, culture, sexual orientation, or religion—have equal access and opportunity in this country. It motivates me to ensure that the next generations of African American children are better off than the present generation. Justice and equality matter; they are fundamental principles of human rights and dignity.

A new beginning

> Why are we here? We are community, gathering itself together—a spiraling movement, a rippling force, a cascading waterfall. We can be a circle of unity to envision the community we want to see, to declare our power together.
>
> We have gathered its people since the beginning of time—and now together in the relationships and efforts this forum is inspiring—we have been, and we are now, organizing to act—to create our future. Because, in our minds, in our spirits we have always known that, as Malcolm X put it, "the future belongs to those who prepare for it today." (Carter, 2009)

As Dr. White and I reminisced about the African American Men Project that summer day in 2007, a new idea began to germinate between us. We realized that one of the key lessons learned involved the need for African American leaders to become engaged, to devise their own solutions to the issues confronting the African American community. We began anew to think about how to construct a movement of African American people who were resolute in their determination to address not only the issues of African American men but African American women as well. In fact, the issues of African American men are inextricably linked and intertwined with those of African American women. We determined to take a more holistic approach.

Dr. White and I postulated that there has been a significant rise in the percentage of African Americans who have moved into the middle class in the past two decades. Unlike prior decades, African Americans now hold prominent positions in nonprofit organizations, government, arts, business, education, and philanthropy. Dr. White and I felt that if we could galvanize these leaders toward a common agenda—one that was not directed by government or county services, but developed and owned by the leaders themselves—then we could begin to build the basis for a new movement within the African American community.

We decided to test our hypothesis by hosting 3-hour luncheons at my house once a month, on Saturday afternoons. These luncheons began in January 2008 and were sponsored by the Northwest Area Foundation. We invited 15 middle-class African American men from different walks of life and different age groups. Some were young and others were more seasoned. They included a newspaper reporter, the head of an economic development group, several psychologists, a preacher, the vice president of a university, an attorney, the head of a local social service agency, a city council member, and several academics.

Dr. White facilitated the discussions, which began by identifying the major values of African Americans. We then began to talk about the nature of leadership and about structuring a common agenda that would allow us to address many of the issues in the African American community. There was a lot of tension in the room. Some members wanted to do something right away; others wanted to have more discussion so that we could agree upon an approach before we began to act. We didn't even agree on what the issues were.

There were some meetings when only seven to nine members would show up. But slowly, momentum started to build. We began to hold each other accountable for both attendance and participation. We began to share our stories. We went through a process of values clarification. We began to bond, and a deep camaraderie soon developed among us. The group took on the unofficial name, the Band of Brothers.

Within 6 months, the group had grown to 20 regular members and moved from my home to the Northwest Area Foundation offices. Over 14 three-hour planning sessions, from December 2007 through January 2009, the Band of Brothers focused on everything from relationship-building and organizing our time to discussions of commonly held values, civic engagement, and community building. The discussion focused not only on crafting an agenda but on how to utilize technology and how to present a tentative agenda to the community and build support.

The Band of Brothers agreed that the major goal of our group was to maximize the potential of African American children. We started to envision an agenda for the African American community, one that contained 5 to 10 fundamental principles that we could agree on, as a people, regardless of what else we disagreed about. Subcommittees were formed to focus on key issues such as education, economic and community development, and family structure. The subcommittees researched each of these areas and brought their ideas back to the group for review and feedback.

At the same time, Dr. White and I started thinking about how we could include women in the equation. I contacted Dr. Yvonne Cheek, whom I have known for many years and who has been a valuable consultant in many other endeavors. I provided Dr. Cheek with the background materials that the Band of Brothers had been working on and asked her to coordinate a series of meetings with about 20 well-known and influential African American women in the community. She put together multiple lists of women, many of whom had done extraordinary service for the African American community and were considered heroes. Others were young, energetic, up-and-coming leaders. Dr. Cheek organized meetings with the help of Cherie Collins, a doctoral candidate at the University of Minnesota. The women's group was charged with reviewing the Band of Brothers draft and developing their own approaches to address issues within the African American community.

The women's group took off. Starting with their first meeting, they asked themselves: Why haven't we ever gotten together like this before? The shared intergenerational knowledge, the ability to talk about common conditions for low-income, African American people, and the realization that each of us owes some part of our success to those who came before all galvanized the group into developing their own ideas about an African American agenda.

We then brought the two groups together to discuss the similarities and differences between their approaches. This meeting of 42 African American leaders became the Twin Cities African American Leadership Forum. Its main goal was to engage African American community leaders in an intentional dialogue to develop a common agenda to do the following:

Mobilize and support community-driven efforts to own (on an individual, institutional, or collective basis) and act on a common agenda to improve the economic and social well-being of the African American community.
Work with leaders to develop a holistic and shared plan that addresses the most critical issues affecting the individual, family, and community wellness of African American people.

Build capacity among community leaders for collective action and community problem-solving.

Identify and leverage the experience, credibility, and influence of community leaders for collaborative efforts and sustainable community change.

Create opportunities for new partnerships and collaborative efforts.

The first meeting of the African American Leadership Forum in April 2009 was moving and inspirational. The keynote speaker was Minnesota Congressman Keith Ellison, who talked about a global paradigm shift in thinking about race and ethnicity. He urged the group to move beyond just thinking locally and to expand our thinking to include a global context. He summoned a group to move out of their silos to maximize our influence on politics and public policy. A number of elder and senior leaders talked about African American leadership in the 21st century. Young leaders were also invited to speak. That day we began to frame a new agenda for the African American community.

The Twin Cities African American Leadership Forum has now grown from 42 members to over 300 members. Forums are now being held in Portland, Oregon and Seattle, Washington. A new forum is now developing in Des Moines, Iowa.

The comprehensive agenda emerging from this process is a product of the community; it is defined and outlined by its leaders. It reflects efforts to heal the rift that has existed between middle-class and low-income African Americans. It is clear that we have a common agenda and a common purpose as a people.

Leaders are now working together across nonprofit, governmental, academic, and business silos to craft an agenda for the urban, African American community in the northwest part of the United States for the 21st century.

It is clear that we have tapped into a deep yearning within African Americans to use their skills, abilities, and knowledge in a collaborative effort to improve the lives of all African American people. As I watch very busy and engaged people give large amounts of their time and emotional energy to this effort, I am moved and humbled. It is clear that we all are motivated to give back something and to build a better future.

The key lesson from the African American Men Project for me was that African American people must galvanize their own power and take charge of their destiny. We have a long way to go before we can determine whether this effort is sustainable, but early indications are promising.

We begin again; out of the ashes of what was, each of us takes up the mantle that was laid down before us. We strive to make the world a better place, not only for ourselves but for our descendents. The breach that was created in the African American community between middle- and low-income African Americans can be healed. Families can be restored. Our children can move from the bottom of the class to the top. Our men can become productive citizens, rather than languish in the criminal justice system. We can set the standards for the next generation. The time is now.

Conclusion

There has been much written about the plight of African American men in recent years. A majority of the literature focuses on programmatic approaches to address long-standing issues of incarceration, unemployment, and underemployment and a host of other social malaise from health disparities to community violence. Like the blind men feeling different parts of the elephant, each describes a different reality and none can see the whole. In many ways, the fragmentation of the literature is a reflection of the fragmentation within the African American community itself.

Much has changed in the past 24 years since William Julius Wilson published his seminal and controversial book, *The Truly Disadvantaged* (1987). Wilson postulated that the decline of the African American family structure is due, in part, to the lack of marriageable African American men.

Although there remains a significant African American underclass today, African American men and women are also strategically positioned in business, government, education, and nonprofit sectors. As a result, these leaders are uniquely positioned to begin the process of changing fragmented relationship structures and the institutional arrangements that maintain the underclass. This provides an opportunity for the African American community to create a new transformational culture and an economic renaissance.

The story of the African American community is also more than just a macroeconomic theory or programmatic responses addressing the vestiges of discrimination and denied opportunity. It is also a human story. And for many African American men that grow up without their fathers, it is a story of deep pain and sometimes redemption.

This chapter shares the story of the creation of the African American Men Project in Hennepin County, Minnesota, and its evolution into the African American Leadership Forum in four urban communities in the United States, against a backdrop of the author's parallel personal journey to find his father and his identity.

Reflective questions

1. Seven strengths of Black males are discussed. What strengths are reflected? Do you agree that these strengths are required? Any others?
2. Cunningham writes about the "State of Emergence for Black Children." Why are some poor Black children successful and others not? What makes a difference for these children?
3. What is the relationship between the history of slavery and the conditions for many African American people today? Are there connections; if so, what are they?
4. Cunningham asserts that there is a need for common agendas among African American leaders and within the African American community. Do you agree with this statement? What would be different in the African American community if there were such a common agenda?
5. The issue of dissention among the "leaders" is discussed. What does this entail, and why is it so important?

Acknowledgments

This chapter would not have been possible without the guidance and mentoring of Dr. Joseph White and Dr. Michael Connor. Joe and Mike have made enormous contributions to uplift African American men, including me. I am also indebted to colleagues Jesse Bower and former National Urban League fellow Eileen Aparis, who each provided support and feedback throughout this project. The *Minneapolis Star Tribune* was also instrumental in allowing me to post portions of this chapter as part of their Your Voices blog at http://www.startribune.com/yourvoices/Gary_Cunningham.html. The feedback and encouragement I received from Your Voices helped to improve portions of this chapter immensely.

References

Anderson, E. (1999). Code of the street: Decency, violence, and the moral life of the inner city. New York: W. W. Norton

Campbell, J. (2010). A Practical Guide to *The Hero with a Thousand Faces* http://www.skepticfiles.org/atheist2.htm (accessed May 2010). Originally published 1949, 1968, 1973, Princeton University Press.

Carter, T. (2009) African American Leadership Forum Speech. Nov. 21.

Gates, H. L., Jr., & West, C. (1996). *The future of the race.* New York: Knopf.

Griffin, S. T. (2000). *Successful African-American men from childhood to adulthood.* New York: Kluwer Academic.

Heifetz, R. A. (1994). *Leadership without easy answers.* Belknap Press/Harvard University Press, p. 14.

Jones, J. (2006, March 26). *Marriage is for White people. Washington Post, Sunday Outlook.*

Libby, D. J. (2004). *Slavery and frontier Mississippi, 1720–1835*. University of Mississippi Press.

National Commission on Terrorist Attacks Upon the United States. (2007). The 9/11 Commission Report: Final Report. Washington, DC: US Government Printing Office.

Phillips, J. A. (1997). Variation in African-American homicide rates: An assessment of potential explanations. *Criminology, 35*, 527–560.

Raspberry, W. (1998). Turning the corner on father absence in Black America. The Morehouse Conference. http://www.americanvalues.org/turning_the_corner.pdf. (accessed Feb. 7, 2011).

Rawls, J. (1971). *A theory of justice*. Cambridge, MA: Belknap Press/Harvard University Press.

Schulte, A. J. (1990). Naming the "father hunger": An interview with Richard Rohr. Retrieved from http://www.malespirituality.org/father_hunger.htm

Spencer, M. B., et al. (2006). Understanding vulnerability and resilience from a normative developmental perspective: Implications for racially and ethnically diverse youth. In C. Chiccetti & D. J. Cohen (Eds.), *Developmental psychopathology: Vol. 1. Theory and method* (pp. 627–672). New York: Wiley.

Staples, B. (1994). *Parallel time: Growing up in Black and White*. New York: Pantheon Books.

Steele, C. M., & Aronson, J. (1995). Stereotype threat and the intellectual test performance of African Americans. *Journal of Personality and Social Psychology 69*(5), 797-811.

Walters, R. W., & Johnson, C. (2000). *Bibliography of African American leadership: An annotated guide*. Westport, CT: Greenwood Publishing Group.

Western, B. (2006). *Punishment and inequality in America*. New York: Russell Sage Foundation.

White, J. L., & Cones, J. H. (1999) *Black man emerging: Facing the past and seizing a future in America*. New York/London: Routledge.

Wilson, W. J. (1987). *The truly disadvantaged: The inner city, the underclass, and public policy*. Chicago: University of Chicago Press.

Wilson, W. J. (1996). *When work disappears: The world of the new urban poor*. New York: Knopf.

chapter five

Debunking the myth
Understanding fathering
in the Black community

Rashika J. Rentie
Howard University
Washington, DC

In psychological literature, when discussing fathers, researchers are referring to biological fathers residing in the same home as their children (Krohn & Bogan, 2001; Lamb, 1975). Much of the literature in the social sciences speaks about African American[*] fathers being absent but neglects the presence of peripheral fathers or father figures in the child's life (Connor & White, 2006). The term *father figure* refers to men who are not biological fathers but assume some of the roles and responsibilities of the father. The omission of these groups has led to a stigmatization of the African American family, specifically African American fathers.

The impact of young men not having a father, or a positive male role model, has received considerable attention in social science research, whereas the impact of fathers on their daughters has just begun to emerge (Bobino, 1986; Krohn & Bogan, 2001; Mitchell, Booth, & King, 2009). As this area of research expands, several researchers have explored attempts to relate the effects of father absence to specific issues in the lives of girls and women. Prior to beginning an analysis on psychological literature that addresses the impact of fathers on daughters, the history of the African American family is discussed, along with relevant literature on fathering.

African worldview and the transition
to "African Americans"

Employing the White family as the standard family model disregards the importance of African American history and culture and commits a

[*] African American and Black will be used interchangeably.

"transubstantive error." A transubstantive error occurs when "one defines or interprets the behavior and/or medium of one culture with 'meanings' appropriate to and consistent with another culture" (Nobles, 1978, p. 683). A true representation of the African American family (before forming an opinion, conducting research, or assessing data validity) must include specific social and historic complexities and recognize the relevance to present-day functioning. If cultural patterns are not considered when researching the African American family, the result is an analysis done solely from the vantage point of European culture. When researching African American families, culture, marriage, and African traditions also need to be studied to understand how they all interlock. After a complete and thorough analysis, all of the information should be used to analyze contemporary African American families.

Understanding the history of family, marriage, and culture for African Americans includes understanding the formation of a traditional African family. Unlike the current Western norm of starting a new family after marriage, traditional African unions served as a joining of families or kinship networks. Knowledge of the structure and functioning of kinship models assists in understanding the concept of African American families and their formation in America (Sudarkasa, 1988). Kinship consists of extended family relationships that have grown out of the wide kinship networks. Africans, both slaves and free, reestablished these networks in America. These kinship networks have historically been more prevalent among Blacks than Whites (Foster, 1983). Extended families and kinship networks form one of the strengths of African American families (Fine, Schwebel, & James-Myers, 1987; Hill, 1999). Although several African family patterns may not have survived the American experience, their transformation and expansion are still evident (Billingsley, 1992).

For African Americans, the institution of slavery is incorporated into their American experience. W. E. B. Du Bois (1908) argued that the constraints of slavery prohibited the replication of African lineage in America because marriages among slaves were not recognized by American society. Yet the values on which kin groups were based and the ideals underlying them led to the emergence of variants of African family life in the form of extended families that developed among the enslaved Blacks in America (Sudarkasa, 1988).

The history of the African family was irrelevant to Western European researchers, which explains why the development of African American family structure, including its roots in African heritage, was a foreign issue to these researchers. Du Bois, one of the first scholars to study African American families, continued to stress the importance of studying Black families in the context of their African origins. Hill (1999) acknowledged Du Bois's perspective by stating that "in order to have a proper understanding of Blacks in America, the influence of historical, cultural, economic, social and political forces need to be assessed" (p. 2). Understanding components of African culture allows for a better understanding of African forms and function in comparison to Western norms. African families exhibit an interdependence or communal cooperation borne out of the necessity of providing a living in a rural, agricultural environment. Africans, once brought to a new country and enslaved, were confronted with a new world in which their norms, values, and ways of life were unacceptable. Africans of different nationalities, who spoke different languages and had different cultures and customs, came to the New World in chains without their families. Others were cut off from their original culture and were not permitted to develop and assimilate into a new culture of their own making. Slaves were stripped of their dignity and converted to property (Billingsley, 1968).

African American family structures conflicted with the generally accepted American family structure as a result of the devastating impact of the institution of enslavement. The slave society included Africans from diverse backgrounds and from different marital and family forms. In addition to the diversity of the African cultures, slaves were forced to adapt to alien European cultural values (Bush, 1990). According to Nobles (1978), culture is a montage of specific ways of thinking, feeling, and acting, which is peculiar to the members of a particular group. A belief system that reflects their worldview and frame of reference is specific to such culture. As a result of being taken from their native land in Africa and being enslaved, African Americans developed a "forced culture" that is unique because of the combination of customs and norms from African and European cultures (Billingsley, 1988; Foster, 1983; Sudarkasa, 1988). This forced transplantation of Blacks into a new environment and lifestyle has led many scholars to address the issue of bicultural socialization. Robert Hill (1999) contends that the residuals of African culture are transmitted from generation to generation by Black Americans through bicultural socialization. He further states that "such patterns of dual socialization facilitate the acculturation of Blacks to mainstream and African American cultural patterns" (p. 54). This biculturalization assists in explaining the differences between Blacks and Whites with reference to family organization (Connor & White, 2006; Foster, 1983).

Theoretical perspectives on the father–daughter relationship

Early literature did not give much attention to the importance of the father in the family, and those who considered men reported little involvement

of the father with the son and completely ignored father–daughter relationships. The mother, the primary caregiver according to the popular
assumption, had the greatest effect on the child and especially on the
daughter. Recently, the role of the father, specifically in reference to the
daughter, and the importance of the father–daughter bond has increasingly gained the attention of researchers (Biller & Meredith, 1972; Bobino,
1986; Boyd-Franklin, 2003; Harris, 2008; Lamb, 1975, 1997; Sherman, 1985;
White & Cones, 1999).

Psychoanalytic perspective on the father–daughter relationship

Psychoanalytic literature emphasized the importance of the relationship
of the children with the mother, while not giving much attention to the
role of the father. "Until recently, the father has been a forgotten parent
in the psychoanalytic and psychological literature" (Ross, 1979, p. 317).
Sigmund Freud, the father of psychoanalytic theory, spoke of the Oedipus
complex, which was an emotional attachment to the mother by the male.
Freud posited the first love object of the female is the mother, until the
child recognizes the male genitalia. When that occurs, the female feels
castrated and blames the mother for this condition. This complex was
later named the Electra complex by Carl Jung, a student of Freud (Bobino,
1986; Trowell & Etchegoyen, 2002). The resolution of the Electra complex
enabled the female child to accept a feminine role and laid the foundation for satisfactory adjustment and interaction with males in adult life
(Leonard, 1966). Despite the mention of the Electra complex, the female
child and her relationship with the father is relatively unmentioned in
psychoanalytic literature (Kieffer, 2008).

According to Trowell and Etchegoyen (2002), until the early 1970s,
mention of fathering, the father–child bond, and fatherhood were lacking
in psychoanalytic literature.

Williamson (2002) made reference to the father being the second object
to hold the infant and the parent to turn to when the child experiences
friction with the mother. Many authors, such as Tucker and Adams (1982),
have ventured to say,

> We have observed repeatedly in clinical work that
> the father's role is generally far from central; his
> absence may scarcely ruffle the good health and
> wellbeing of the family; his presence is often only
> a limp existence within the body of the family unit;
> and at times his presence is so destructive to the
> welfare of wife and children that the family mem-
> bers would do far better without papa. (p. 24)

The same article stated that "the father is sometimes a better guide than the mother to worldly-wise matters, adding useful perspective on a girl's affairs of the heart" (Tucker & Adams, 1982, p. 26). Although the view of Tucker and Adams may not be the popular contemporary view, it points out the relative lack of focus on the father historically in psychology and how that view has changed.

Although there is no complete and consistent body of theory about fatherhood in the psychoanalytic literature, recent literature points to the father's influence on his children in the pre-oedipal stage and extending into latency, with ramifications in adulthood. The father also contributes to the daughter's formation of personality as well as to the ability to form and maintain healthy relationships with the opposite sex in adulthood (Balsam, 2008; Sherman, 1985; Trowell & Etchegoyen, 2002).

Attachment theory and the father–daughter relationship

Attachment theory was first discussed by Bowlby while studying the infant–mother relationship. Bowlby developed attachment theory to account for pathology and phenomena in personality development that were not explained by other psychoanalytic theories. Bowlby monitored infants' reactions to temporary separation from their normal caregivers and given to unfamiliar people in an unfamiliar environment—a phenomenon that is currently referred to as separation anxiety (Colin, 1996).

Previous research on attachment theory speaks about the father as a playmate for the child and not as a figure for which the child develops the same attachment as to the mother (Lamb, 1975, 1997). Early developments in attachment theory questioned whether attachments were developed between the father and the infant. Colin (1996) made reference to the existence of earlier cultures in which most infants had to be in close proximity to the mother for survival purposes. "Prior to the introduction of agriculture, and even when gardening began, most of a mother's work could be done with an infant tied to the mother's back or side or playing nearby" (Colin, p. 168). Additionally, Colin noted the necessity for breast-feeding, which centered the mother in a more caregiving role. Recent research has revealed the importance of the father as well as the attachment that develops from infant to father. Kotelchuck, Ross, Kagan, and Aelazo (1975) observed that the absence of the father elicited the same response by the child as the absence of the mother. Although there was a difference in intensity, the baby's comfort level in the presence of the father and the disturbance in the absence of the father clearly portrayed the father as one who was able to provide a secure base and one for whom the baby had developed an attachment. Research also points to the adjustment of adult attachments based on the childhood relationships these adults formed

(Colin, 1996; Hoffman, 1995; Lamb, 1978; Main & Weston, 1981; Simpson, 1990). Further research concluded that infants who had a secure attachment to the father were more curious in exploring their environment and adjusted more positively to novel stimuli (Biller & Meredith, 1972).

Social learning and the father–daughter relationship

Social learning theorists such as Albert Bandura emphasized the importance of modeling. Bandura believed we acquire personality by observing others and seeing if our modeled behaviors are reinforced. Some of the characteristics involved in learning are modeling those with similarities in gender, the power of the model, observation reinforcement, how attentive the child is, and the amount of exposure and rehearsal the child receives. The first characteristic, the similarity of gender, specifically refers to the mother serving as a model for the daughter and the father serving as a model for the son. All other characteristics speak to the contributions of the father in relation to the daughter's gender role development.

Interactions between mother and father reinforce feminine roles and behaviors for the daughter and discourage masculine ones. Fathers also affect the gender role development of daughters by being nurturing, participating in rearing, and reinforcing the essence of beauty (Lamb, 1981). The first role models for males are fathers or the significant males in their lives. Daughters look to fathers or significant males to show them what they value in women. "If a father thinks his daughter is beautiful and feminine, she may be inclined to see herself that way. But if a father rejects his daughter as unattractive, she may carry problems associated with self-image into adulthood" (Adams, 2004, p. 53). The emphasis of observational learning by social learning theorists further elaborates on the father's role in the development of the daughter, "Through her relationship with her father she will learn to relate to male expectation in general, and this would seem to be vital importance to her later psychological happiness" (Williamson, 2002, p. 210).

Father absence

The literature on fathering and their presence or absence in the home concludes that a father's absence can result in daughters being unmotivated, promiscuous, and eager to seek male attention (Adams, 2004; Hetherington, 1972; Krohn & Bogan, 2001). The effects of the absence may vary depending on whether the cause of the absence is death, divorce, or separation. Within the African American community, fathers have usually been viewed as being absent or noninvolved by researchers. "Live away" fathering and elements of peripheral fathering were established for African American men centuries ago during the institution of slavery (Adams, 2004; Hamer, 2001). Peripheral fathers may play a substantial role in the lives of their children but are often overlooked by researchers. According to Liebow (1967), "Some fathers are not always absent and some are less absent than others" (p. 73). Connor and White (2006) further elaborated on the issue of peripheral or social fathers by stating, "Men who live outside the home and who father and the manner in which they father are routinely ignored" (p. 3).

Father figures represent another type of fathering in the African American community. Father figures may be relatives, family friends, neighbors, or stepparents who fulfill some of the aspects of the parental role when the biological father is not present (Boyd-Franklin, 1985; Connor & White, 2006; Staples, 1985). The presence of father figures may allow children to develop positive self-concepts through this social interaction (Cooley, 1962). Connor and White (2006) spoke about father figures as social fathers. The authors contended that there is confusion about fathering in the African American community that is due to a lack of understanding of the role of fathering and the narrow scope of the traditional definition of a father. To more fully grasp the essence of fathering in the African American community, the concept is extended beyond the traditional definitions to include father figures, since kinship or extended family forms incorporate their presence.

The effect of fathers or father figures on girls and women is just as important as the presence of a male role model for men. African American girls, much more than boys, constantly have to maintain their self-esteem and sense of beauty. Black fathers work on breaking traditional gender conventions that foster continuation of female subordination and male dominance. Such a role is pivotal in child and adolescent development and has future implications in a woman's life (Adams, 2004). African American girls look to their fathers to show them what men value in women (Cochran, 1997).

According to Western psychological theory, the absence of a biological father in the home will have a detrimental effect on the overall development of children, specifically girls (Biller & Meredith, 1972; Milne, Myers, Rosenthal, & Ginsburg, 1986; Salem, Zimmerman, & Notaro, 1998). Girls raised without a father may gravitate toward men who do not personify what they would like in a man (Saunders, 1983). According to Krohn and Bogan (2001), females that have minimal contact with their fathers, particularly during their adolescent years, and did not have the benefit of the father–daughter relationship to use as a model, had difficulty forming lasting relationships with men. Previous studies on father presence or absence have neglected to discuss how involved the father is. The presence of a father is not, by itself, enough to have a significant positive impact on the child. "Ironically it may be better for a child to have no father at all than one living with him but uninvolved in this upbringing" (Biller & Meredith, 1972, p. 18).

Research on decisions regarding sexual health and the lack of male interaction for African American women in their childhood years augments the desire for interaction with and acceptance by members of the opposite sex. According to Gail Wyatt, an expert in the study of African American women and sexual health, family socialization is associated with women's responsiveness about sexual relationships (Wyatt & Rowe-Lyons, 1990). Adolescent females raised in fatherless homes are more likely to engage in promiscuous sexual activity, have low self-esteem, have abortions, cohabitate, have unwanted pregnancies or become pregnant before marriage, and experience difficulty in forming and maintaining romantic relationships (Ellis et al., 2003; Krohn & Bogan, 2001; Lohr, Legg, Mendell, & Reimer, 1989; McLanahan & Schwartz, 2002).

The health of African American women has recently become an issue of concern as a result of the incidence of sexually transmitted diseases, acquired immune deficiency syndrome (AIDS) and human immuno-deficiency virus (HIV). According to the Centers for Disease Control and Prevention (CDC, 2005), in 2004 the rate of chlamydia among African American females in the United States was more than 7 times that of White women. The rate of gonorrhea in 2004 for African American women ages 15 to 19 was 2,790.5 per 100,000, whereas the rate for White women of a similar age range was 201.7. The incidence of primary and secondary syphilis among African American women ages 20 to 24 was 13.4 cases per 100,000. This rate was more than twice the rate of Whites. Clearly these numbers illustrate a racial discrepancy in regard to safe sexual practices and the transmission of sexually transmitted diseases.

"Girls with absent fathers grow up without the day-by-day experience of attentive, caring and loving interaction with a man. Without this continuous sense of being valued and loved, a young girl does not thrive, but rather is stunted in her emotional development" (Krohn & Bogan, 2001, p. 602). Most of the literature that speaks to the effects of absent fathers on African American women refers specifically to biological fathers being absent from the home. However, it disregards social fathers, or father figures, and the impact of the kinship network often practiced in Black families. This is problematic because of the complexity of family structures and differences in rearing practices across cultures. Baumrind (1968) conducted a study observing African American fathers and White fathers. Baumrind found significant differences between African American and White fathers with respect to parenting styles, values, expectations, and socialization.

Hunt and Hunt (1977) looked at the difference between White and Black females, social class, sex role, and self-esteem. The results yielded a difference between White and Black females in the area of dating. For White females, dating frequency was lower when fathers were absent but was enhanced for Black females when fathers were absent.

Females of both races with an absent father experienced lower self-esteem. Hunt and Hunt neglected to research family background and gave a narrow scope of possible reasons for the differences in the results. The authors stated that overall the impact of father absence is more apparent in White girls than Black girls. One of the reasons stated for that conclusion is the long-standing tradition of the male being the stable breadwinner in the White family. Yet for Black girls, "in contrast to the White-world pattern of stable male breadwinners and differentiated sex roles, the status realities of Blacks have meant greater exposure to conditions that fragment families, making father absence a more frequent and normal feature of Black life" (Hunt & Hunt, 1977, p. 100). The notion that Black girls have become accustomed to not having a father around because it is a "normal feature of Black life" is absurd. While there are greater social, political, and legal conditions that may lead to a fragmented "nuclear" family in the traditional sense, the long-standing history of interdependence among Black families may serve as a moderator to the negative effects that are purported to surface if one does not have an active father in the home.

Another study examined whether father absence placed daughters at special risk for early sexual activity and teen pregnancy (Ellis et al., 2003). This study was done cross-culturally in the United States and New Zealand. The sample in the United States was 81% White and predominately from a middle-class background. The results of the study indicated that father absence does place daughters at special risk for teen pregnancy and sexual activity. Although the study yielded consistent results with the populations in the United States and New Zealand, the lack of diversity of the United States sample does not qualify it for generalizability across cultures. Despite the limitations of this study, the results are clear and have yielded support from more recent literature, indicating fathers can be an important influence on daughters' sexual behavior (Wilson, Dalberth, & Koo, 2010). The theories on father absence in the African American community are so common they are published in mainstream and popular literature (Barras, 2000; Boyd-Franklin, 2003; Feiler, 2010).

The importance of appropriate guidelines for social science research with a diverse population is an area that has received attention from the

American Psychological Association (2003) in its Division 45 guidelines. According to these guidelines, the recognition of multicultural sensitivity and understanding of racial difference should be taken into consideration when conducting research on individuals from a background that is racially different from that of White Americans. Although these guidelines were not available for researchers in the past, they set the precedent for current and future research.

To understand the complexity of the African American family, there is a need to understand the different components of its family structure. The African American family structure does not solely fit the nuclear or extended model, but instead combines several models that encompass the totality of the family. The operational definition of the African American family is one reflecting a "kinship model that is composed of parents, children, siblings, friends and neighbors involved in relationships of co-parenting and reciprocity. Non-kin may become part of the family when they assume familial roles" (Baer, 1999, p. 342). Parham et al. (1999) noted that the Black extended family or kinship network is an intergenerational group. Not all members of the family reside in the same household but are part of a social-familial network that functions like a mini-community.

A greater understanding of the African American family, its history, and its many complexities is warranted. It is the hope of this author that out of an in-depth study of the Black family, one may be able to understand the importance and the impact of kinship networks and its utility in the Black family. Fathers—whether biological, peripheral, or a father figure—are present in the Black community and have an impact on both males and females. However, the rigid definition of a father as defined by European researchers does not fit the networks in the Black community. This results in false statements such as "fathers are absent in the Black community" and leads to fathers often being mislabeled and overlooked. Furthermore, the need to refrain from the use of a deficiency model toward the use of a strength-based perspective has been demonstrated and will yield greater results.

Conclusion

African American fathers have been stigmatized throughout literature; however, the importance and impact of their presence on their daughters' development of healthy psychological and interpersonal relationships is beginning to emerge. Whereas the effect of a father's presence has been disregarded historically in psychological literature, the impact of their absence has been magnified. This magnification has led to further stigmatization of the African American family and has disregarded the importance of kinship networks and the cultural essence of interdependence. The acknowledgment of the interdependent nature of the African American family includes recognizing the importance of peripheral fathers or father figures.

Fathering, whether biological, peripheral, or father figures, is a role that requires men to be active in their daughters' lives from birth. The presence of a father or father figure does not solely affect childhood behaviors but also has implications for future behaviors and decision making in adulthood. Specifically, research has contended the presence or absence of a father can impact a daughter's self-esteem, decisions regarding employment, and future mate selections, to name a few. Presently, researchers are starting to highlight that the bond a father develops with his daughter is different from a mother–daughter bond but is just as imperative. The recognition of fathers and father figures, their role in child-rearing, and the importance of the father–daughter bond is key to understanding fathering in the African American community.

Reflective questions

1. How does the Eurocentric framework for definitions, customs, and norms affect one's perspective of Black families and the nature of fathering?
2. Do biological relationships make a difference when considering the impact fathers have on female children?
3. Considering the consequences researchers report regarding the effects of "absent" fathers, is a daughter who is not residing with her father or a father figure destined for failure? Why or why not?

References

Adams, K. R. (2004). Influences of childhood/adolescence paternal relationships on African American women's expectations and needs for adult emotional (heterosexual) intimacy. (Doctoral dissertation, Loyola University, 2004). *Dissertation Abstracts International, 65*(3-A), 1112.

American Psychological Association. (2003). Guidelines on multicultural education, training, research, practice and organizational change for psychologists. *American Psychologist, 58*(5), 377–402.

Baer, J. (1999). The effects of family structure and SES on family process in early adolescence. *Journal of Adolescence, 22*(3), 341–354.

Balsam, R. H. (2008). Fathers and the bodily care of their infant daughters. *Psychoanalytic Inquiry, 28*, 60–75.

Barras, J. R. (2000). *Whatever happened to daddy's little girl? The impact of fatherlessness on Black women.* New York: Ballantine.

Baumrind, D. (1968). Authoritarian vs. authoritative parental control. *Adolescence* 3(11), 255–272.

Biller, H. B., & Meredith, D. L. (1972). The invisible father. *Sexual behavior, 2*(7), 16–22.

Billingsley, A. (1968). *Black families in White America*. Englewood Cliffs, NJ: Prentice-Hall.

Billingsley, A. (1988). *Black families in White America* (1st Touchstone ed.). New York: Simon & Schuster.

Billingsley, A. (1992). *Climbing Jacob's ladder*. New York: Simon & Schuster.

Bobino, R. F. (1986). African American fathers and daughters: The adult developmental consequences of the retreat of fathers during their daughters' adolescence. (Doctoral dissertation, The Wright Institute, 1986). *Dissertation Abstracts International, 46*(7-B), 2452.

Boyd-Franklin, N. (1985). A psycho-educational perspective on parenting. In H. P. McAdoo & J. L. McAdoo (Eds.), *Black children* (pp. 119–140). Thousand Oaks, CA: Sage.

Boyd-Franklin, N. (2003). *Black families in therapy: Understanding the African American Experience* (2nd ed.). New York: Guilford Press.

Bush, B. (1990). *Slave women in Caribbean society*. Kingston, Jamaica: Heinemann.

Centers for Disease Control and Prevention. (2005, November 16). Trends in reportable sexually transmitted diseases in the United States, 2004. Retrieved February 13, 2006, from www.cdc.gov/std/stats04/trends2004.htm

Cochran, D. (1997). African-American fathers and focus groups: A group approach to increasing visibility in research. *Social Work with Groups, 20*(3), 75–88.

Colin, V. L. (1996). *Human attachment*. Philadelphia: Temple University Press.

Cooley, C. H. (1962). *Social organization: A study of the larger mind*. New York: Schocken Books.

Connor, M. E., & White, J. L. (2006). *Black fathers, an invisible presence in America*. Mahwah, NJ: Erlbaum.

Du Bois, W. E. B. (Ed.). (1908). *The Negro American Family*. New York: Harper.

Ellis, B. J., Bates, J. E., Dodge, K. A., Fergusson, D. M., Horwood, L. J., Pettit, G. S., et al. (2003). Does father absence place daughters at special risk for early sexual activity and teenage pregnancy? *Child development, 74*(3), 801–821.

Feiler, B. (2010). *The council of dads: My daughters, my illness, and the men who could be me*. New York: HarperCollins.

Fine, M., Schwebel, A. L., & James-Myers, L. (1987). Family stability in Black families: Values underlying three different perspectives. *Journal of Comparative Family Studies, 18*(1), 1–23.

Foster, H. J. (1983). African patterns in the Afro-American family. *Journal of Black Studies, 14*(2), 201–232.

Hamer, J. (2001). *What it means to be daddy: Fatherhood for Black men living away from their children*. New York: Columbia University Press.

Harris, A. (2008). "Fathers" and "daughters." *Psychoanalytic Inquiry, 28*, 39–59.

Hetherington, E. M. (1972). Effects of father absence on personality development in adolescent daughters. *Developmental Psychology, 7*(3), 313–326.

Hill, R. B. (1999). *The strengths of African American families*. New York: Oxford University Press.

Hoffman, N. H. (1995). The father-daughter bond and intimate relationship outcomes in women (Doctoral dissertation, University of Pittsburgh). *Dissertation Abstracts International, 55*(7-B), 3015.

Hunt, J. G., & Hunt, L. L. (1977). Race, daughters and father-loss: Does absence make the girl grow stronger? *Social Problems, 25*(1), 90–102.

Kieffer, C. (2008). From self objects to mutual recognition: Towards optimal responsiveness in father and daughter relationships. *Psychoanalytic Inquiry, 28*, 76–91.

Kotelchuck, M., Ross, G., Kagan, J., & Aelazo, P. (1975). Separation protest in infants in home and laboratory. *Developmental Psychology, 11*(2), 256–257.

Krohn, F. B., & Bogan, Z. (2001). The effects of absent fathers have on female development and college attendance. *College Student Journal, 35*(4), 598–609.

Lamb, M. E. (1975). Fathers: Forgotten contributors to child development. *Human Development, 18*, 245–266.

Lamb, M. E. (1978). The father's role in the infant's social world. In J. H. Stevens & M. Matthews (Eds.), *Mother/child, father/child relationships* (pp. 87–108). Washington, DC: National Association for the Education of Young Children.

Lamb, M. E. (1981). Fathers and child development: An integrative overview. In M. E. Lamb (Ed.), *The role of the father in child development* (2nd ed., pp. 1–70). New York: Wiley.

Lamb, M. E. (1997). Fathers and child development: An introductory overview and guide. In M. E. Lamb (Ed.), *The role of the father in child development* (3rd ed., pp. 1–18). New York: Wiley.

Leonard, M. R. (1966). Fathers and daughters: The significance of "fathering" in the psychosexual development of the girl. *International Journal of Psychoanalysis, 47*, 325–334.

Liebow, E. (1967). *Tally's corner: A study of Negro street corner men.* Boston: Little, Brown.

Lohr, R., Legg, C., Mendell, A., & Reimer, B. (1989). Clinical observations in interferences of early absence in achievement of femininity. *Clinical Social Work, 17*(3), 351–365.

Main, M., & Weston, D. (1981). The quality of the toddler's relationships to mother and father: Related to conflict behavior and readiness to establish new relationships. *Child Development, 52*, 932–940.

McLanahan, S., & Schwartz, D. (2002). Life without father: What happens to the children? *Contexts, 1*(1), 35–44.

Milne, A. M., Myers, D. E., Rosenthal, A. S., & Ginsburg, A. (1986). Single parents, working mothers, and the educational achievement of school children. *Sociology of Education, 59*, 125–139.

Mitchell, K. S., Booth, A., & King, V. (2009). Adolescents with nonresident fathers: Are daughters more disadvantaged than sons? *Journal of Marriage and Family, 71*, 650–662.

Nobles, W. W. (1978). Toward an empirical and theoretical framework for defining Black families. *Journal of Marriage and the Family, 40*(4), 679–688.

Parham, T. A., White, J. L., & Ajamu, A. (1999). *The psychology of Blacks: An African centered perspective.* Upper Saddle River, NJ: Prentice-Hall.

Ross, J. M. (1979). Fathering: A review of some psychoanalytic contributions on paternity. *International Journal of Psychoanalysis, 60*, 317–327.

Salem, D. A., Zimmerman, M. A., & Notaro, P. C. (1998). Effects of family structure, family process, and father involvement on psychosocial outcomes among African American adolescents. *Family Relations, 47*(4), 331–341.

Saunders, M. (1983). Fathers and daughters. *Essence Magazine, 14*, 85–86.

Sherman, M. T. (1985). Daughters' views of fathers from a developmental perspective (Doctoral dissertation, Bryn Mawr College). *Dissertation Abstracts International, 46*(2-B), 1359.

Simpson, J. A. (1990). Influence of attachment styles on romantic relationships. *Journal of Personality and Social Psychology, 59*, 971–980.

Staples, R. (1985). Changes in Black family structure: The conflict between family ideology and structural conditions. *Journal of Marriage and the Family, 47*, 1005–1014.

Sudarkasa, N. (1988). Interpreting the African heritage in Afro-American family organization. In H. P. McAdoo (Ed.), *Black families* (2nd ed., pp. 27–43). Newbury Park, CA: Sage.

Trowell, J., & Etchegoyen, A. (2002). *The importance of fathers: A psychoanalytic reevaluation.* New York: Brunner-Routledge.

Tucker, C., & Adams, P. L. (1982). Her father, her self. *American Journal of Social Psychiatry, 2*(1), 24–28.

White, J. L., & Cones, J. H. (1999). *Black man emerging.* New York: W. H. Freeman.

Williamson, M. (2002). The importance of fathers in relation to their daughters' psychosexual development. *Psychodynamic Practice, 10*(2), 207–219.

Wilson, E. K., Dalberth, B. T., & Koo, H. P. (2010). "We're the heroes!" Fathers' perspectives on their role in protecting their preteenage children from sexual risk. *Perspectives on Sexual and Reproductive Health, 42*, 117–124.

Wyatt, G. E., & Rowe-Lyons, S. (1990). African American women's sexual satisfaction as a dimension of their sex roles. *Sex Roles, 22*(7/8), 509–524.

chapter six

The impact of fathers' absence on African American adolescents' gender role development[*]

Jelani Mandara
Northwestern University
Evanston, Illinois

Carolyn B. Murray and Toya N. Joyner
University of California
Riverside, California

Gender role development is a well-studied area of psychological research that refers to schemas or beliefs about one's masculinity and femininity, the feelings associated with those attributes, and one's perceptions of one's similarity to others of one's gender (Egan & Perry, 2001). Although a great deal is known about the development and consequences of gender role orientations (Bussey & Bandura, 1999; Marsh & Byrne, 1991; Ruble & Martin, 2000), the effects of different cultures and diverse family environments are highly debated (Harris, 1996; Hilton & Haldeman, 1991; Hofferth & Anderson, 2003; Hunter & Davis, 1992; Ruble & Martin, 2000).

For example, there is great debate about the effects of living in a fatherless home on gender role development (Beaty, 1995; Leve & Fagot, 1997; Stevens, Golombok, Beveridge, & ALSPAC Study Team, 2002; Stevenson & Black, 1988). Many have argued that fathers are important to the psychosocial development of children and adolescents (Adelson, 1980; Amato, 1991; Beaty, 1995; Hilton & Desrochers, 2002; Mandara & Murray, 2000), whereas others have argued that the importance of fathers to child development is questionable at best (Silverstein & Auerbach, 1999; Stevens et al., 2002). Given that a large percentage of African American children are now reared

[*] Reprinted with kind permission from Springer Science+Business Media: *Sex Roles*, "The Impact of Fathers' Absence in African American Adolescents' Gender Role Development," Vol. 53:3, 2005, pp. 207–220, Jelani Mandara, Carolyn B. Murray, Toya N. Joyner.

in predominately single-mother-headed households (Fields, 2003; Tucker & Mitchell-Kernan, 1995), the differences between father-absent and father-present African American adolescents are at the center of this debate (Mandara & Murray, 2000). It is surprising that very few researchers have specifically examined gender role differences between father-absent and father-present African American adolescents. The purpose of this chapter is to fill this void and to explore the effects of fathers' absence on the current and ideal gender role development of African American adolescents.

Fathers' influence on gender role development

As the structure of American families began to change, several researchers examined the effects of paternal absence on both masculine and feminine gender role development. The general trend suggested that boys who were not primarily raised with their fathers were more passive and exhibited more feminine and fewer masculine traits, such as rough and competitive play, than did father-present boys. However, no effects appeared for girls (Adelson, 1980; Beaty, 1995; Hetherington, 1966, 1972; Kodandaram, 1991; Stephens & Day, 1979; Stevenson & Black, 1988). For instance, an early study found that African American and European American boys whose fathers were not living with them by the age of 5 years were less aggressive, participated less in physical games, and generally had fewer gender-typed traits than did father-present boys (Hetherington, 1966). Other researchers found no gender-typing differences between father-absent and father-present girls (Hetherington, 1972) or between girls living with their fathers only, with their mothers only, or in two-parent homes (Stephens & Day, 1979). A meta-analysis of several early studies confirmed this and showed that father-present boys were more stereotypically gender-typed (i.e., masculine) than were father-absent boys and that there were no such differences for girls (Stevenson & Black, 1988).

More recent studies have shown similar trends. In a study of 40 boys who had been arrested for various delinquent acts, the 20 father-absent boys were significantly higher on femininity than were the 20 father-present boys (Kodandaram, 1991). Research even suggests that the rough-and-tumble play, stricter discipline, and focus on achievement and overcoming obstacles that is typical of fathers' relationship with sons (Parke, 1996) may produce an increase in boys' self-confidence in their masculinity, and it may actually impact the boys' hormone levels. For instance, a study of the hormone profiles of men and women in a rural Caribbean village showed that adult men who had experienced father absence during childhood exhibited significantly lower levels of testosterone than men who were raised with a father (Flinn, Quinlan, Decker, Turner, & England, 1996). Because testosterone influences observable differences in characteristics such as physical strength, growth of facial hair, voice changes, and other signs of physical and behavioral masculinization (Schaal, Tremblay, Soussignan, & Susman, 1996), boys' levels of testosterone may influence self-perceptions of masculinity.

Although it is not clear if the hormonal differences observed in men generalize to differences in boys, other anecdotal evidence suggests this may be the case. Beaty (1995) conducted a study in which 40 junior high school boys rated each other on 15 words associated with masculinity. Results showed that the father-absent boys rated the father-present boys as being significantly more masculine than the father-present boys rated the father-absent boys. Another study showed that feminine boys' fathers had spent less time with them in infancy than had the fathers of masculine boys (Green, Williams, & Goodman, 1985). Therefore, on average, father-present boys likely had more traits associated with masculinity than did father-absent boys.

These findings have been interpreted in many ways (see Ruble & Martin, 2000, for a review), but the main explanation is that boys are more affected than girls are by their fathers' absence because father-absent boys do not have a prominent role model of masculinity, whereas father-absent girls do have a prominent role model of femininity (Beaty, 1995; Ruble & Martin, 2000). Boys have other men as role models, but they are usually not as close or important as a parent (Hofferth & Anderson, 2003). Furthermore, mothers, and especially fathers, differentially treat and talk to their girls and boys (Jackson, 1993; Jenkins & Guidubaldi, 1997; Leaper, Anderson, & Sanders, 1998; Leve & Fagot, 1997; Siegal, 1987; Starrels, 1994). Mothers are also more likely to encourage androgyny in their children, whereas fathers are more likely to stress masculine traits in their sons and feminine traits in their daughters (Leve & Fagot, 1997; Parke, 1996; Popenoe, 1996; Price-Bonham & Skeen, 1982; Starrels, 1994). However, there are several limitations in the family structure and gender role development literature.

Conceptual and methodological issues

One unresolved issue is the effect of race and culture on gender role development. For instance, some have argued that gender role socialization in African American homes is less gender-typed than is the case in European American homes (Harris, 1996; Hunter & Davis, 1992; Reid & Trotter, 1993). Thus, African American women are more likely to be masculine or androgynous than are European American women (Binion, 1990; De Leon, 1993; Harris, 1996). Also, because of the traditional extended nature of African American families (Kamo, 2000; Scott & Black, 1989), they may be able to depend on other men to fulfill the father's traditional role in gender role development (McAdoo & McAdoo, 2002). Furthermore, given that single mothers have headed a significant percentage of African American families since the 1960s (Tucker & Mitchell-Kernan, 1995), single African American mothers may have learned to supplement the role of fathers in the lives of their children. Therefore, it is possible that father absence does not have the same effect on African Americans as it is does on other populations.

The cultural and socioeconomic context of African American fathers also greatly impacts their ability and decision to be actively involved in the socialization of their children (Bowman & Forman, 1997; Johnson, 1998, 2001; Lawson & Thompson, 1999; McAdoo & McAdoo, 2002). According to Bowman and Sanders (1998), "As employment problems among Black fathers shifted from underemployment in menial jobs to joblessness, corresponding increases have occurred in family provider role problems, unmarried teenage pregnancies, mother-headed households, and the feminization of family poverty in Black communities" (pp. 1–2). In support of this, data from the National Survey of Black Americans show that married fathers have higher personal income than formerly married fathers, who in turn have higher personal income than never married fathers (Bowman & Forman, 1997). Furthermore, fathers' marital status and provider role problems impact their ability to be actively involved in the day-to-day socialization of their children (Bowman & Forman, 1997; Johnson, 2001; McAdoo & McAdoo, 2002).

Many researchers have even argued that the actual physical presence of the father is not as important as the added financial resources he brings to the family (McLanahan, 1985; McLeod, Kruttschnitt, & Dornfeld, 1994). This implies that the father's primary role is a financial provider, and, if the father's income producing role is somehow supplemented, then the children living in the average father-absent family will be the same as those living in the average father-present family. Whether this family income perspective is accurate or not is debatable (Mandara & Murray, 2000). However, it is clear that socioeconomic status may account for many of the differences between father-absent and father-present families.

Another limitation of most previous father absence and gender role studies is the lack of family functioning measures (Scott & Black, 1989; Stevens et al., 2002). The most consistent finding in family research is that the quality of family functioning is the main predictor of child and adolescent development for both genders (Coley, 1998; Maccoby & Martin, 1983; Mandara, 2003; Mandara & Murray, 2002). Therefore, if fathers influence their adolescents' psychosocial development, it is likely that they do so by impacting the dynamics of the family environment. Several authors have made this argument (Florsheim, Tolan, & Gorman-Smith, 1998; Heiss, 1996;

Mandara & Murray, 2000; McLoyd, Cauce, Takeuchi, & Wilson, 2000). This implies that if a single mother can facilitate a family environment that is similar to that of a traditional father-present environment, then she can mitigate any negative consequences of her children not having the day-to-day presence of a father. Thus, her adolescents should have the same psychosocial development, including gender role orientations, as those in father-present homes.

There are also some methodological concerns with the father absence and gender role development literatures. One issue is the difference between how participants perceive themselves as behaving and how they would like to behave. Although studies show the effects of fathers' absence on one's current gender role development, researchers have not examined how participants would like to be or the discrepancy between these behaviors. The ideal represents a desired state or goal that a person may wish to achieve. The discrepancy between the ideal and current behaviors implies unhappiness with current levels that cannot be uncovered only by assessing current behavior (Ruvolo & Veroff, 1997; Waugh, 2001). Therefore, for the researchers to make more detailed statements about the effects of fathers' absence on gender role development, adolescents in this study were asked what their current gender role orientations are and what their ideal orientations are.

Another methodological issue with previous studies is that the individual's personal definition of masculinity or femininity was not taken into consideration. Because most previous researchers used standardized measures of gender role development, whether people consider themselves to be masculine or feminine (i.e., whatever it means to them) may be lost. Although standardized measures have many advantages (Nunnally & Bernstein, 1994), they also have some disadvantages. It is possible that most emotionally stable women are high on the masculinity and low on the femininity scales of Bem's Sex Role Inventory (thus being considered masculine by standardized measures), but they may consider themselves to be feminine. For instance, a recent study of elementary and middle school children showed that feeling like a typical member of one's gender was positively correlated with psychosocial adjustment for girls and boys (Egan & Perry, 2001). However, researchers who have used standardized measures have found null or negative correlations between femininity and adjustment for girls (Barrett & White, 2002; Whitley, 1985). This may be because their perceptions of what femininity is do not conform to the same stereotypes underlying the development of standardized measures. In the current study, Q-sort methodology was used to ask adolescents how "manly, masculine" and "ladylike, feminine" they believe they are now and how they would ideally like to be.

In an earlier study of the current sample, it was found that father-present boys had significantly higher levels of self-esteem than did father-absent boys, even when family functioning and family income were statistically controlled (Mandara & Murray, 2000). Because self-esteem is positively related to standardized measures of masculinity in both male and female adolescents (Adams & Sherer, 1985; Burnett, Anderson, & Heppner, 1995; Long, 1989; Marsh, Antill, & Cunningham, 1987; Ruble & Martin, 2000; Whitley, 1985), it is highly likely that self-esteem mediates the relationship between father's absence and gender role development. This may be particularly true for adolescent boys because their perceptions of masculinity are so intertwined with their self-esteem (Berrenberg & Deyle, 1989; Burnett et al., 1995; Long, 1989; Whitley, 1985). Therefore, we also examined the effects of self-esteem on gender role development in the current study.

Theory and hypotheses

Given the literature reviewed earlier, it was expected that the old saying in African American communities that "Mothers love their sons and raise their daughters" would hold true for the average, or most typical, African American family. This theory argues that many African American mothers have different discipline styles and generally different parental goals and expectations for their sons and daughters (Hill & Zimmerman, 1995; Mandara & Murray, 2000; McLoyd, 1990; Radziszewska, Richardson, Dent, & Flay, 1996; Staples & Boulin-Johnson, 1993). Because African American mothers "love" their sons, they tend to be more permissive and less demanding of their sons. However, they spend more time guiding and pressuring their daughters to be independent and achievement-oriented. For instance, a qualitative study of 35 low-income African American mothers who have a child suffering from sickle cell disease showed that mothers of sons were more involved, more protective, and generally more worried about their children's ability to deal with the disease than were mothers of daughters with the disease (Hill & Zimmerman, 1995). Daughters were given more freedom, encouraged to go on with their lives as if they didn't have the disease, and trusted to care for themselves more than the sons. The authors concluded that mothers saw their girls as valiant (i.e., strong and independent) and their boys as vulnerable (i.e., weak and dependent).

In contrast, African American fathers tend to be more controlling, guiding, achievement-oriented, physically rougher, and more involved in the day-to-day activities of their boys than their girls. They are also more permissive and less demanding of their girls (Leaper et al., 1998; Leve & Fagot, 1997). For instance, Wilson (1992) found differences in children's and mothers' perceptions regarding African American fathers' socializing strategies of their girls and boys. Specifically, mothers, grandmothers, daughters, and sons perceived the fathers of sons as using more controlling, demanding, and supporting parental behaviors than did fathers of daughters. Fathers of sons were also perceived as more involved with their children than were fathers of daughters.

Therefore, in the average two-parent African American household, where the parents have relatively equal influence on their children, the mothers' tendency to raise their daughters and love their sons would be balanced by the fathers' tendency to do the opposite. In this case, children of both genders receive a balanced amount of control and warmth (i.e., raising and loving), even though the actions are coming primarily from different sources. However, in the average single-parent home, this balance may become upset, and the family environment can become skewed in the direction of the single parent. Given this balance theory, two hypotheses were deduced. First, because father-absent boys are missing the traditional father socialization that stresses masculinization, it was expected that they would have lower perceptions of both their current and ideal masculinity and higher perceptions of both their current and ideal femininity than would father-present boys. Given the permissive socialization and feminization fathers try to promote in their girls, it was also expected that father-present girls would perceive themselves to be higher in both current and ideal femininity compared to father-absent girls.

Methods

One hundred and six 15-year-old African American adolescents (53% girls; 47% boys) participated in the study. Seven of the parents were fathers. Fifty percent of the parents were married. There were 25 father-absent boys, 25 father-present boys, 27 father-absent girls, and 29 father-present girls. Approximately 20% of the sample earned less than $20,000, and 35% earned more than $35,000 annually. Information regarding the perceptions of gender role development (Aguilar, Kaiser, Murray, & Ozer, 1998; Block & Block, 1980), self-esteem (O'Brien & Epstein, 1988), and family functioning (Moos & Moos, 1986) was obtained from the adolescents (see Tables 6.1 and 6.2); all other demographic information was obtained from their parents.

Results and discussion

The first hypothesis was that boys in father-present homes would have higher current and ideal perceptions of their masculinity and lower levels of current and ideal femininity than would father-absent boys. Results

Table 6.1 Descriptive Statistics for Boys' Gender Role Development Variables

	m	sd	1	2	3	4	5	6	7	8	9
1. Current femininity	1.46	1.13	1								
2. Current masculinity	4.66	1.72	-.04	1							
3. Ideal femininity	1.66	1.24	.64**	-.24	1						
4. Ideal masculinity	5.18	1.60	-.06	.26	-.33*	1					
5. Family income	5.69	2.83	-.09	-.04	-.02	.42**	1				
6. Family relations	1.57	.15	.17	.12	.07	.12	.13	1			
7. Family growth	1.65	.11	.04	.28	-.17	.33*	.22	.33*	1		
8. Family systems	1.66	.16	.00	.05	-.10	.11	.23	.05	.27	1	
9. Self-esteem	3.47	.39	-.05	.18	-.17	.25	.21	.20	.50**	.46**	1

Note: *p-values < .05, **p-values < .01.

Table 6.2 Descriptive Statistics for Girls' Gender Role Development Variables

	m	sd	1	2	3	4	5	6	7	8	9
1. Current femininity	4.71	1.76	1								
2. Current masculinity	2.03	1.64	-.40**	1							
3. Ideal femininity	5.52	1.42	-.11	-.06	1						
4. Ideal masculinity	1.81	1.25	-.08	-.05	-.60**	1					
5. Family income	6.36	3.27	.22	-.22	.02	-.10	1				
6. Family relations	1.59	.18	.26*	-.37**	-.08	-.02	.16	1			
7. Family growth	1.64	.13	.19	-.24	-.10	-.18	.19	.39**	1		
8. Family systems	1.64	.14	.32*	-.07	.13	-.29*	-.23	.31*	.40**	1	
9. Self-esteem	3.57	.43	.24*	-.15	-.17	.04	.28*	.50**	.40**	.03	1

Note: *p-values < .05, **p-values < .01.

Table 6.3 Boys' Gender Role Development by Family Structure Before and After Controlling for Self-Esteem, Family Income, Family Relationships, Family Growth, and Family Systems

Gender role (raw scores)	Family structure		F (1,48)	η
	Father-present (n = 25)	Father-absent (n = 25)		
Current femininity	1.44 (1.3)	1.48 (0.9)	0.02	.02
Current masculinity	5.12 (1.7)	4.20 (1.6)	3.80*	.27
Ideal femininity	1.52 (1.2)	1.80 (1.3)	0.65	.11
Ideal masculinity (adjusted scores)	5.72 (1.2)	4.64 (1.8)	6.32*	.34
Current femininity	1.46	1.46	0.00	.00
Current masculinity	5.36	3.96	5.83*	.35
Ideal femininity	1.61	1.71	0.48	.10
Ideal masculinity	5.48	4.88	1.36	.17

Note: *p < .05. The means are adjusted for the covariates. Standard deviations are in parentheses and are given for raw scores only.

partially supported this prediction. Even after adolescents' self-esteem, family income, and three dimensions of family functioning were controlled, father-present boys had higher levels of current masculinity than did father-absent boys (see Table 6.3). These results corroborated those of most of the previous studies in this area with European American boys. However, after we controlled for the other variables, the boys no longer differed on ideal masculinity. Therefore, father-absent boys perceived themselves to be lower in masculinity, but they wanted to be as masculine as the father-present boys wanted to be. Counter to the prediction and to previous researchers' use of standardized measures (Kodandaram, 1991), the boys did not significantly differ on current or ideal femininity (although the trends were in that direction). Both groups tended to perceive themselves as low in femininity, and they did not want to be more or less feminine (see Table 6.3).

These findings have many implications for future research. For one, they show that the average African American boy from father-absent homes has a different perception of his masculinity than does the average father-present African American boy. Because income, self-esteem, important family functioning factors, or the everyday presence of their mothers cannot fully explain this result, this difference is most likely due to some remaining difference between the two groups. The everyday presence of fathers in the lives of the two-parent boys is the most likely factor. This implies that there is something unique about fathers' everyday presence in the lives of their sons that cannot be accounted for by the fathers' income or by general family functioning (see Tables 6.1 and 6.3).

Although it is still possible that the socialization differences between single and married mothers are the main cause of the gender role differences, this is still probably due to single mothers' attempts to compensate for the lack of everyday socialization from fathers. Therefore, it could still be the lack of everyday socialization from fathers for the father-absent boys that influences the differences between the boys. Future researchers need to examine this differential socialization in more detail.

The differences that remained in current masculinity after the controls may also be accounted for by previous findings that indicate that father-present boys might actually be physically more mature than father-absent boys (Beaty, 1995). Thus, when many single African American mothers "love" their sons by attempting to protect them from perceived environmental dangers (Cunningham, Swanson, Spencer, & Dupree, 2003), they may inadvertently prevent them from physically maturing at the same rate as father-present boys. In fact, Cunningham et al. (2003) found that parental monitoring was higher for physically less mature African American boys than for more physically advanced boys of the same age. Those boys who had high parental monitoring also experienced fewer stressful events associated with high-risk neighborhoods. These stressful events may cause the boys' bodies to respond by developing faster, or fewer stressful events may cause slower physical maturity. Either way, if there are actual physical differences between the boys, they will undoubtedly impact boys' perceptions of their masculinity. Because the traditional socialization strategies of fathers facilitate a more physically demanding environment for boys, the extra years of receiving this type of socialization every day (e.g., rough-and-tumble play, pushing to achieve, making boys work through pain) may have slowly increased the physical differences between the boys.

The second set of hypotheses stated that father-absent girls would have lower current and ideal perceptions of their femininity (Table 6.4). Given previous research in this area, we expected both groups of girls to perceive similarly low levels of current and ideal masculinity. The results were somewhat different than the hypotheses. Even though the girls did not differ in their perceptions of current levels of femininity, they both wanted to be more feminine. However, the father-present girls wanted to be more feminine than the father-absent girls wanted to be (see Table 6.4). This is probably due to fathers' tendency to feminize their girls by rewarding behavior they deem to be feminine (Leve & Fagot, 1997; Parke, 1996).

The most unexpected finding was that father-absent girls had higher perceptions of their current masculinity than did father-present girls (see Table 6.4). This is interesting because previous researchers have found that

Table 6.4 Girls' Gender Role Development by Family Structure Before and After Controlling for Self-Esteem, Family Income, Family Relationships, Family Growth, and Family Systems

| | Family structure | | | |
Gender role (raw scores)	Father-present (n = 29)	Father-absent (n = 27)	F (1,54)	η
Current femininity	4.66 (1.5)	4.52 (2.0)	0.08	.00
Current masculinity	1.52 (0.8)	2.63 (2.2)	6.70*	.33
Ideal femininity	5.93 (1.2)	5.17 (1.6)	4.31*	.26
Ideal masculinity (adjusted scores)	1.54 (0.7)	2.03 (1.6)	2.32	.20
Current femininity	4.39	4.80	0.62	.11
Current masculinity	1.60	2.60	3.71*	.26
Ideal femininity	6.07	5.04	5.32*	.32
Ideal masculinity	1.50	2.00	1.90	.18

Note: *p < .05.

The means are adjusted for the covariates.

Standard deviations are in parentheses and are given for raw scores on.

although father-absent adolescent girls tend to be less feminine (Stevenson & Black, 1988), they are not necessarily more masculine. However, in retrospect, this finding could be predicted by the balance theory as well, because father-absent girls are similar to father-present boys. They both are pushed to be independent and accept many responsibilities (e.g., babysit younger siblings, cook, clean, do yardwork). Consequently, girls in this situation would tend to be assertive, confident, self-reliant, and acquire many other traits traditionally associated with masculinity. Furthermore, because their brothers (i.e., father-absent boys) are not as masculine as some other boys, and because their brothers are likely to be their main models of masculinity, these girls may think of themselves as more masculine than father-present girls because they think of themselves as being just as capable of doing many traditionally masculine activities as the boys their age.

Another related possibility is that father-absent girls are physically more mature than father-present girls, and they perceive this physical maturity as masculinity. This may explain the finding that father-absent girls experience menarche at younger ages and are more sexually precocious than father-present girls (Belsky, Steinberg, & Draper, 1991; Ellis et al., 2003). Furthermore, when fathers are present in the home, girls are less likely to have to do many of the manual labor chores and take on many of the other traditionally masculine duties that they would have to do if a father were not present (Hilton & Haldeman, 1991). Therefore, it is likely that both male and female bodies respond to the physical demands of the environment in which they grow. Because, according to the balance theory, father-absent girls have more physical and psychological demands placed on them, it makes sense that they would be physically more mature than girls of the same age who have experienced fewer physical demands.

The finding that father-absent girls perceive themselves as being more masculine than do father-present girls is also interesting because the groups of girls did not differ on their perceptions of ideal masculinity (see Table 6.4). In fact, father-absent girls were the only group in the study who wanted to be significantly less masculine than they perceived themselves to be. Thus, father-absent girls perceived themselves to be more masculine than did father-present girls, but they did not want to be so. This implies unhappiness with traits considered more masculine than those of the traditional stereotype of adolescent girls.

This unhappiness may be best understood by considering the reality of the stereotypic portrayal of single African American women as overly independent and assertive (Fordham, 1993). Instead of perceiving these traits as positive and adaptive, as studies have shown them to be (Burnett et al., 1995; Whitley, 1985), society has labeled them as atypical and problematic for women. Thus, it is not surprising that some girls are unhappy with traits society deems to be masculine and desire to be more of what society considers to be feminine.

Conclusion

In general, father absence is related to gender role development in both male and female African American adolescents. Father-present boys perceive themselves as more masculine than do father-absent boys. Father-absent girls also perceive themselves to be more masculine than do father-present girls, but they did not desire to be so masculine. We argued that this difference is primarily due to the absence of father's traditional socialization strategies in father-absent homes, but these were not directly assessed in the current study. However, if fathers do indeed place more physical demands on their sons and reduce the physical demands placed on their daughters, as many studies have indicated (Hilton & Haldeman, 1991; Wilson, 1992), then this is likely one of the mechanisms by which fathers' absence impacts gender role development. If this is the case, then the lack of everyday socialization from fathers will place father-absent boys at risk for not developing traits such as independence and assertiveness. Although many father-absent girls will develop these traits, the negative emotional toll of not having a close relationship with their fathers (Amato, 1991; Mandara & Murray, 2000) and their tendency to seek out the loving they missed from their fathers in babies and other men (Belsky et al., 1991; Ellis et al., 2003) must not be discounted. Therefore, researchers and social service providers must impress upon single and married African American mothers and fathers the necessity of both raising and loving their boys and girls.

Reflective questions

1. "Mothers love their sons and raise their daughters." What does this mean, and what is the impact on the Black community?
2. How does the above childrearing strategy differ for Black fathers?
3. In what ways do father-absent homes differ from father-present homes in terms of adolescent gender role development (male and female)?

References

Adams, C. H., & Sherer, M. (1985). Sex-role orientation and psychological adjustment: Implications for the masculinity model. *Sex Roles, 12,* 1211–1218.

Adelson, J. (1980). *Handbook of adolescent psychology.* New York: Wiley.

Aguilar, M. L., Kaiser, R. T., Murray, C. B., & Ozer, D. J. (1998). Validation of an adjective Q-Sort as a measure of the Big Five personality structure. *Journal of Black Psychology, 24,* 145–163.

Amato, P. R. (1991). Parental absence during childhood and depression in later life. *Sociological Quarterly, 32,* 543–556.

Barrett, A. E., & White, H. R. (2002). Trajectories of gender role orientations in adolescence and early adulthood: A prospective study of the mental health effects of masculinity and femininity. *Journal of Health and Social Behavior, 43,* 451–468.

Beaty, L. A. (1995). Effects of paternal absence on male adolescents' peer relations and self-image. *Adolescence, 30,* 874–880.

Belsky, J., Steinberg, L., & Draper, P. (1991). Childhood experience, interpersonal development, and reproductive strategy: An evolutionary theory of socialization. *Child Development, 62,* 647–670.

Berrenberg, J. L., & Deyle, R. (1989). Type A behavior, masculinity, and self-esteem: Achievement disclosure as a moderating variable. *Journal of Social Behavior and Personality, 4,* 389–399.

Binion, V. J. (1990). Psychological androgyny: A Black female perspective. *Sex Roles, 27,* 487–507.

Block, J., & Block, J. H. (1980). *The California Child Q-set.* Palo Alto, CA: Consulting Psychologists Press.

Bowman, P. J., & Forman, T. A. (1997). Instrumental and expressive family roles among African American fathers. In R. J. Taylor & J. S. Jackson (Eds.), *Family life in Black America* (pp. 216–247). Thousand Oaks, CA: Sage.

Bowman, P. J., & Sanders, R. (1998). Unmarried African American fathers: A comparative life span analysis. *Journal of Comparative Family Studies, 29,* 39–56.

Burnett, J. W., Anderson, W. P., & Heppner, P. P. (1995). Gender roles and self-esteem: A consideration of environmental factors. *Journal of Counseling and Development, 73,* 323–326.

Bussey, K., & Bandura, A. (1999). Social cognitive theory of gender development and differentiation. *Psychological Review, 106,* 676–713.

Coley, R. L. (1998). Children's socialization experiences and functioning in single-mother households: The importance of fathers and other men. *Child Development, 69,* 219–230.

Cunningham, M., Swanson, D. P., Spencer, M. B., & Dupree, D. (2003). The association of physical maturation with family hassles among African American adolescent males. *Cultural Diversity and Ethnic Minority Psychology, 9,* 276–288.

De Leon, B. (1993). Sex role identity among college students: A cross-cultural analysis. *Hispanic Journal of Behavioral Sciences, 15,* 476–489.

Egan, S. K., & Perry, D. G. (2001). Gender identity: A multidimensional analysis with implications for psychosocial adjustment. *Developmental Psychology, 37,* 451–463.

Ellis, B. J., Bates, J. E., Dodge, K. A., Fergusson, D. M., Horwood, L. J., Pettit, G. S., & Woodward, L. (2003). Does father absence place daughters at special risk for early sexual activity and teenage pregnancy? *Child Development, 74,* 801–821.

Fields, J. (2003, June). *Children's living arrangements and characteristics: March 2002.* Current Population Reports, P20-547. Washington, DC: U.S. Census Bureau.

Flinn, M. V., Quinlan, R. J., Decker, S. A., Turner, M. T., & England, B. G. (1996). Male-female differences in effects of parental absence on glucocorticoid stress response. *Human Nature, 7,* 125–162.

Florsheim, P., Tolan, P., & Gorman-Smith, D. (1998). Family relationships, parenting practices, the availability of male family members, and the behavior of inner-city boys in single-mother and two-parent families. *Child Development, 69,* 1437–1447.

Fordham, S. (1993). "Those loud Black girls": (Black) women, silence, and gender "passing" in the academy. *Anthropology & Education Quarterly, 24,* 3–32.

Green, R., Williams, K., & Goodman, M. (1985). Masculine and feminine gender identity in boys: Developmental differences between two diverse family groups. *Sex Roles, 12,* 1155–1162.

Harris, A. C. (1996). African-American and Anglo-American gender identities: An empirical study. *Journal of Black Psychology, 22,* 182–194.

Heiss, J. (1996). Effects of African American family structure on school attitudes and performance. *Social Problems, 43,* 246–265.

Hetherington, E. M. (1966). Effects of paternal absence on sex-typed behaviors in Negro and white preadolescent males. *Journal of Personality and Social Psychology. 4,* 87–91.

Hetherington, E. M. (1972). Effects of father absence on personality development in adolescent daughters. *Developmental Psychology, 7,* 313–326.

Hill, S. A., & Zimmerman, M. K. (1995). Valiant girls and vulnerable boys: The impact of gender and race on mothers' caregiving for chronically ill children. *Journal of Marriage and the Family, 57,* 43–53.

Hilton, J. M., & Desrochers, S. (2002). Children's behavior problems in single-parent and married-parent families: Development of a predictive model. *Journal of Divorce & Remarriage, 37,* 13–36.

Hilton, J. M., & Haldeman, V. A. (1991). Gender differences in the performance of household tasks by adults and children in single-parent and two-parent, two-earner families. *Journal of Family Issues, 12,* 114–130.

Hofferth, S. L., & Anderson, K. G. (2003). Are all dads equal? Biology versus marriage as a basis for paternal investment. *Journal of Marriage and the Family, 65,* 213–232.

Hunter, A. G., & Davis, J. E. (1992). Constructing gender: An exploration of Afro-American men's conceptualization of manhood. *Gender & Society, 6,* 464–479.

Jackson, A. P. (1993). Black, single, working mothers in poverty: Preferences for employment, well-being, and perceptions of preschool-age children. *Social Work, 38,* 26–34.

Jenkins, J. E., & Guidubaldi, J. (1997). The nature-nurture controversy revisited: Divorce and gender as factors in children's racial group differences. *Child Study Journal, 27,* 145–160.

Johnson, W. E., Jr. (1998). Paternal involvement in fragile, African American families: Implications for clinical social work practice. *Smith College Studies in Social Work, 68,* 215–232.

Johnson, W. E., Jr. (2001). Parental involvement among unwed fathers. *Children and Youth Services Review, 23,* 513–536.

Kamo, Y. (2000). Racial and ethnic differences in extended family households. *Sociological Perspectives, 43,* 211–229.

Kodandaram, P. (1991). Sex-role identification in father absent juvenile delinquents. *Journal of Personality and Clinical Studies, 7,* 63–65.

Lawson, E. J., & Thompson, A. (1999). *Black men and divorce.* Thousand Oaks, CA: Sage.

Leaper, C., Anderson, K. J., & Sanders, P. (1998). Moderators of gender effects on parents' talk to their children: A meta-analysis. *Developmental Psychology, 34,* 3–27.

Leve, L., & Fagot, B. (1997). Gender-role socialization and discipline processes in one and two-parent families. *Sex Roles, 36,* 1–19.

Long, V. O. (1989). Relation of masculinity to self-esteem and self-acceptance in male professionals, college students, and clients. *Journal of Counseling Psychology, 36,* 84–87.

Maccoby, E. E., & Martin, J. (1983). Socialization in the context of the family: Parent child interaction. In E. M. Hetherington (Ed.), *Handbook of child psychology: Vol. 4. Socialization, personality, and social development* (4th ed., pp. 1–101). New York: Wiley.

Mandara, J. (2003). The typological approach in child and family psychology: A review of theory, methods, and research. *Clinical Child and Family Psychology Review, 6,* 129–146.

Mandara, J., & Murray, C. B. (2000). The effects of parental marital status, family income, and family functioning on African American adolescent self-esteem. *Journal of Family Psychology, 14,* 475–490.

Mandara, J., & Murray, C. B. (2002). Development of an empirical typology of African American family functioning. *Journal of Family Psychology, 16,* 318–337.

Marsh, H. W., Antill, J. K., & Cunningham, J. D. (1987). Masculinity, femininity, and androgyny: Relations to self-esteem and social desirability. *Journal of Personality, 55,* 661–685.

Marsh, H. W., & Byrne, B. M. (1991). Differentiated additive androgyny model: Relations between masculinity, femininity, and multiple dimensions of self-concept. *Journal of Personality and Social Psychology, 61*, 811–828.

McAdoo, H. P., & McAdoo, J. (2002). The dynamics of African American fathers' family roles. In H. P. McAdoo (Ed.), *Black children: Social, educational, and parental environments* (pp. 3–12). Thousand Oaks, CA: Sage.

McLanahan, S. S. (1985). Family structure and the reproduction of poverty. *American Journal of Sociology, 90*, 873–901.

McLeod, J. D., Kruttschnitt, C., & Dornfeld, M. (1994). Does parenting explain the effects of structural conditions on children's antisocial behavior? A comparison of Blacks and Whites. *Social Forces, 73*, 575–604.

McLoyd, V. C. (1990). The impact of economic hardship on Black families and children: Psychological distress, parenting, and socioemotional development. *Child Development, 61*, 311–346.

McLoyd, V. C., Cauce, A. M., Takeuchi, D., & Wilson, L. (2000). Marital processes and parental socialization in families of color: A decade review of research. *Journal of Marriage and the Family, 62*, 1070–1093.

Moos, R. H., & Moos, B. S. (1986). *Family environment scale manual.* Palo Alto, CA: Consulting Psychologists Press.

Nunnally, J. C., & Bernstein, I. H. (1994). *Psychometric theory.* New York: McGraw-Hill.

O'Brien, E. J., & Epstein, S. (1988). *The Multidimensional Self-Esteem Inventory: Professional manual.* Odessa, FL: Psychological Assessment Resources.

Parke, R. D. (1996). *Fatherhood.* Cambridge, MA: Harvard University Press.

Popenoe, D. (1996). *Life without father.* New York: Free Press.

Price-Bonham, S., & Skeen, P. (1982). Black and White fathers' attitudes toward children's sex roles. *Psychological Reports, 50*, 1187–1190.

Radziszewska, B., Richardson, J. L., Dent, C. W., & Flay, B. R. (1996). Parenting style and adolescent depressive symptoms, smoking, and academic achievement: Ethnic, gender, and SES differences. *Journal of Behavioral Medicine, 19*, 289–305.

Reid, P. T., & Trotter, K. H. (1993). Children's self-presentations with infants: Gender and ethnic comparisons. *Sex Roles, 29*, 171–181.

Ruble, D. N., & Martin, C. L. (2000). Gender development. In W. Damon & N. Eisenberg (Eds.), *Handbook of child psychology: Vol. 3. Social, emotional, and personality development* (pp. 933–1016). New York: Wiley.

Ruvolo, A. P., & Veroff, J. (1997). For better or for worse: Real-ideal discrepancies and the marital well-being of newlyweds. *Journal of Social and Personal Relationships, 14*, 223–242.

Schaal, B., Tremblay, R. E., Soussignan, R., & Susman, E. J. (1996). Male testosterone linked to high social dominance but low physical aggression in early adolescence. *Journal of the American Academy of Child and Adolescent Psychiatry, 35*, 1322–1330.

Scott, J. W., & Black, A. (1989). Deep structure of African American life: Female and male kin networks. *Western Journal of Black Studies, 13*, 17–23.

Siegal, M. (1987). Are sons treated more differently by fathers than by mothers? *Developmental Review, 7*, 183–209.

Silverstein, L. B., & Auerbach, C. F. (1999). Deconstructing the essential father. *American Psychologist, 54*, 397–407.

Staples, R., & Boulin-Johnson, L. (1993). *Black families at the crossroads: Challenges and prospects.* San Francisco: Jossey-Bass.

Starrels, M. (1994). Gender differences in parent-child relations. *Journal of Family Issues, 15*, 148–165.

Stephens, N., & Day, H. D. (1979). Sex-role identity, parental identification, and self-concept of adolescent daughters from mother-absent, father-absent, and intact families. *Journal of Psychology, 103*, 193–202.

Stevens, M., Golombok, S., Beveridge, M., & ALSPAC Study Team. (2002). Does father absence influence children's gender development? Findings from a general population study of preschool children. *Parenting: Science and Practice, 2*, 47–60.

Stevenson, M. R., & Black, K. N. (1988). Paternal absence and sex-role development: A meta-analysis. *Child Development, 59*, 793–814.

Tucker, M. B., & Mitchell-Kernan, C. (1995). Trends in African American family formation: A theoretical and statistical overview. In M. B. Tucker & C. Mitchell-Kernan (Eds.), *The decline in marriage among African Americans* (pp. 3–26). New York: Russell Sage Foundation.

Waugh, R. F. (2001). Measuring ideal and current self-concept on the same scale, based on a multifaceted, hierarchical model of self-concept. *Educational and Psychological Measurement, 61*, 85–101.

Whitley, B. E. (1985). Sex-role orientation and psychological well-being: Two meta-analyses. *Sex Roles, 12*, 207–225.

Wilson, M. N. (1992). Perceived parental activity of mothers, fathers, and grandmothers in three-generational Black families. In K. Burlew, C. Banks, H. P. McAdoo, & D. A. A. Azibo (Eds.), *African American psychology: Theory, research, and practice* (pp. 87–104). Thousand Oaks, CA: Sage.

chapter seven

Finding yourself when you're not at home

William D. Allen
Healing Bonds
Minneapolis, Minnesota

Introduction

This chapter explores strategies for effective clinical work with African American youth. It specifically addresses the therapeutic needs of African American males in various types of foster care (both familial and nonfamilial) or in the process of being adopted. Some of the developmental and relational dynamics presented here may also apply to African American girls and young women, but the author has chosen to focus on boys and young men as this book is about the lives of Black fathers.* Fatherhood is a role that many of these young males will move into over the course of their lives. As such, it is important for those seeking to help these youth to consider these future roles as they provide current services.

These young men present a unique set of challenges for clinicians working with them in individual counseling or other programmatic settings (Kortenkamp & Ehrle, 2002). These include the possibility of their having experienced traumatic events earlier in their lives, current (and often past) familial disruptions, ongoing conflicts family conflicts, and a variety of unresolved developmental problems (Halfon, Mendonca, & Berkowitz, 1995; Reams, 1999). The youth and their families also bring ongoing issues, such as conflicts between biological and custodial parents, familial estrangement, and instability in their current home settings. As we will see, layered on top of these structural issues, these youth face the challenge of developing healthy, Black male identities in a variety of social contexts.

* The terms *African American* and *Black* are used interchangeably in this chapter.

Therapeutic success with these youth raises several important issues for clinicians. They must be grounded personally and professionally, especially in terms of their knowledge about child and adolescent development, as some of these young males are difficult to engage in therapy. The clinicians must also understand the importance of culture in shaping these youth's lives. For this reason, cultural competence (Sue & Sue, 2007) is a critical requirement if the therapy is to be effective. Knowledge about the child welfare system in their state is also useful, as there are regional differences that can affect if and when reunifications with biological parents can occur or how youth can eventually become emancipated as young adults. Clinicians must also carefully consider their suitability to work with African American youth and families, taking into account the cross-cultural strengths and weaknesses they bring to the work.

This chapter will attempt to answer many of these questions based on the author's clinical experiences with African American youth and families in a large, Midwestern city over the past two decades. The chapter is intended to provide suggestions for therapeutic and collaborative approaches that have proven effective with Black males in foster care, rather than an exhaustive survey of research or programs on this topic. It will leave readers with a greater appreciation of how their work can assist Black youth in addressing the complex developmental needs they bring to therapy.

The unique challenges of supporting African American youth

The majority of African American children are still raised by at least one of their biological parents in families including one or more siblings (Kreider, 2007; Taylor, Tucker, Chatters, & Jayakody, 1997). However, a disproportionate number of young, African American children spend a portion of their lives in the nation's child welfare system (U.S. Government Accountability Office, 2007). For example, in one Midwestern state, Black children experience more out-of-home placements as well as longer durations of those placements than their peers in other ethnic groups (Minnesota Department of Human Services, 2010); this is a condition typical of the experience of Black children in foster care throughout the United States. A small but significant group of these children eventually "age out" of the system at ages ranging from 18 to 21, often to uncertain futures (Harris, Jackson, O'Brien, & Pecora, 2009; Iglehart & Becerra, 2002). Regardless of their specific child welfare experience(s), most of these youth progress into adulthood with relationship skills honed earlier during the first two decades of life. These young men become fathers with or without their natal partners and form new marital and nonmarital households. Thus, the therapeutic needs of young, African American males in foster care are relevant in the wider discussion of the lives of African American males across the life span.

Successfully supporting African American families in the nation's child welfare system can be difficult considering the multiple pressures on these families (Simms, Dubowitz, & Szilagyi, 2000), including the various social support agencies they must negotiate. In addition to institutions such as school and health care, more restrictive forces such as child protection services and the criminal justice systems are often involved. These shape the individual developmental and family processes of these families in ways that are not always apparent but important to assess when seeking to provide assistance.

Though African American youth and their families are disproportionately involved in child welfare systems across the United States, it is not because African American families are necessarily more abusive or neglectful of their children. When adjusted for other demographic factors such as socioeconomic status, the incidence of child maltreatment is similar across ethnic groups (Ards, Myers, Chung, Malkis, & Hagerty, 2003). The disparity appears to be one aspect of a larger constellation of disproportionate representations for African Americans. These include disproportionately poorer health outcomes and greater involvement in the juvenile and criminal justice systems. Thus, to achieve success with this population, it is essential that practitioners understand both the wider ramifications of the problems they are dealing with and the potential benefits to the African American community (and society at large) of effective work with these youth.

Foundations

There are several foundational concepts underpinning this chapter. The first of these is an assumption that a primary task for young African Americans is establishing stable, authentic identities. These must include awareness of and comfort with their gender and ethnicity. In this discussion of young Black males, it means they need to develop a balanced sense of their masculinity, avoiding the hypermasculine trappings in much pop culture (as exemplified in much gangsta rap music) while gaining the emotional maturity they will need throughout life. Just as important, it means embracing a complex ethnocultural heritage that begins on the African continent but that in most cases weaves through time across many cultures and ethnic groups. African American boys and adolescents must develop healthy gender and ethnic identities in order to function effectively as healthy, productive African American men later in life.

This process is difficult enough, given the normative physical and emotional changes of adolescence, but it can be a more complex developmental task for these youth. They are developing these identities in the absence of their biological fathers, who, for many Black male children, provide a prototypical model of African American manhood. They must also accomplish the process outside of their families of origin, who, along with extended family and fictive kin, ideally provide supplementary cues about what Black men are and what they do for their families. Though out-of-home placements may be supportive, the effects of familial disruption may still place additional strains on the foster youth's process of identity formation. These strains may become insurmountable, as some of these youth must be moved from one foster placement to another. Much more could be (and has been) said on the topic of identity development among Black youth (Boyd-Franklin, Franklin, & Toussaint, 2000; Kunjufu, 2007), but we will simply reiterate here that it is a foundational concept in the care of these youth and their families.

This leads to a second foundational concept regarding ethnicity, which the author believes is an organizing principle in individual psychology, family process, and society. To quote Cornel West, "race matters" (West, 1993). It is important in shaping the emergent personality of young males developing internal models of what Black men/fathers are supposed to be, while being bombarded by mass media images of what some segments of society think they are. Black boys and adolescents are often keenly aware that they are ethnically different than other youth. Their perceptions about the significance of these differences can shape their motivations and behaviors in various social settings, most notably at home and in school. For example, if they believe that school is an environment where they are expected to succeed, it is more likely they will be motivated to attend and succeed in school. The converse is equally true: If they perceive that school is primarily "for Whites," they are not likely to be motivated to do well.

Ethnicity is also significant in the lives of both biological and fostering families (although the degree to which this is true varies from family to family). As noted, ethnicity plays an important role in determining which children experience foster care and the duration of those experiences. It can also affect the extent to which Black youth can be successfully integrated into foster households, since the ethnic experiences and parenting styles of foster parents may not align perfectly with those of biological parents. This is particularly true in the case of transethnic or interracial placements. Thus, ethnicity (aka race) is a component of the therapeutic process for all African American boys and adolescents in foster care, regardless of whether it is addressed explicitly or remains implicit.

For this reason, clinicians seeking to assist Black youth in foster care must be dedicated to practicing cultural competence (defined here as being knowledgeable, skilled, and comfortable working across ethnic and cultural boundaries). Cultural competence begins with understanding of one's own ethnicity and how it shapes one's worldviews and behaviors. The process continues through expanding one's knowledge of other ethnic groups and cultures, including possible similarities and differences between oneself and others (as well as awareness that similarities and differences occur within groups). Culturally competent clinicians then use these knowledge bases to help them and their clients find common grounds upon which to build therapeutic engagement. These clinicians also develop an informed capacity to know the limits of their ability and, if necessary, utilize service networks that can extend their expertise.

A final foundational concept for this discussion of Black youth in foster care is the suggestion that all therapeutic work with African American youth must be systemic. This means taking an ecosystemic view of the child, his physical and emotional needs, and those of both biological and fostering families. It applies to all phases of care from assessment and diagnosis to treatment. The reason for assessing the entire ecosystem is not for a single clinician to attempt to treat it *in its entirety*. The objective is to gain a thorough knowledge of the presenting problems the young male brings to therapy as well as the identification of resources available for addressing those problems.

These youth typically have multiple relationships with family members and social service providers outside of their primary foster households. It is important to incorporate these often significant relationships (and their potential effects) into the therapeutic process. Keeping a systemic view can help clinicians working with these children avoid the possibility of the therapy collapsing into a persistent set of problematic behaviors. When this happens, clinicians miss many of the resources within the ecosystem, including skills the youth may be using more or less effectively in various settings.

Characteristics of the population

African American young males and adolescents who are currently in (or have been) in foster care are as diverse as the general population of African American youth. With this in mind, several typical characteristics of foster children will be explored as well as some of their challenges.[*] These should provide a suitable backdrop for the discussion of suggested approaches to working with these youth and their families.

---

[*] The sample of youth the author has encountered in his practice is by no means a scientific one, but these youth can be considered typical examples of African American boys and adolescents in foster care, as well as their presenting problems.

Black youth in foster care must often deal with feelings of separation from biological parents, even if their time with birth parents was limited. Attachment theory suggests that early disruption of parent–child bonds can have negative consequences for children later in life. An example of this may be the internal struggles regarding inclusion that some in foster or adoptive care face. (Inclusion is the sense that one belongs to a specific group or place; inclusion is the glue that holds groups like families together.) Black youth in foster care deal with inclusion questions on several levels, including "To which parents do I belong?" "Where is my real home?" and "Am I included in a society in which I am an ethnic minority?"

It is a given that many of these young males have experienced some degree of trauma during their lives. They may have been the victims of neglect, physical abuse, or sexual abuse. Even if they were not victimized themselves, they may have witnessed the victimization of others. However, most of these youth typically do not perceive these experiences as traumatic, and they may be unaware of the effects they may be having in their lives at present. For some, separation from other family of origin members may feel like a more significant trauma than the events that precipitated their entering foster care. Even when allegations of neglect or abuse have been substantiated (and biological parents have been found guilty), many foster children still feel a deep sense of allegiance to their biological parents that makes outplacement and the resulting family estrangement problematic.

Some of these youth (and their siblings) may have experienced informal adoption or fostering by other family members. In some cases, these informal adoptions may avoid subsequent extrafamilial placement or at least postpone it. But when they occur in distressed family systems, these informal adoptions may represent another step in a downward progression toward eventual outplacement and permanent foster care. In these cases, the "failed" adoptions (formal or informal) may simply add to their trauma history, especially when accompanied by maltreatment by the foster or adoptive parents. Lack of stability in foster or adoptive placements may be the result of poor training (as a foster parent), inadequate preparation, or unrealistic expectations on the part of the foster parent, the placing authority, or even the child. Placements also tend to fail if the foster households have familial or social problems that cause their homes to be instable (e.g., other children with severe behavioral problems).

Many of these young men may also have experienced other types of family disruptions, such as relational conflict between their biological parents, including separation and divorce. These disruptions may or may not be accompanied by domestic violence. In some cases, the familial conflicts may have been severe enough to prompt the youth's removal from the biological parents' care. Other familial problems that might precipitate disruption include one or both parent's chemical dependency, problems with the criminal justice system, or mental health problems. Although these problems pose serious difficulties for all families, they often precipitate more serious child welfare interventions in African American families.*

In addition to family *disruption*, there may be ongoing familial *conflict* that may reach beyond the child's biological family of origin. Examples of this would be poor relationships between parents and siblings, parents and grandparents, or other combinations extending into fictive kin networks. These relational problems tend to make it difficult for these youth to formulate what healthy, familial relationships look like. Conflicts between their biological and custodial families can present problems for some youth despite the best preparation by child welfare workers. If not outright conflict, there are often resentments (on the part of biological parents) or feelings of mistrust (by foster parents) that affect the youths' relationships with both households. This type of cross-household conflict can make the task of negotiating attachment and inclusion issues for African American foster youth even more difficult.

A final characteristic that seems a typical feature of many of these youngsters is the potential that they are struggling with undiagnosed developmental or psychological problems (Clausen, Landsverk, Ganger, Chadwick, & Litrownick, 1998). Although being in foster care does not predict that a child will have psychological problems, the probability of such problems is increased given the presence of some of the typical traumas discussed earlier. Because a disproportionate number of African American children live in poverty (Moore, Redd, Burkhauser, Mbwana, & Collins, 2009), when these children enter foster care, they are also more likely to have experienced or witnessed these traumatic events. These children are also less likely to have had their own developmental or psychological needs attended to, as evidenced by widely acknowledged health disparities.† It can also be the case that problematic behaviors of foster youth are attributed solely to their "troubled background," when in fact

---

* This is due to several factors, including that (a) many African American families experience multiple risk factors that may facilitate conditions that lead to neglect or abuse; (b) these same risk factors expose Black families and children to higher levels of public scrutiny (e.g., mandatory reporting); and (c) Black families typically have fewer resources to shield them from child protection services (e.g., legal representation) and are afforded fewer opportunities to access less intrusive interventions, such as residential treatment, diversion programs, or psychotherapy.

† Although there is some debate about the underlying causes of health disparities between European Americans and African Americans on a range of health measures, there is little disagreement that they exist or that they are not entirely mitigated by socioeconomic factors such as household income, education level, or employment status.

they may be suffering from a developmental delay or mental illness co-occurring with trauma related to the familial disruption(s).

Therapeutic approaches

The work of individuals and agencies in the child welfare system influences the psychosocial development of African American youth in foster care. The influence can be beneficial or harmful, depending on the planning and execution of the specific intervention or services delivered over time. Clinicians who work with these children and their families have an obligation to consider therapeutic approaches that minimize the negative effects of out-of-home placement while maximizing these children's potential to develop as competent participants in future relationships. Their work should help these youth develop healthy gender and ethnic identities. It should also enable these boys to develop the relational skills they will need to be successful in relationships as friends, coworkers, and neighbors, and in close relationships as partners, husbands, and fathers. The probability that therapeutic work will be beneficial increases when it is *strategic* (i.e., planned and coordinated) rather than haphazard, and when it is *systemic* rather than narrowly focused on problems. The chances of success also increase when clinicians work from a culturally competent as opposed to a "color blind" perspective.

Clinicians working with African American foster youth must be able to tolerate these youth's initial resistance to therapy. If successful, the resistance will give way to more trusting attitudes. Many of these young males have been in therapy before, often unsuccessfully. They bring to the therapeutic encounter a wariness that can often feel to the clinician like direct challenges to their competence or the utility of therapy. It is critical that clinicians avoid interpreting this reticence as a personal attack but rather use it as an opportunity to demonstrate openness, commitment to the youth, and tolerance for the ambiguity inherent in beginning therapeutic relationships. Getting past the turbulence of the first couple of sessions can also demonstrate to these youth that they can build relationships with others despite differences or even disagreements.

Patience and endurance are important assets to have in working with this population for several reasons. Young Black males are sometimes brought to therapy with expectations of brief "miracle cures," or magical cessations of long-standing problems. Typically, it takes time to build therapeutic relationships that are sturdy enough to support the work of assessing and treating such problems. This may run counter to arbitrary timelines dictated by funding sources (e.g., managed care) or other considerations (such as court dates). Approaches that maximize adherence to technical standardization over the quality of the therapeutic relationship are also likely to be less successful. Fighting for sufficient time to establish such trusting relationships may be as difficult as the therapy itself, but it is a fight worth winning. Trust (and specifically, determining who to trust) is a significant concern of African American youth, including those in foster care. Gaining and maintaining their trust is one of the most effective strategies for success in this work.

Support to foster youth

Therapeutic work with Black children in foster care is, by its very nature, multifaceted. Clinicians must assess not only the child's needs but the needs and capabilities of the child's parents and often other siblings. The foster parents and their needs must be factored into the assessment as well. There are several tasks that the author has found are essential components for effective work with African American boys and adolescents in therapy as part of their foster care. They include (a) facilitating growth, (b) providing stability, (c) building a safe, trusting therapeutic environment, and (d) modeling openness.

Facilitating growth

Because the lives of many African American youth in the child welfare system have been punctuated by numerous family and relational disruptions, their emotional and psychological development is often negatively affected by these events. Thus, an important clinical objective is to assess where these youth are in their individual and social development. One way in which therapeutic work influences these youth is its capacity to influence how they perceive themselves in terms of gender and ethnic identity. It can also affect how they assess their ability to enter into and, perhaps more important, sustain close relationships throughout their lives. Developing the personal awareness and relationship skills required to do so is an important part of these youth's psychological development.

African American foster adolescents struggle with the same tensions between wanting familial security and desiring independence that all adolescents do. This is made even more complex by the fact that the "nest" in this case is almost always not the one into which they were born. Thus, many of the emotional anchors that other adolescents typically rely on as they gain autonomy and increasing self-confidence (e.g., the belief that parents will always love them no matter what) are often unavailable to Black youth in foster care, or at least they may not perceive them to be as accessible. Layered on top of these normative, developmental tasks is the struggle to forge healthy, ethnic identities in the face of societal forces that, at times, directly (e.g., overt bias) and indirectly (e.g., negative media images) undermine this process.

As members of a distinct ethnic group, African American youth develop identities in a sea of influences that shape their self-concept. These include cultural messages from other African Americans (e.g., family, neighbors, etc.) as well as from members of other ethnic groups. The messages may also come from sources close to the youth as well as from more distal influences such as the mass media. Given their interpretive role, clinicians are in a unique position to help African American youth examine the meaning of these messages as they relate to ethnic identity formation. Development of positive, ethnic identity should be an explicit aspect of any treatment plan (regardless of the ethnicity of the clinician).

One approach to facilitating identity development is through articulation of the narrative or story of how the child came to be in foster care. These stories are sometimes explicit and part of the child's awareness and written record. However, stories can also be implicit in that they are not openly discussed or are even hidden. Whether explicit or implicit, clinicians should consider whether the stories explaining how youth entered foster care *help* or *hinder* their development. When youth are told that their parents' chemical abuse led to their abandonment, or that their parents' incarceration for violent crime necessitated placement, what do these young people make of these stories? Clinicians may need to help these youth place the circumstances that led to their out-of-home placement in contexts that don't perpetuate feelings of shame, inevitable doom, or denial.

For example, a young man who had experienced several foster placements over the first decade of life was now in a stable placement with experienced African American foster parents. However, he continued to have angry outbursts at home and problems fighting peers in school. In discussing his "story," the young man explained his resignation to the fact that both of his parents were angry, violent people and that this was simply "in his blood." Helping him understand that his parents' relational problems (and other unrelated failings, such as chemical dependency) did not predetermine his ability to build healthy relationships with others laid the groundwork for a dramatic improvement in his behavior.

Providing stability

As previously discussed, African American youth typically experience more frequent out-of-home placements and longer durations in those placements, and the circumstances leading to outplacement may also have involved trauma. The instability attending these disruptions does not facilitate the development of durable relationships with parents, siblings, and other significant people in these young people's lives. Moreover, many of these children struggle to find a sense of permanency on which to build individual self-esteem and reach out to others in healthy relationships. Thus, a primary clinical objective should be to help establish and nurture as much stability in the therapeutic system as possible while simultaneously promoting stability in other parts of the child's ecosystem. This begins with finding a predictable, mutually agreed upon time and place for therapy. This may not always be in the therapist's office or agency, and may need to accommodate the schedules of other stakeholders involved with the child and family. Many youth and their families who hold dim views of social service providers do so because they consider the latter to be inflexible (and thus perceived as uncaring). Working collaboratively to provide stability for African American foster youth is a critical link in the process of developing strong therapeutic bonds between the youth and their clinicians.

Families in the foster care system often have competing obligations that make it difficult to find a regular meeting time. This is made even more difficult when the needs of additional children must be considered. Clinicians also have scheduling constraints that restrict options for when and where they can see a child. Despite these potential obstacles, it is very important to establish a consistent, predictable relationship with Black children in foster care. A consistent schedule can help these youth develop a level of trust that can facilitate therapeutic engagement. The therapeutic relationship (if eventually solid enough) can mitigate some of the ambiguity many of these children initially experience in placement. The consistency may also be helpful to foster parents in organizing household activity and, as discussed later, in providing support for their custodial efforts. Because African American families are typically extended in nature, therapy can also become a quasi-familial substitute for kin relationships that have been disrupted.

Building a safe, trusting therapeutic environment

Building a safe, trusting environment is an essential part of all successful therapy, but it is even more important when working with African American youth for two reasons. As noted earlier, frequent relational disruptions tend to make many of these children mistrustful of others. They are understandably unsure of how long relationships with caregivers or service providers will last. In addition, some of the relationships they have experienced have been abusive or neglectful. Because they likely will have been in the child welfare system more often and for longer periods of time, clinicians may need to work harder with African American boys and adolescents to demonstrate that the therapeutic encounter can be trusted to as a place where their experiences (positive or negative) will be honored.

These young clients will open up about their lives and their perceptions about current concerns if they feel they can trust the provider to listen empathically, to be genuine when critical, and to be a credible resource. Unlike therapy with other ethnic groups, many African Americans may perceive uninvolved, "clinically objective" therapeutic styles as uninterested and thus unlikely to generate the levels of trust necessary for successful engagement.

A second reason that focus on developing safety and trust is critical is that, in many cases, the clinicians working with African American boys and adolescents will be European Americans or some other ethnicity than African American. The ethnic and cultural differences may or may not seem relevant to clinicians, but they typically hold significance for African American youth and their families because the clinicians may be perceived as agents of larger systems of social control (e.g., child protection). This may make developing trust initially more difficult.*

Modeling openness

Openness is a quality that can help these young men in many areas of their lives. The term *openness* is used here in a number of contexts. Modeling openness can also be a useful strategy for building trust. Clinicians can clearly communicate that they are open to learning more about the youth than what appears in their written files. Openness can also connote willingness to understand the youth's perception of the presenting problem(s).

Clinicians may need to demonstrate to young clients that the structure and process of therapeutic sessions can be flexible and open to change. For example, if a young client comes in and doesn't want to communicate *at that given moment*, clinicians may want to avoid labeling the youth as resistant. Instead, a change of the therapy in the form of a walk around the block may be instrumental in helping the young man disclose what is on his mind either then or at a later date. Openness to change is both a coping mechanism for those in the midst of change, as well as a skill for learning from new experiences and environments. Helping these youth develop self-confidence in the midst of the ambiguity attending the many changes in their lives may facilitate their ability to be open to the therapeutic process.

---

* This may be the case regardless of the clinician's ethnicity, but the problem can be more acute when the ethnic differences resonate with power and privilege disparities related to institutional racism.

Young African American males often feel uncomfortable acknowledging the range of their human emotions. Like their peers in other ethnic groups, most of these boys and adolescents have generally been socialized to repress their emotions, with the notable exception of anger. It may initially be difficult for them to express feelings of fear, abandonment, loneliness, regret, grief, or depression, much less joy, anticipation, excitement, and other, more positive emotions. The youth may perceive many of the latter as "uncool" or "weak," and they are unlikely to display them to others unless they feel they will not be ridiculed for being childish or unmanly. By discussing these emotions as normative, clinicians can broaden the repertoire of emotional response for these youth and increase their chances of developing deeper, more authentic relationships.* Self-disclosure and modeling during the session can facilitate this learning process while also enriching the therapeutic bond.

Support to foster parents

In addition to addressing the needs of the African American foster youth, clinicians need to consider how best to support the foster parents with whom the youth reside. This can begin with clear affirmation of the challenges in fostering children and adolescents who are temporarily or permanently separated from their parents. Clinicians should continue to express explicit support for foster parents work throughout the therapeutic relationship, using parents' interactions with the youth in the home as an extension of the therapy session. Regularly scheduled check-in sessions with the foster parents, and family therapy including parents and youth together may also be appropriate depending on the severity of presenting problems in the case. These can be useful opportunities for prospective problem solving as well as celebrating successes (and strategizing how to build upon them).

Just as cultural competence is a critical factor in the delivery of therapeutic services, foster parents of African American youth should be encouraged to consider how best to facilitate these youth's ethnic identity while promoting their ability to coexist with others in a multicultural society. It is particularly important to openly discuss characteristics such as ethnicity, religion, and country of origin in the case of transcultural, foster placements or adoptions. Even if either the foster parents or the children are initially uncomfortable with broaching the topic, clinicians should try to help them understand that pretending that these cultural

---

* Male clinicians (particularly African American males) may be in a uniquely advantageous position to do this with African American boys and adolescents.

characteristics and dynamics don't exist is potentially more harmful than the temporary discomfort of discussing them.

A typical example of how ethnicity can cause unnecessary problems for a foster family is the example of a European American family in a predominantly White, rural part of a Midwestern state that decides to foster a pair of African American siblings from a nearby city. The White family may mistakenly believe that discussing ethnicity or class (or even differences between urban and rural life) would be uncomfortable for them or the children. The children might also believe that bringing up questions on these topics might be interpreted by their foster parents as ingratitude. In this scenario, both parties would be underestimating the power of institutional racism to affect their lives and (in the case of the White family) may be unaware of their own White privilege. Addressed or unspoken, questions regarding differences would still exist. In addition, members of the extended family, neighbors, and other members of the community (not to mention members of the children's social network) would undoubtedly have many of the same unanswered questions. Rather than try to avoid or ignore these questions, clinicians may offer therapy as a safe place for the children and their foster family to discuss these important aspects of their lives together.

Clinicians should counsel foster parents to avoid taking foster youth's testing behaviors personally. Although it is prudent to take problematic behaviors seriously, it is not helpful to perceive them as personal attacks. The latter approach can lead to fatigue and frustration, and may eventually leave foster parents unmotivated to do the hard work of foster care. In that vein, a specific infraction or the accumulated weight of a series of problems may cause foster parents to express frustration about the status of the placement to the foster child. Changes in placement arrangements need to be thoroughly discussed among members of the treatment team before they are shared with the youth to avoid unnecessarily triggering feelings of insecurity in the youth regarding their placement. For example, telling the foster youth that bad behaviors mean "they are turning out like their (biological) parents" might reignite past feelings of shame while also heightening fears of (re)abandonment.

Like their peers residing at home, when foster children act out behaviorally, it is partially because they feel comfortable and secure enough to do so. Such "reframing" of negative behaviors does not minimize the seriousness of the problems. Instead, it gives parents (and clinicians) a more empowered perspective from which to co-develop solutions with the youth.

Another challenge for parents providing foster care is distinguishing between normative (developmentally appropriate) behavior problems and abnormal problematic behaviors. Whereas talking back is annoying and often a sign of disrespect, it is a fairly common behavior for adolescents. Morbid curiosity about fire and persistent fire-setting in the home may be signs of much more serious (and potentially dangerous) psychological problems. Similarly, the foster parent who fears his or her 15-year-old son's refusal to clean his room is a confirmation that he has Oppositional Defiant Disorder may be casting a normative, adolescent behavior as a psychological problem.

Finally, clinicians should work hard to engage both the foster parents and (if possible) the biological parents in support of the Black foster youth in therapy. When the biological family is involved with a child in foster placement, it is important to avoid conflicts between the biological and foster families. This is sometimes made more difficult because the circumstances seem to pit the two sets of parents (and family members) against each other. Clinicians should strategize with both families to find approaches for keeping appropriate family members in contact with the youth, including joint family activities when possible.

For example, an urban, African American couple had three young children removed from their home based on a single report of sexual abuse from a school-based, mandated reporter. The children were placed together in a suburban, European American household. After both biological parents complied fully with court-mandated anger management and parenting classes, and seeing no further evidence of maltreatment, the child welfare authorities were considering how best to reintegrate the children with their parents. The family therapist began by working with the children to help them cope with their conflicted feelings about their removal from their parents. Next, both sets of parents were counseled to see the critical importance each held for the children. As a result, the biological parents appreciated the love and care the foster parents had provided their children during the separation. For their part, the foster parents let go of their repulsion of the alleged abuse in favor of empathizing with the biological parents as loving parents who, for a complex set of reasons, found themselves in a catastrophic situation. Therapy concluded with a picnic occurring a month after reunification, indicating both parents' intention to continue the relationship.

This example also demonstrates the importance of encouraging foster parents to build out their "villages."* Extended support networks of family and friends are helpful for all families but may be especially important resources for foster families. In the case of transethnic placements or adoptions, these networks may provide pathways for African American youth to meet and socialize with other members of the African American community. They may also give non–African American foster parents the

---

* In the sense of the African proverb, "It takes a village to raise a child."

chance to obtain culturally specific services (e.g., hair care) for the Black foster children in their care. Clinicians should consider assessing relationships between foster parents and their extended families (e.g., siblings, grandparents, etc.) as well as friends (e.g., neighbors, faith communities, etc.) in order to develop strategies that leverage these social resources.

Suggestions for further research

More research is needed on African American males who as children spent time in foster care, particularly those who may have been in cross-cultural foster placements. These men could help us understand the pathways they traveled to establish positive gender identities as males/fathers, ethnic identities as people of African descent, and secure familial attachments later in life. Researchers at universities and nonprofit agencies (e.g., the Casey Foundation) have begun to look into this line of research as essential to facilitating better outcomes in later life for African American youth who previously experienced foster care.

Although quantitative data suggest that youth who have spent time in foster care typically become sexually active earlier than their non–foster care peers, it is not clear why this appears to be the case. Similarly, these youth are statistically more likely to become parents at earlier ages than other youth, but we know relatively little about how they perceive these early transitions to parenthood (e.g., whether they are seen as positive or negative events or potential determinants of life trajectories). More qualitative study is needed of the family formation decisions these youth make throughout late adolescence and early adulthood.

Of particular interest to readers of this book would be further research on young African American males' ideas and values regarding the appropriate timing for sexual activity and reproduction, as well as a better understanding of how youth in foster care develop their understanding of what fatherhood means. How do young men emerging from foster care who were abandoned by their own fathers build internal models of fatherhood to emulate? What is the influence of having several "social fathers" throughout one's life (as opposed to the primary influence of a biological father)? How might all of this differ from the situation of similar youth whose fathers were not involved or available to them *but who were raised in one household by their biological mothers*?

Finally, this chapter has briefly discussed the complex developmental task facing African American foster adolescents who must attempt to build durable gender *and* ethnic identities while often moving between multiple foster placements. The literature on the many pathways Black males follow on their way to becoming fathers has grown significantly over the past two decades. However, there is relatively little research documenting the factors that promote (or hinder) the unique "dual" development process these African American foster youth must successfully pursue if, later in their lives, they are to become successfully involved with their procreated families. In addition, there are few studies that present proven practices that clinicians can use to assist Black youth in this process. Attention to these issues is urgent, given the fact that most of these youth will go on to become fathers themselves, and in other ways involved in the lives of women and children (e.g., boyfriends, stepdads, etc.).

Conclusion

This chapter has focused on the specific challenges clinicians face in working with African American youth in foster care or otherwise involved in the child welfare system. These young men often come into counseling or therapeutic settings with similar psychological needs for gender and identity development. In addition, each has his own unique blend of life histories that often combine with factors in his foster settings to produce the diagnostic puzzle clinicians must decipher. Several ideas have been presented here to help clinicians understand what they are dealing with as well as how best to identify and harness therapeutic resources for assisting these youth and other significant stakeholders in their lives. Throughout the chapter, we have been mindful of the likelihood that many of these young Black males will become principal members of their own families and households at some point. It is therefore critical that clinicians keep in mind the long-term effect their work can have in shaping these youth's paternal aspirations and later behaviors.

We would be remiss in not pointing out that there is a need for the training and retention of more African American clinicians to work with African American youth. Although many of the concepts in this chapter can be mastered by qualified clinicians of other ethnic groups, we believe that African American youth in foster care may benefit from working with African American providers. African American men, in particular, may be able to help these youth work on their gender and ethnic identity issues while addressing the emotional and psychological problems that typically bring them to therapy. Black male therapists may also provide more credible models of what familial involvement looks like, whether it be as a father, son, boyfriend, or other significant familial role.

Concern over the disproportionately higher involvement of African American families and children in the nation's child welfare system has been growing recently. This includes more scrutiny by federal and state agencies that are beginning to demand more effective planning to reduce racial/ethnic disparities in out-of-home placement of African American children. Although the rates of outplacement have moderated and in some cases declined, a significant number of African American boys and adolescents across the nation face the prospect of spending a portion of their lives in foster care. Thus, improving their access to effective, culturally competent mental health services must be a national priority. It is hoped that readers will find this chapter useful in their continuing education as providers to this population, and as supportive resources in the lives of other stakeholders such as foster parents. In this way, those of us who work with African American boys and adolescents in foster care can help them understand not only who they are and where they came from but also who they have the potential to become.

Reflective questions

1. What do I know about African Americans, and in particular, African American children in foster care?
2. What do I know about male identity development in boys and adolescents?
3. What do I know about ethnic identity development?
4. What can I do to prepare Black males in foster care for successful familial roles later in life?
5. What constitutes the best therapeutic care for Black youth in foster care?
6. How systemic are my therapeutic case conceptualizations?
7. Do I work collaboratively with other stakeholders?

References

Ards, S., Myers, S., Chung, C., Malkis, A., & Hagerty, B. (2003). Decomposing differences in child maltreatment. *Child Maltreatment, 8*(2), 112–121.

Boyd-Franklin, N., Franklin, A., & Toussaint, P. (2000). *Boys into men: Raising our African American teenage sons.* New York: Dutton Press.

Clausen, J. M., Landsverk, J., Ganger, W., Chadwick, D., & Litrownick, A. (1998). Mental health problems of children in foster care. *Journal of Child and Family Studies, 7,* 283–296.

Halfon, N., Mendonca, A., & Berkowitz, G. (1995). Health status of children in foster care: The experience of the Center for the Vulnerable Child. *Archives of Pediatrics and Adolescent Medicine, 149,* 386–392.

Harris, M., Jackson, L., O'Brien, K., & Pecora, P. (2009). Disproportionality in education and employment outcomes of adult foster care alumni. *Children and Youth Services Review, 31,* 1150–1159.

Iglehart, A., & Becerra, R., (2002). Hispanic and African American youth: Life after foster care emancipation. *Journal of Ethnic & Cultural Diversity in Social Work, 11*(1/2), 79–107.

Kortenkamp, K., & Ehrle, J. (2002). *The well-being of children involved with the child welfare system: A national overview* (Series B, No. B-43). Washington, DC: Urban Institute.

Kreider, R. M. (2007, February). *Living arrangements of children: 2004.* Current Population Reports, P70-114. Washington, DC: U.S. Census Bureau.

Kunjufu, J. (2007). *Raising Black boys.* Chicago: African American Images.

Minnesota Department of Human Services, Children and Family Services. (2010). *Minnesota child welfare disparities report* (Rep. No. DHS-6056-ENG). St. Paul, MN: Author. Retrieved from https://edocs.dhs.state.mn.us/lfserver/Public/DHS-6056-ENG

Moore, K. A., Redd, Z., Burkhauser, M., Mbwana, K., & Collins, A. (2009). *Children in poverty: Trends, consequences, and policy options* (Research Brief Publication No. 2009-11). Washington, DC: Child Trends.

Reams, R. (1999). Children birth to three entering the state's custody. *Infant Mental Health Journal, 20,* 166–174.

Simms, M., Dubowitz, H., & Szilagyi, M. (2000, October). Health care needs of children in the foster care system. *Pediatrics, 106*(4), 909–918.

Sue, D. W., & Sue D. (2007). *Counseling the culturally diverse: theory and practice* (5th ed.). Hoboken, NJ: Wiley.

Taylor, R. J., Tucker, M. B., Chatters, L., & Jayakody, R. (1997). Recent trends in African American structure. In R. Taylor, J. Jackson, & L. Chatters (Eds.), *Family life in Black America* (pp. 14–62). Thousand Oaks, CA: Sage.

U.S. Government Accountability Office. (2007, July). *African American children in foster care* (Report to the Chairman, Committee on Ways and Means, House of Representatives, GAO-07-816). Washington, DC: Author.

West, C. (1993). *Race matters.* Boston: Beacon Press.

section two

Father stories

chapter eight

Man-to-boy becoming man-to-man

A son's reflection

Bedford E. Frank Palmer II
Southern Illinois University
Carbondale, Illinois

In my experience, Black fathering comes from many different sources. Uncles, brothers, cousins, the men that one interacts with in the neighborhood, all have a part to play in the development of children (Boyd-Franklin, 2003; Parham, White, & Ajamu, 1999). In my case, this fathering came primarily in the form of my biological father, who has been both active and present throughout my life. In this chapter, I will attempt to give the reader an understanding of how his presence has been a constant instigator of personal growth and development. And although I focus on my father's contribution to my development, I also acknowledge the equal influence of my mother, as I was lucky enough to be raised by two people who resolved to be good parents, whether I liked it or not.

My father, who I have always affectionately referred to as either "Dad" or "Pops," was born in December 1945, in a small house that time has reduced to a brick foundation. His mother tended the house and his father was a porter for the railroad. By the time my dad turned 12, his family had moved to San Diego, California, and both of my grandparents had died. He spent his adolescence moving between the homes of his 12 siblings, attending Catholic school, playing sports, and generally hustling to get by. He spent a short time in the U.S. Air Force, married my mother in 1967, and had my older sister in 1969. By the time that I was born in 1978, and my younger sister in 1982, my parents had worked hard enough to move our family to a middle-class suburb of San Diego.

Early lessons

Some of my first memories of my father revolve around play. One of the earliest, which I remember clearly, happened at a time when I was so small that my father had to squat down for me to reach his hands. I remember him showing me how to make a fist and telling me to punch his open hands, and the feeling of accomplishment that I felt when I was able to hit his hand and make it move. I remember him laughing and pretending that the blows that I leveled, with a fist he could easily engulf in his own, could actually cause his hands to fly backward and cause him to sometimes lose his balance. Looking back, this memory is important for multiple reasons. In that simple game, my father was able to begin to teach me lessons that would help to shape me as a person and prepare me for life as a Black man.

I find it somewhat ironic that as an activist, my first memory of my father consists of being taught to fight. Boyd-Franklin (2003) explains the "Black macho role" as the tendency of Black fathers to teach their sons not to show weakness. I believe that this was one of the core lessons that my father sought to teach me from a young age. Using this game of "hit-my-hands" as an example, my father began to teach me to become comfortable with asserting myself physically. With each punch, my father reinforced the belief that I was a strong person. He bolstered my confidence by acting as though I was strong enough to overwhelm the strongest person that I knew. Although some might contend that this was a lesson in how to be violent, I would counter that a young Black man, living in a White community, who did not know how to fight would soon learn how to take a beating. This type of play/training continued throughout my childhood, and I will revisit it later in the chapter.

Along with these early lessons in toughness, my father also taught me to use restraint. During my childhood, it was a rare and quite jarring event for my father to exhibit unrestrained anger. This would invariably be expressed in the form of one or two sentences of reproach roared with a level of intensity that, in my ears, would have garnered the respect of any fully maned lion that I saw on PBS. However, unlike those lions, these exclamations only seemed to manifest when he perceived some sort of real risk to our family. An example of one such event was when, in a moment of adolescent angst, I made the mistake of saying "I hate her [my sister]," after being tattled on.

My younger sister and I had the type of contentious relationship that seems to be reserved for siblings who are close in age. We argued over toys, television shows, privacy, and just about anything else that we could think of. My mother and father would tolerate this, as long as we kept our hands to ourselves and kept the arguing to a low din. I think that they understood that our behavior was normal, as they had both grown up in large families. Yet, even in their tolerance of our intolerance of each other, they made it clear that we were expected to treat one another as family. In terms of my outburst, my father made it clear that the word *hate* was inappropriate, when referring to my sister, and that I would love her whether I liked her or not. He reminded me that there was a difference between liking things about a person, or liking what a person does, and loving them.

In many ways, I feel that my parents were deeply practical in their view of familial interactions. My sisters and I were taught that we did not always need to like or approve of our family members. If a family member wronged another family member, we were not asked to sweep that wrong under a rug or to immediately forgive that wrong. In fact, it was our duty to call out bad behavior and try to remedy the situation. However, we were taught to never do this through violence. Nor were we to confuse the temporary negative feelings that came of bad situations, with the permanent negative appraisal that came with the word *hate*. In essence, one does not have to get along with family, but one must never make family into an enemy.

In terms of general restraint, I learned both directly and vicariously from my father. As I stated earlier, "the lion" made relatively few appearances. In terms of physical violence, my father and mother explained that there was a difference between starting fights and self-defense. Specifically, they made it clear that I was not to provoke physical altercations. However, they also made it clear that I not only had a right to defend myself but, as a rule, I should do so if threatened. In explaining this rule, my father made it clear that there would be stiff consequences if I was found to be the aggressor. Moreover, physical aggression was absolutely prohibited between me and my sisters.

Though I took these rules to heart, it was the example that my father set that truly taught me the benefit of taking a calm and reasoned approach to interpersonal interactions. In all my years, I have never seen my father raise his hand to strike another. And although, as an adult, I know he has been in his share of scrapes, real violence was not something that he was willing to expose me to. Instead, when conflicts would occur, I was able to watch as my father defused volatile situations with a mixture of sternness, knowledge of his rights, and a generally friendly and respectful demeanor.

My father's approach to conflict was most salient when he modeled this behavior in the interactions that occurred between him and me. I learned early that I would be more successful in negotiating with my father if I was able to back up my request with a reasonable argument. I remember one such discussion, where I was attempting to negotiate payment for cleaning and organizing his work van. I remember explaining to him that the work that would be necessary to properly clean his van would far exceed the usual amount of work that I regularly invested in the household. Of course, being around 12 years old, it is more likely that I stated this argument by telling my dad that cleaning his van was too much work and that it was "unfair."

I was able to make up for my primary stance by backing it up with the fact that people paid me for mowing lawns. I explained that since cleaning the van was extra work, I should be paid to do it. I remember my father smiling and agreeing that my argument made sense. He offered to pay me the steep sum of $10 for my extra work. This was, of course, a major boon for me, which translated into a burst of confidence. To my chagrin, this overconfidence provided my father with another opportunity to provide me with one of my most salient learning experiences.

Having been successful in my endeavor to be paid for the extra work, I forgot to attend to the reality of the power dynamic between my dad and me. This error in judgment led me to making the mistake of trying to negotiate with my father, to convince him that a higher payment would be fairer. I attempted to explain to him that based on my estimate, it would take 2 hours to get the job done, and that the neighbors paid me $5 for the 30 minutes that it took for me to mow their lawn, a fairer wage would be $20 for the van clean-up. My father responded by agreeing that my argument was reasonable. And then he presented me with a counteroffer of $8. When I tried to explain that that was less than the first offer, he smiled and agreed with me, then changed his offer to $5. In confusion and panic, I said, "But ..." and he responded by saying, "You're right, you should just do it for free, because I said so." From this interaction I learned two main lessons. The first lesson was that I should never lose sight of my actual power in a given situation, as the consequences might be catastrophic. The second lesson was simply to know when to stop talking, a lesson that I often to have to remind myself.

The early lessons that my father shared with me have helped to shape me into the person that I am today. In the examples that I have presented, my father provided a foundation for the way in which I should view myself and my family. He also provided me with guidance, in terms of dealing with people interpersonally, both casually and when trying to come to an agreement. Beyond these more concrete lessons, my father taught me that I should deal in reality, with an understanding that the world was not fair, yet it could be successfully navigated. These lessons have prepared me for many of the struggles that I have faced over the course of my life, and I am sure that they have helped me to find some success in a system that is antithetical to such outcomes for Black men.

Building a relationship

The Western conceptualization of the parenting relationship has been elaborated in terms of three possible strategies. These strategies have been described as (a) authoritarian, which has been described as taking on the role of the strict disciplinarian, who provides for the material needs of his family while neglecting the more nurturing aspects of parental relationships in nature; (b) permissive, which has been described as taking on a friendship role, with a goal of avoiding conflict and being liked by one's child at the expense of behavioral boundaries; and (c) authoritative, which has been described as taking on a parental role, with the goal of providing guidance and reasonable boundaries for one's children, while respecting their growing autonomy (McAdoo, 1988). Over the course of my childhood, it would be fair to say that my father oscillated between these strategies; however, it seems to me that he spent most of his time as an authoritative father.

At age 31, I am happy to be able to state that my father and I share a close friendship; however, this was not always the case. As a child, there was never a time when I could have confused my relationship with my dad as anything other than a parent–child relationship. As with many families, my mother took on the role of the day-to-day manager of the family's business, not the least of which was keeping my sisters and me in line. My father, on the other hand, was cast in the role of the not-so-secret weapon. There have been few times in my life that rival the times when my mother would utter the words, "Wait 'til your father gets home," in terms of sheer fear and apprehension. For me, those words inspired adolescent prayers for mercy, the acquisition of some sort of super power, or at the very least, that one of my sisters would do something to pull the heat off of me. Yet, looking back, through all the threats, anticipation, and general dread of my dad bursting through the wall, having grown two feet taller and shooting fire from his eyes, I never received more than a stern talking to and an occasional grounding.

I recall an incident that occurred when I was around 14 years old. My childhood best friend, Hiriam, and I were invited to hang out with a young lady and some of her friends from our high school. As with many 14-year-old boys, an invitation to hang out with girls was about as important an invitation as one could be given. With this in mind, I approached my dad with a finely crafted argument for why I was responsible enough to be trusted to hang out on a school night. I explained that I had completed my homework and that I would be back before 9 p.m., which was our general family bedtime. I let him know that Hiriam would be with me and that we would watch out for each other. Most important, I neglected to tell him that that we were meeting all girls and that their parents would not be home.

To my surprise, he consulted with my mother, and they agreed that it would be OK for me to spend some time with friends on a school night. My father explained to me that it was important that I be home before 9 p.m. and then asked me for the house address. After agreeing, and providing the address, I whispered a thank-you to the universe and got out of the house before he changed his mind. I met up with Hiriam and had a completely uneventful night with the girls, as well as with the other people who attended what we had not understood was actually a party. As the night wore on, and 9 p.m. got closer, I tried to calculate the latest time that I could leave and get home by curfew. To make a long story short, I calculated wrong. At 9:15 I was about a block away from my house, and my father pulled up next to me and told me to get into the car.

I remember being nervous on that ride home. After we walked into the house, my father narrowed his eyes and asked me what time it was. I muttered the time and tried to make an excuse about forgetting the time. This my father ignored. He explained to me that he had expected better from me and informed me that I would have a fair amount of time to think about what I had done wrong. He explained that he had been worried and that I should have at least called to tell him and my mother that I was OK. Then he told me that I was grounded for a month, which was the longest punishment that I had ever received. This seemed to be a bit much for 15 minutes, yet I have to admit that I was never late without calling again.

Once, as an adult, I asked my father about that interaction. I asked him why he was so harsh for such a small infraction. He explained that he and my mother were worried about me, but moreover, that they were worried what would happen if I made a pattern out of that type of behavior. He told me that he was harsh because he did not want to have to revisit, in the future, the issue of me keeping them apprised of my whereabouts. Then my father shared something with me that surprised me. He told me that he had to force himself to ground me for that month and that it had been a particularly difficult thing for him to do. He shared with me that he was afraid that I would resent him for it and that he was thankful that it worked out the way it did, as he was unsure that he would have been able to level a similar punishment again. In that moment of self-disclosure, I began to understand that at the core of my father's strong exterior lies a deeply sensitive man, who cares profoundly about the feelings of his family. Through many conversations, including the one just mentioned, it has become clear to me that he cares, primarily about our general well-being; however, it is also clear that he cares deeply about what we think and how we feel about him.

My father expressed this caring through both word and action. In mainstream media images of fathers, a common theme is the aloof father, who has a difficult time expressing emotions. In my family, this was not the case. Expressing our love for each other has become something of a family value, one that my father helped to promote. Whether he was telling me good night, leaving for work, or ending a conversation on the telephone, with few exceptions, my dad always ended the interaction with a "love ya boy," "love ya kid," or my favorite, "love ya son." In fact, on the few occasions where a proper "love ya" was not conveyed, there would usually be a follow-up telephone call to rectify the situation. Along with this family tradition of verbally expressing affection, we are also a family that hugs. And in this arena, my dad was able to shine. Looking back, I remember him scooping me up as a child, then as I grew giving great bear hugs, which might end in a head lock, and most recently shaking hands and embracing as friends. However, these overt expressions of love were not the most poignant.

In truth, these direct expressions of love tend to serve more as a reminder of the nurturing relationship that my parents provided. In terms of my father, this nurturing took many forms, not the least of which was his presence at times when I needed him. One such time occurred while our family was traveling across the United States. We were traveling back to California from West Virginia, and passing through Colorado. At the time I was 7 years old, had developed asthma, and found that I needed reading glasses during the preceding year. There are many stories that could be shared about this trip: like how my father taught me how to read a road map and allowed me to navigate; or how he showed me that being farsighted could be a strength, by asking me to take off my glasses so that I could read the signs farther up the road; or even how my father, my older sister, and I shared a game hen and some homemade biscuits, driving out of West Virginia, using only our hands for utensils. However, the memory that seems to be most cogent occurred while we were crossing through Colorado's high country.

As stated earlier, at the time, I had recently begun to suffer from asthma. My family knew that it was a bad idea for me to do too much running or to be exposed to too much pollen or dust, but being that we lived at sea level, in San Diego, we had not had the occasion to think about the possible dangers of high elevation. Therefore, it was a surprise to my family when I began to take ill as we drove across the Colorado plateau, which has an average elevation of 6,800 feet above sea level. I remember the pain and tightness in my chest as my lungs began to fill with fluid, as well as the panic on my parents' faces as they looked for the closest hospital. Yet more than anything, I remember being in the hospital examination room with the medical staff and my dad. I do not remember whether they were taking blood or placing an IV, but somehow I found the needle that they were bringing toward me more distressing than the pain in my chest. I believe that my father must have seen the panic building in my eyes because he moved to the opposite side of the bed, took my hand, and told me not to pay attention to the needle but to look him in the eye. On a lighter note, this completely backfired, as I was able to see what the doctor was doing through the reflection in his glasses, yet it was his presence that made the difference. In that moment, my dad was there for me. And that was all that mattered.

Understanding that the parent–child relationship between my father and me was clearly defined, both in terms of nurturing and discipline, the existence of that power differential did not prelude opportunities for building a deeply caring relationship. Throughout my childhood, and on into adulthood, I have found that my father and I are similar in many ways. We are similar both in appearance and in temperament, yet early on, it was our shared affinity for the learning about the natural world as well as a fascination with space and science fiction, which led to some of my most cherished memories.

I remember being around elementary school age, my father would turn the television to a nature program or to our favorite science fiction show, *Star Trek*, and we would just sit quietly and watch together.

For me, this was a special time, as it was one of the only times that I could spend time alone with my father. This was facilitated by the fact that my mother and both of my sisters seemed to have a special dislike for science fiction and would tend to leave us be while it was on. Others may have had a similar experience around watching sports, but for us it was science fiction. In fact, as my mother and sisters are bigger sports fans than I am: Sunday football was more about the whole family than a time for the guys. It was during our time watching television that my father and I were able to begin a running dialogue that has continued through-out our relationship. It started with my questions about nature, science, things that were real, and things that were not. Yet it evolved into a rela-tionship where we spoke to each other on an increasingly even (young adult to adult) level.

Within this dialogue, I found myself challenged to think deeper about things than I had before. It was the first place I was allowed to stretch my intellectual abilities without the threat of judgment or reproach. It was an honest space where I was able to have a true conversation with an adult, which did not consist of being instructed or being given directions. During these conversations, I began to appreciate the simple pleasure of knowing things and being able to use that knowledge. And over time, it became a place where I was able to find the confidence to realize that there were things that I knew that my father did not. It was in this realization, and my father's reaction to my first attempts to share this knowledge, which gave me the confidence to question and contradict information given by other people in authority. You see, my father did not react with defensiveness, nor did he dismiss my input off-hand. Whenever I was able to catch him in a bit of broken logic, or offer a bit of nuance, or rattle off a fact that I had recently learned, my father would encourage me to tell him more, or debate the point, or just smile and shake his head. He treated me as someone important enough to listen to, and later I learned that he took pride in every sign of my continued development.

Guidance toward manhood

In any beginning counseling course, one of the first things that a counselor in training will learn is the importance of providing his or her clients with an environment of unconditional positive regard. Rogers (2007) explained that unconditional positive regard refers to the act of placing one's personal feelings aside and providing a nonjudgmental environment for the client to grow within. This concept seems to provide a useful frame for understanding the environment that my father provided for me, as I developed and grew into a man. Over the course of my life, I cannot recall a time when my father made his love contingent upon any particular choice or achievement that I might make. Even when he was unhappy with a particular aspect of my behavior, or when we disagreed, or even when life events pushed us apart, my father never closed himself to me. There was, in fact, no time in my life that I believed that my dad did not care about me.

One major way that my father was able to provide this nonjudgmental environment was in the way that he buffered me from the judgments of the outside world. Both he and my mother were zealous defenders of their children, in public. Parham et al. (1999) discussed the tendency for Black children to find themselves in educational settings where they are expected to do poorly. Boyd-Franklin (2003) explained that Black children who attend majority White schools can be exposed to educationally and socially challenging situations around being "the only one." These descriptions ring true in terms of my personal experience as one of few Black children who attended the predominately White schools that were available in my neighborhood. Though there was little that my parents could do about the social challenges presented by my White and Asian American classmates, my parents were able to stand between me and the more institutional level threats.

While in elementary school, there were a number of times when my mother and father were forced to assert themselves in my defense. Earlier in this chapter, I alluded to the need for a Black boy to know how to defend himself, living in a predominately White neighborhood. Though I would not consider myself a person that is prone to physical altercations, I found that, between Grades 3 and 7, some of my peers refused me the choice. This became more problematic in that the administrators at my elementary schools had a tendency to punish the person they see first, and not necessarily the one who started the fight. My parents took exception to this unofficial policy, and on multiple occasions, my father visited the school to insist on a fairer approach. This is not to say that there were not consequences to be had at home; it was just that my parents refused to let me be mistreated by the school. Boyd-Franklin (2003) explained that Black parents who make a habit of insisting things to school personnel could be labeled as troublemakers. From my teachers' reactions, I believe that this label was given to my father. Lucky for me, my father did not care.

Along similar lines to social institutions, my father has also been protective of me in social situations. Although one might find dissenting opinions within my current group of friends and colleagues, I have always been a shy and thoughtful person. As a child, I was just as comfortable playing alone, if not more so, than I was interacting with groups. This was especially apparent when I was placed in new situations, and it was particularly evident when I was in the presence of other Black men. For me, the "Black macho role" was just not immediately apparent. This is why, when my father took me to Harvey's Barber Shop for the first time, when I was around 10 years old, the guys around the shop focused on me as though I was the proverbial sore thumb.

I remember sitting in the barber chair, with Harvey, the shop's owner, giving me the first professional haircut that I remember. I have to admit that it was an intimidating environment, with the guys talking "smack" (i.e., trading personal insults in a way that challenged each other to respond with a more clever retort, while giving the impression that you were not affected by the comments of others) at a level that was just beyond me. However, as intimidating as the barber shop might be, it was also a space where everyone was included. This meant that both my dad and I were open game, and Harvey started in on both of us. He talked about how I flinched when he tried to comb my hair and compared me to my father, explaining that he was "tender headed" too, when he was my age. Then he joked with my father about the trouble that he used to get into. I remember how my dad just laughed and talked about how old Harvey was, and I began to realize that although there was a large amount of smack talk, people were mostly getting along.

The moment that most stuck with me about this event was when someone was speaking to my dad and said to him, "He's a quiet kid, isn't he?" referring to me. This was not meant to be an insult, nor was it taken as such, yet it was a definitive moment for me, in terms of my persona in that particular social setting. More than that, it was a rare moment when I would be able to hear what my father actually thought about me. His response was to tell the other man, "Not really.... he's just not used to you guys, but he'll talk your ear off when he gets to know you." In that short statement, my father provided me with the room to grow into that particular social environment without having to fight the expectations and assumptions that came with being a "quiet kid." But more than that, my father showed me that he understood my way of being, and he provided me with a template for how to acculturate myself into a community of Black men.

Although, like at the barber shop, my father provided implicit guidance in terms of how I might grow into my own, I never felt that he pressured me to move in any direction other than forward. I have seen many of my friends spend a great deal of energy attempting to follow in one of their parent's footsteps. For some it may be in terms of career; in others it might have to do with sports or some other parental expectation. In terms of my parents, the only real push was toward doing well in school, but even that was kept to a reasonable level. My father seemed to be more interested in providing me and my sisters with opportunities to try new things than in choosing what those things would be. Humorously enough, even without pressure from him, my path seemed to converge with his in many aspects of my life. An example that comes to mind is that of when I began to play football in the ninth grade.

I remember being afraid to ask my dad for the money to play Pop Warner football. I honestly do not understand why I was worried, as he had agreed to pay for my earlier Kung Fu lessons, and before that the Boy Scouts, and before that for my saxophone, and so on. At the time, it just seemed like it would be too expensive to do. Yet to my surprise, he not only let me sign up, and helped me convince my mother that I would not get hurt, but he became one of the main boosters for our team. He seemed to approach my football experience with the same level of enthusiasm that was usually reserved for the local professional football franchise. I remember having a conversation with him about how he felt about me playing football during my first season. We were driving somewhere, maybe to practice, and I asked him if he played football when he was a kid. To my surprise, he not only played football, but he was very good at it. He explained to me that he had always wanted get me into the sport but that he did not want to be one of those parents that make their kids follow after them.

In that one statement, my father made it clear that I could do whatever I wanted with my life. I learned that he would cheer for me regardless of the activity, even if he would cheer somewhat louder for the ones that he particularly enjoyed. What continues to strike me is that this was an intentional style of interaction. My father was not just acting on instinct and personality traits; he intentionally checked his personal feelings and placed my goals before his. More than building a nonjudgmental environment, I have come to realize that behind his nonpressuring stance laid an underlying level of trust. My father trusted me to make my own way, not in some aloof or ambivalent shirking of responsibility, but instead with a resolution to support me and provide guidance when the occasion presented itself.

Conclusion

As I conclude, I cannot help but to reflect on one of my favorite moments from *The Cosby Show*, in my opinion, one of the first truly positive representations of the Black family in media. In this moment, we find Theo (the son) and Cliff (the father) playing basketball in their backyard. Theo makes his winning shot, beating his father for the first time in his life. It reminds me of the concept of "coming of age," whereby a young person takes his first true steps into adulthood. Earlier in this chapter, I recounted some of the first sparring matches that I had with my father. Over the course of my childhood, these early lessons transformed into a playful wrestling, which, without fail, would end with my father pinning me. He'd call out, "Say uncle!" And I would yell "Uncle!" Then he would reply, in a snide voice, "I'm not your uncle, I'm your dad!" After which, I would yell "Dad!" and he would let me up. It was not until I was 15 years old that I could finally pin him. I yelled, "Say uncle!" He replied, "Uncle!" Then I said, "I'm not your uncle, I'm your son!" That was the last time we wrestled, and it was not long afterward that he began to treat me as a young man.

Over the course of this chapter, I have tried to illustrate the approach that my father took to being a parent, as well as how that approach affected me in positive ways. It was my hope to present a strength-based narrative of Black fathering, which would help to provide a window into the experience of having a father who is not only present but completely active in one's life. Though I understand that this is not the case for the majority of Black families, it is a blessing that can be reproduced as we move into the future. My father taught me how to feel strong in a way that inspired protectiveness as opposed to aggression. He helped me to form my basic understanding of how to relate to my family and the world at large. My father showed me that a man can be both a provider and a nurturer. He helped me to understand that having less power did not mean that I was less of a person. I learned from him that a father should place himself between dangerous forces and his children, but also that trusting your children to embody the values that you taught them can help them grow. And as I grew, my father allowed our relationship to grow into a friendship, which in turn helped me to cherish the interactions that would always be father-to-son.

Reflective questions

1. When you think about being present or spending time with your child, what is the quality of that interaction? Does it have to be a big thing?
2. What is your parenting style? How should adults and children interact?
3. Are your expectations for your child in line with their personal aspirations? How could you find out?

References

Boyd-Franklin, N. (2003). *Black families in therapy: Understanding the African American experience* (2nd ed.). New York: Guilford Press.

McAdoo, J. L. (1988). Changing perspectives on the role of the Black father. In P. Bronstein & C. Cowan (Eds.), *Fatherhood today: Men's changing role in the family* (pp. 79–92). Oxford, UK: Wiley.

Parham, T., White, J. & Ajamu, A. (1999). *The psychology of Blacks: An African centered perspective* (3rd ed.). Englewood Cliffs, NJ: Prentice-Hall.

Rogers, C. (2007). The necessary and sufficient conditions of therapeutic personality change. *Psychotherapy: Theory, Research, Practice, Training, 44*(3), 240–248.

chapter nine

Birthright
Anecdotes of fatherhood, race, and redemption

Ivory A. Toldson
Howard University
Washington, DC

At 37 years old, I have grown content knowing that I do not know exactly who I am. I understand that, by nature, humanity is a confused species with a language that is filled with contradictions. We define ourselves by singularities—one name indicating you or I, when no one is one person, and everybody is everything, but nobody understands everything—so, no one truly knows himself or herself. Therefore, our keys to life come from identifying with everything and nothing at the same time. In other words, we have to accept failing, without becoming a failure and losing without being a loser. We make mistakes, but mistakes do not make us. Thus, the answer to the perennial question, "Who am I?" was best answered when Moses asked God his name, and God said, "I am who I am."

Like "A Father's Call: Father-Son Relationship Survival of Critical Life Transitions" (Toldson & Toldson, 2006), this is a collection of autobiographical essays, which detail my experiences coming of age while discovering the gifts, conflicts, and responsibilities I inherited from my fathers. I use *fathers* in the plural, not because I grew up with both my biological and stepfather. Rather, because recently, I have grown to understand that fathers change. My father, Dr. Ivory Lee Toldson, today is a different man than he was when I was a child. Not better or worse, but different in ways that allow me to experience his love, guidance, and wisdom in very novel ways. Since I wrote, "A Father's Call," my stepfather, Dr. Imari Obadele (Brother Imari), moved on to the afterlife, so I honor his memory with this chapter, understanding that I extend his mortality every time I write his name.

A second reason that I use *fathers* in the plural is because I have grown to understand that the Black community needs communal fathering in order to sustain. Good fathers should expand their role outside of the home, as well as open their homes to the wisdom of other fathers. I will try to reinforce this point throughout this chapter.

The first section of this chapter, "Child of the Black Revolution, Part 2," will continue the essay and will draw from my stint as a psychology intern at a federal prison where I encountered Black Power era inmates who worked directly with my stepfather and War on Drugs era inmates, who were in my peer group. The second section of this chapter, "Talk to the Kids! The Impact of Black Fathers" will highlight the 3 years I spent working with my father at a residential group home for males in state custody, as well as results of my research on Black fathers. The final section, "Lessons Learned," will discuss the birth and development of Makena, my only child. The chapter also recaps lessons learned and discusses my affiliation with a parent cooperation program at the Superior Court of the District of Columbia.

Child of the Black revolution, part 2

In 1971, two years before I was born, the police department of Jackson, Mississippi, conspired with the Federal Bureau of Investigation (FBI) to raid a settlement legally occupied by the Republic of New Africa (RNA). In the ensuing gun battle, a police officer was killed, a federal agent was wounded, and 11 RNA members were arrested and detained. My stepfather, Dr. Imari Obadele, among seven to be convicted, served 4 years in the U.S. Penitentiary in Atlanta, Georgia, before being exonerated. About 25 years after the U.S. government released Brother Imari, both he and I found it amusingly ironic when I was matched to the U.S. Penitentiary for a yearlong predoctoral prison psychology internship. On the brink of indefinitely extending the mortal paths of my two fathers, I was less than a year away from receiving the same degree as my biological father (a Ph.D. in counseling psychology) from my stepfather's alma mater (Temple University), while conducting my dissertation research at a penal repository for my fathers' less fortunate comrades of the 1970s and their bastard sons who became casualties to the modern War on Drugs.

The year was 2000. I was one of three psychology interns for the 2000–2001 class; the other two were White females. Of a psychology staff of nine, only two of us were Black, and I was the only Black male. During our training, which we shared with all new correctional personnel, the assistant warden demanded, "Never forget, you are a correctional officer first." He explained the inherent dangers of working with inmates, regardless of the nature of our position. My office was on the second floor of Cell Block D, next to an elder inmate minister who occupied a private cell. I was the only intern on a cell without a supervising psychologist, so the staff and inmates treated me as if I was already a psychologist.

At 27 years old, I was troubled by the large number of young Black males who were incarcerated, particularly the ones who had children. One day, I visited an inmate in the special housing unit at the request of one of my internship classmates. My cohort suspected he requested counseling because he was attracted to her. When I appeared, he smirked and conceded to his shenanigans but proceeded to talk about his nine children. He was younger than 30 years old.

Days later, I met another inmate who was genuinely interested in self-reflection. He was also younger than 30 years old and had 11 children. He told me he was concerned that his children were so close in age and proximity, and knew so little about him, that he feared one of his sons and daughters could become unwittingly intimate, unaware that they were siblings. Interestingly, at the time, he was writing a novel that dramatized the potential accidental incest. Within 9 years of his 25-year sentence, he had handwritten 10 books that were popular among other inmates.

A star basketball player in high school, as a teenager, he had had a friendly competition with a good friend of mine who received a Ph.D. in psychology 2 years before me. My friend remembered him well, recollecting that they were on similar paths growing up in a very poor neighborhood with single mothers. They were both being recruited for colleges, while flirting with the new opportunities to sell drugs, which had become ubiquitous in their community. How one became a successful psychologist and the other an inmate with a quarter-century sentence was merely happenstance.

As prison personnel, I was keenly aware of several high-profile inmates. One, Dr. Mutulu Shakur, was particularly intriguing for several reasons. First, he was the stepfather of Tupac Shakur. Second, after reading his presentencing investigative report (public record), I learned that he had a story that was strikingly similar to my stepfather's. He adopted the last name Shakur from an elder from Philadelphia and married Afeni Shakur when Tupac was very young. Dr. Shakur was a member of the RNA in the 1970s, obtained a doctorate in acupuncture therapy, and operated the first Black acupuncture clinic in New York. In 1986, he was arrested for planning the Brinks armored truck bank robbery in New York and assisting in the escape of Assata Shakur, who is currently in exile in Cuba under political asylum. Dr. Shakur maintains his innocence and insists that he and Assata were targets of COINTELPRO[*] because of their political beliefs.

---

[*] COINTELPRO is an acronym for Counter Intelligence Program, an FBI-initiated program designed to investigate, disrupt, and neutralize domestic organizations deemed to be dissenting to the United States.

I first met Dr. Shakur when he entered my office on his own recon-
naissance. Although I fully expected our paths to cross, I was unsure of
what he knew of me, or my family. When he entered my office, he formally
introduced himself and maintained a scrutinizing posture. After about
5 minutes of awkward small talk I asked, "Do you know Imari Obadele?"

In a tone that was somewhat smug and haughty, he replied, "Yes,
that's my president."

I immediately acknowledged, "That's my stepfather."

He then proceeded to utter words in another language before saying,
"This is the best thing that's happened to me since I've been incarcerated."

Admittedly, after Dr. Shakur expressed his glee, my heart started to
accelerate. Although pleased that the tension was lifted, I did not fully
grasp what he believed to be the circumstance or potential of my being
there. I had undergone a rigorous background investigation to acquire the
position, which entailed agents visiting old teachers and other acquain-
tances to determine my propensity for deviance or subversive activity. On
the application, I explicitly remember responding "no" to the question,
"Has any of your family members been incarcerated in the federal prison
system?" At the time, I conveniently rationalized that my stepfather was
not technically related to me. But sitting face-to-face with his former com-
rade made the question seem far less trivial.

Fortunately, over the year I spent at the prison, it became clear that
Dr. Shakur's initial response to my disclosure was not connected to any
base desire to exploit the relationship for his personal benefit. Throughout
the year, Dr. Shakur endeared himself to me, sharing his political perspectives, as well as his challenges remaining connected to his family and
community while being incarcerated.

Inherently, I was an important legacy to Dr. Shakur's political past,
regardless of the extent to which I ascribed to his beliefs. I was only 2 years
younger than Tupac, the son he had lost 4 years earlier. My stepfather
recalled bouncing Tupac on his knee more than a decade before he knew
I existed. Also the godson of Geronimo Pratt, Tupac was surrounded by
staples of the Black Power movement throughout his childhood. A deeper
examination of Tupac's music reveals the strong connection he had to the
Black Power movement in general, and Dr. Shakur specifically. Dr. Shakur
once recorded a cameo for one of Tupac's songs from the prison phone.
Much of Tupac's earlier recordings were laced with esoteric allusions to
the Black Power movement, which I greatly appreciated as a teen. However, West Coast style gangsta rap and thug life became the public face of
Tupac's music in the year preceding his death.

Most hip hop enthusiasts appreciated the Shakespearean conflict of
Tupac's lyrics, as he vacillated between "conscious" and "gangsta" rap.
Also present in the subtext of Tupac's music was an unhinged resentment

toward his father. A phrase from Tupac's (1995) hit single, "Dear Mama," seemed to resonate with a generation of young Black males who felt estranged from their fathers:

> No love from my daddy cause the coward wasn't there
> He passed away and I didn't cry, cause my anger
> wouldn't let me feel for a stranger

As a teen, Tupac's venom toward his father quietly stoked my own smoldering dissatisfaction with my father. Unfortunately, the song also explained, and rationalized, the role that drug dealers played as surrogate fathers for a generation of fatherless Black males. Through my interactions with Dr. Shakur, I wondered why the father who Tupac never really knew appeared more prominently in his music than the stepfather with whom he interacted throughout his life. He seemed to love his stepfather with a whisper and hate his biological father with a bullhorn.

Dr. Shakur once revealed that the conversations he had with me brought him a level of solace that compared to a period in which he and Tupac spoke almost daily. He shared the same experience with *The New Yorker* reporter Connie Bruck, who detailed it in the article, "The Takedown of Tupac" (Bruck, 1997). Dr. Shakur revealed that he and Tupac had nearly daily telephone conversations at a time in which Tupac was trying to craft his public identity. At the time, Dr. Shakur believed that Tupac had the potential to regenerate the hip hop generation into a force that harnessed the principles of Black liberation, to confront modern issues in the Black community.

In the midst of what Dr. Shakur believed to be a breakthrough in his quest to help Tupac rebrand his image and solidify his role to Black youth, he was transferred to a super-max penitentiary, where he was locked in a cell for 23 hours a day. Connie Bruck reported that in a memorandum written in February 1994, "the warden of Lewisburg argued that Mutulu needed 'the controls of Marion', in part because of his 'outside contacts and influence over the younger black element'" (Bruck, 1997). Dr. Shakur maintains that by the time he was released to the general population of the penitentiary, Tupac was firmly in the clutches of the criminal justice system and ultimately under the control of Death Row Records, at the time, the nation's most notorious gangsta rap label.

At the time of Tupac's death in 1995, I had become disenchanted with his image but nonetheless a fan of his music. I remember trying to quell the venom of my younger cousin, Kendall, who vehemently blamed Biggie Smalls and Bad Boy Records for Tupac's death. I found it unfortunate that Tupac's music could inspire Black-on-Black resentment among teens; however, my discussions with Dr. Shakur help me to see the situation through a different lens.

In many ways, Tupac was a mortal enemy of the state. He was a living vestige of a movement that the FBI spent millions to suppress in the 1960s and 1970s, and his persona was infectious. Bearing the surname of a Black American clan, which includes active political prisoners and an exile in a country with an embargo, and the given name of a Peruvian communist guerilla group, Tupac was born to breed consternation to agents of the status quo. Like the generation that preceded him, Tupac probably became a target when he became a symbol of armed civil resistance among disenfranchised Black Americans. Many of his contemporaries believed that he became a government mark when he was acquitted of shooting two off-duty police officers in self-defense. Whatever the forces—corporate, government, street, or a combination of the three—Tupac quickly entered a world in which his vices and fears were relentlessly being used to manipulate his behavior; this was an overwhelming burden for someone in his early 20s.

After examining details and nuances, the East Coast versus West Coast feud, featuring Tupac and Biggie Smalls, seemed to have the trappings of the feud between Black Panthers from New York and those from California. By the time COINTELPRO-BPP* officially dissolved in 1971, an estimated 7,500 Black Panther members were government informants. In 1969, the FBI paid out an estimated $7.4 million to Black Panther informants (Churchill & Vander, 2002). By 1970, the wave of informants within the Black Panthers ultimately led to a culture of paranoia within the organization, culminating with a public feud between Huey Newton and Eldridge Cleaver, and genuine animosity and violence between East and West Coast Panthers.

As the FBI's two primary targets, both Newton and Cleaver showed emotional scars from years of harassment, intimidation, and psychological trickery. By 1971, the once flourishing Black Panthers was reduced to a small, predominately female-led group of Newton loyalists in California (Theohris, 2004). The FBI's annihilation of the Panthers affected the poor Black community in many ways. The FBI's reliance upon social degenerates within the Black community to infiltrate the Panthers, in effect, marginalized the leadership of principled Black men and increased the capacity of criminals and drug dealers in the Black community.

The explosion of Black men in the criminal justice system, the rise of crack and subsequent War on Drugs, and the marginalized presence of

---

* COINTELPRO-BPP began in 1967. According to FBI files, the purpose was to expose, disrupt, misdirect, discredit, or otherwise neutralize the activities of Black Nationalist, hate-type organizations and groupings, their leadership, spokesmen, membership, and supporters, and to counter their propensity for violence and civil disorder.

Black male leadership in the poor Black community are the natural degenerative effects of the federal government's overthrow of Black liberation movements. In many ways, the War on Drugs was the government's effort to clean up the ashes from the Black Power movement. The aggressive tactics used to catch drug dealers had striking similarities to COINTELPRO, especially the use of informants. The instigation of government informants and other infiltration activities often exacerbated violence and instilled a manic paranoia of "snitchers" in the Black community. The most violent and sinister members of the Black community were able to slither through the system while exploiting the communities' disillusionment, as petty dealers peddling crack from the corner were given 15 years to life.

By the time I became a prison psychology intern, the nonviolent drug offender population had eclipsed all of the violent offenders in the federal prison system, in number and length of sentence. The inmates with whom I worked, some former college students, entrepreneurial geniuses, artists, and a host of other talents, were keenly aware of the system they served. Many could trace their demise to state-sponsored efforts to build the capacity of the anti-communist Contras in Nicaragua through crack revenue from poor Black communities. After the dust settled from the Iran-Contra scandal, the War on Drugs continued to function as the middle passage between poor Black neighborhoods and prison industries that thrived on cheap prison labor. Inmates with better health and lower security risk typically worked for a prison industry called UNICOR for about 23 cents per hour. From this, one can surmise that a system that gives longer prison sentences to less violent offenders can generate a healthy profit. In 2008, UNICOR reported $854.3 million in sales, nearly twice their earnings of 1996.

As COINTELPRO and the nomenclature of the War on Drugs fades into infamy, I reflect on something an inmate told me. As if he had rehearsed his lines for days and had been building up the nerve to express his point, without reserving anything, he marched into my office, sat on the seat before me and said, "I see you walking in here every day, wearing a suit with your briefcase, looking like you've done something with yourself. When I was growing up, I never saw anyone look like you in my neighborhood—a young Black man with a profession. When I was growing up, all I saw was hustlers and dealers and drug fiends. Maybe if I saw you back then, I wouldn't be here today. So, what I really came here to tell you is: Talk to the kids!"

Enamored with the line, "Talk to the kids," I repeat it often in public speeches. However, I am not naive to the fact that the Black community needs much more. As an optimist, I believe many problems will be corrected through the universal potential of Black empowerment and the undaunted spirit of a community responding to oppression. Every day I wonder how this will actually look.

Talk to the kids! The impact of Black fathers

The year after I completed my Ph.D. in psychology and my internship at the federal penitentiary, I became my father's, Dr. Ivory Lee Toldson's, junior colleague at Southern University and his clinical director for a group home that he recently opened called the Manhood Training Village. I had many advantages at Southern University. Besides having my father's guidance and contacts, my stepfather, Brother Imari, had recently retired from Prairie View University and moved in with my mother to run his publishing company, House of Songhay Commission for Positive Education, full time.

Early in my tenure at Southern University, my father and I began to publish research on the Black experience. We used the principles described in one of our publications as the theoretical basis for the treatment program of the group home we ran together. Working with the children at the Manhood Training Village was very rewarding to me. However, I was often unsettled by standard practices and politics within the social service system that I felt were not conducive to the children's growth. Notwithstanding, I am proud of the services that we provided and pleased that my father continued to operate the group home after I left Baton Rouge to join the faculty at Howard University.

During the same period, I became more active with Brother Imari's publishing company. I was very intrigued with Brother Imari's sophisticated models of academic liberation. He maintained his own journal and published his own books; therefore, he never had to compromise his intellectual property. When I wrote *Black Sheep: When the American Dream Becomes a Black Man's Nightmare* (Toldson, 2004), Brother Imari allowed me to publish it through the House of Songhay. We became business partners, as he taught me how to obtain ISBN and LOC numbers, and I taught him how to generate barcodes, design book covers with Photoshop, and use social media to market products. We sold books together at conferences, and he seemed proud to usher in a new era of leadership to his publishing house.

Both of my fathers enthroned me with important tools that I used when I relocated to Washington, D.C., to advance my career. However, I left Baton Rouge feeling like my work was incomplete. By leaving, I compromised my position as the natural heir to both of my fathers' empires, but, being a lifelong student of life, it was a chance that I was willing to take.

I also regretted leaving the young men at the group home. However, leaving the group home help me to escape a quandary, which nagged me nearly every day when lived in Baton Rouge. Throughout my years as clinical director, I felt that I was making a difference most when I was doing something extratherapeutic, such as taking the young men to work with me, or helping them with their homework, or visiting their school. However, after 10 years studying psychology, I could not find the therapeutic technique, psychological assessment, standard of care, or psychotropic medication that I felt truly made a difference in the children's lives. Functionally, the teenagers that I worked with had less than half of a parent. Most had no father and an inadequate mother, whose pattern of abuse, neglect, and personal failings prompted the state to intervene. However, for all of the trifling behaviors of the mother, her pedestal will always shine in contrast to an absent father.

As a psychology professor, I remain optimistic that we in the academic community will find solutions to problems described, including absentee fathers and children. Throughout my work in the psychology field, the most important lesson I learned was that the Black community needs principled leaders and mentors for children. The large number of children with incarcerated fathers underscores the need for Black men to step away from the confines of their home and share the responsibility to protect the next generation.

Research on Black fathers

Over the past 2 years, I have conducted extensive research on Black male achievement. A research question that often surfaces is "What is the impact of Black *fatherlessness* on Black boys?" Any answer to this question, besides "no impact," is likely to further depress the Black community. The question in and of itself, however, is misguided. It is very difficult to measure the dose impact of fatherlessness, because fatherlessness is difficult to define.

Reflect on the question of whether President Barack Obama was fatherless. To most, only seeing your father once your entire life and having very minimal contact with him before he passes at a relatively young age would certainly qualify as fatherless. Yet, Obama went on to become the first African American president of the United States. He might be an anomaly, or more likely he had resources, such as his grandfather and mentors, who helped him to compensate for his father's absence. Thus, the more appropriate research question is "What is the impact of Black *fathers* on Black boys?" With this question, we seek transferrable characteristics that can be harnessed to help all young Black people, regardless of their relationship to their biological father.

For my research in *Breaking Barriers: Plotting the Path to Academic Success for School-Age African-American Males* (Toldson, 2008), I used the Health

Behavior in School-age Children (HBSC; U.S. Department of Health and Human Services, National Institutes of Health, & National Institute of Child Health and Human Development, 2001) and the National Survey on Drug Use and Health (NSDUH; U.S. Department of Health and Human Services, Substance Abuse and Mental Health Services Administration, & Office of Applied Studies, 2007) to determine the impact of fathers on the academic success of young Black males. The HBSC surveyed 11-, 13- and 15-year-old children's attitudes and experiences concerning a range of health-related behaviors. The U.S. sample included 664 schools, in a stratified, two-stage cluster sample of classes at Grades 6 through 10.

The NSDUH used a stratified 50-state design with a multistage area probability sample for each of the 50 states and the District of Columbia. The study population included youth, aged 12 to 17 years, sampled in the NSDUH. Survey instruments primarily measured the scope and correlates of drug use in the United States. Correlates explored in the present study primarily involved "youth experiences," which covered a range of topics, including neighborhood upbringing, unlawful activities, peer associations, social support, extracurricular activities, and exposure to substance abuse prevention and education programs.

Impact of father in the household on academic success

One-way ANOVA was used on the HBSC data set to determine if a father's presence in the household improved academic success among school-age African American males. Respondents who reported that their father was present outperformed those with no father in the household. Among students who had a father present, 62% reported good or very good grades, compared to 55% for students with no father present. When comparing students who had both parents present to those with one parent present, the results were almost identical (63% versus 55%), suggesting that most students with a father present lived in a two-parent home. Among the students who reported having neither their mother nor father in the home, only 45% reported making good or very good grades in school.

Incidentally, African Americans were the only ethnic group that was more likely to live in a fatherless home than to live with a father in the home. Analysis of the HBSC data set showed that 60% of African American children live in fatherless homes, compared to 15% for Asian American, 25% for White, and 34% for Hispanic children. The NSDUH data set validated these findings. When cross-tabulating the item "Father in Household" with race, 56% of African American adolescents reported living in fatherless homes, compared to 13% for Asian American, 20% for White Americans, and 29% for Hispanic Americans.

Impact of father's education on academic success

The HBSC data set was used to test the relationship between fathers' and mothers' education and academic achievement among African American males. Pearson correlations revealed a linear relationship between school-age African American males' and fathers' educational attainment. Participants who reported having a father who graduated from college were significantly more likely to also report making good grades in school ($p < .01$). No such relationship existed between mothers' education and academic achievement for boys. However, when performing the same Pearson correlations for African American girls, academic achievement had weaker ($p < .05$) significance for fathers' education. Interestingly, African American girls were significantly ($p < .01$) more likely to report good grades when their mothers had a higher educational attainment.

Findings on the relationship between African American males' academic achievement and fathers' education gain context when comparing fathers' education across ethnic groups. Forty-three percent of European American students and 51% of Asian American students reported having a father who completed college. Only 26% of African American students reported having a father who completed college.

The impact of the relationship of fathers to Black children

When responding to the question, "How easy is it for you to talk to your father about things that really bother you?" in the HBSC survey, African American males students who responded "very easy" were significantly more likely to have good grades ($p < .001$). Across all levels of academic achievement, Black males found it easier to talk to their fathers than Black females ($p < .001$). When asked the same questions about the mother, the results were similar. Black males who found it easy to talk to their mothers had higher levels of academic achievement than those who reported that talking to their mothers was "very difficult" ($p < .001$).

Not surprisingly, caretakers of Black students who perform poorly in school reported that the child often "bothers" and angers them and that they are generally sacrificing more to care for the child. These relationship dynamics could signal that the parent is frustrated with the child's performance in school or that the parent has a low threshold for frustration, which is interfering with the child's abilities. Children of the aggravated parents may also have general special needs, such as alternative learning styles or social challenges.

Another aspect of parenting that had a significant impact on Black males' academic progress was a parent's involvement with school. Parents who helped their kids with school-related problems were comfortable talking to teachers, encouraged their children to do well in school, and maintained high expectations had higher performing children. When analyzing similar parenting practices with a separate data set, the strongest parenting indicators of academic success were holistic factors: (a) parents who often told children they were proud of them, and (b) parents who let students know when they did a good job. Interestingly, although probably important for other aspects of development, restricting children's behavior, such as time spent with friends or watching TV, did not produce significant effects on grades.

Impact of fathers on college aspirations

In a related study, using the HBSC, I looked at the impact of fathers on the college aspirations of Black males (Toldson, Braithwaite, & Rentie, 2009). College aspiration was measured with the question, "What do you think you will be doing when you finish high school?" Survey participants were given the following options: 4-year college/university, 2-year community/junior college, technical or vocational school, apprenticeship/trade or on-the-job training, working, armed forces/military, unemployed, and don't know. The responses from the original questionnaire item were reconfigured to simplify the analyses. Four-year college remained an independent option to form the category "College Aspirations;" "Unemployed" and "Don't know" were combined to create the category "No Plans," and all remaining response options were combined to create the category "Other Plans."

Findings on family factors demonstrated that social modeling plays an important role in promoting college aspirations among Black adolescent males. Father's education had a significant impact on Black males' college aspirations, ranking second overall to academic achievement. The effect size for fathers' education was considerably greater than it was for mothers' education. Mothers' education was not significantly different across races; however, White males reported higher educational attainment among their fathers than Black males. Interestingly, when comparing all three groups, Black males with "other plans" reported mothers with the lowest educational levels. This finding suggests that some Black males may be making post–high school plans based on economic situations and a need to provide income for the family. Ease of communication with fathers and mothers was also important in promoting college aspirations. However, Black males with other plans reported the highest level of ease when communicating with their fathers, when comparing them to college aspirants and students with no plans.

Lessons learned on becoming a father

On July 27, 2007, my wife, Marshella, gave birth to an extraordinarily beautiful baby girl named Makena. She was our first child and the first grandchild of her maternal grandparents and her paternal grandmother. She was my father's first granddaughter; his first grandson was born to my half-sister in 2001. I literally cried out when the doctor pulled my daughter from my wife's belly. Nothing could have prepared me for the overwhelming rush of emotion that I experienced the day of her birth. Every day, I continue to be amazed by the rapid changes in her size, temperament, and abilities.

Approaching fatherhood, I embraced certain perceived advantages I had over the generation before me. First, at 34 years old, I was beginning the journey at an older age. Surely, my relative maturity would give me a social advantage over my father, who had his first child when he was about 10 years younger. Second, I was equipped with communication devices, such as cell phones and e-mail, which allowed me to have constant contact with my wife throughout the pregnancy. Finally, in the information age, I had infinite "on-demand" resources through the Internet. In seconds, I could tell you the advantages of breast-feeding, whether it is safe to paint the nursery less than a month before delivery, or which car seat has the highest safety rating.

Several months into the pregnancy, neither my maturity, nor communication devices, nor information could rescue me from the chaos of conflicting doctors' orders, early contractions, weekly doctors' visits, medications, and months-long bed confinement for my wife that shattered her wits and sent me into a tailspin. In our quasi-advanced society, both the doctors and I had too much and not enough information at the same time: knowledge of too many risks but not enough knowledge to know how to mitigate them.

At the same time, I realized challenges that were unique to my generation. Most notably, the 21st-century cyber office demanded nearly 16 hours per day attention. As the boundaries between work and home blurred, physical proximity became overshadowed by mental distance, as I responded to e-mails and tried to meet deadlines at midnight. As hyperinflation normalized in society, a single salary for a primary provider seemed obsolete. I found myself juggling multiple jobs to meet the material needs of my family, often at the expense of my emotional availability and sanity.

Nearly 3 years later, my wife and I have survived some of the most significant challenges of our marriage. Through it all, we have learned how to endure, forgive, and build upon the long-standing love, respect, and admiration we have for one another. Our daughter gives us a reason to keep our relationship strong, but not an excuse to stay together. We understand that we must love one another and love our daughter—not love one another *because* we love our daughter. For her part, my daughter has given everything I do a higher purpose and a deeper meaning. The journey of helping her to reach new milestones, as she expresses her appreciation through timeless affection, is beautiful and rewarding.

Hope for the future

Approximately twice per month, I teach parent cooperation classes for the Program for Agreement and Cooperation (PAC) in child custody cases for the Family Court of the Superior Court of the District of Columbia. Participants of the class are men and women who are involved in a custody dispute over one or more child. At the onset of the class, tensions are typically high. Many, who are more familiar with a traditional custody dispute process, resist our attempts to steer them into a system that allows them, rather than a judge, to determine the fate of their child. Already war worn, most are clearly ready to continue to fight. Expecting the jury lounge where class is held to be a combat zone, they instead find something more akin to the Truth and Reconciliation Commission.

However, when I begin my class, all of the grumbles fade into oblivion when I summarize the experience I shared in "No Tears, No Fears" (Toldson & Toldson, 2007). Listening to my personal testimony of my parents' conflict driving me to act out suicidal gestures as a toddler does a great deal to allay the defenses in the group. Above their bitterness toward one another, the vast majority are truly interested in the health and well-being of their children.

Many of the fathers are no older than 25 years old, and less than half were ever married to their child's mother. Experienced or imagined, most of them expect to be treated unfairly in the custody case, because they feel as though the court will be naturally biased toward mothers. Through all of the hostilities, shortsightedness, and innuendos against their children's mothers, I appreciate them for fighting to remain involved in their children's lives. After working in the federal prison and being the director of a group home, I find it rewarding to be a part of a public system that I believe is truly functioning in the best interest of citizens. The fathers and mothers involved with the program have the opportunity to avoid costly, time-consuming, and emotionally damaging custody battles, and work together through mediation to draft an agreement to share their most important responsibility: raising their children.

As I conclude this chapter on Black fathers, I reflect on a young man I met in the PAC program. He looked no older than 21 years old and sat in the fourth row in the very large room. He was dressed casually with a large, wild, and untamed Afro that probably had recently been in corn-rows. He did not say much during class, but I remember him smiling and nodding in agreement consistently throughout the 3-hour class. His posi-tive demeanor seemed inconsistent with his unruly hairstyle. Days later, I saw the young man push through a crowded street to greet me. I did not immediately recognize him because he had cut his hair very low.

Smiling ear to ear he said, "We did it! We had our sessions, and I'm gonna raise my kid! Thank you!" Internally, I thanked him. He repre-sented the hope of Black fathers who look significantly different from me. The hope of young fathers, working poor fathers, fathers reentering society after periods of incarceration, unwitting fathers who "slipped up" during a sexual escapade, and the unseen fathers of the children at the Manhood Training Village.

Conclusion

The high mortality rate among Black men and explosion of the Black male inmate population over the past 30 years has conceivably contributed to the alarming number of Black children in fatherless homes and fathers with less education. Lack of Black male models can have a profound academic impact on Black children's social and academic prospects. The Black com-munity specifically, and society, must organize social capital, policy advo-cacy, and social services to strengthen Black fathers who are present and compensate for those who are absent. Following are specific strategies.

First, current revisions of 25-year-old criminal justice policies and remedial efforts should consider the relationship between inmates and parolees and their children. Educational programs that allowed inmates to obtain degrees in prison should be reintroduced. In addition, barri-ers that deny men from pursuing education and employment after they have been released from prison should be eased.

Second, funding for fatherhood programs and mentoring programs is supported by the observations presented in this chapter. In addition, healthy marriage initiatives, which help Black people to understand the material and immaterial value of marriage and family, are important for developing a culture that is more conducive to academic success. Family values are virtues that should be understood and promoted in a more bipartisan way than they are currently presented in the United States.

Third, parent education and parenting organizations should stress aspects of positive parenting that has translated into academic success. A premium should be placed on the good things students do, as restrictions are placed on the negative things they do. The findings support a "positive referral" system in school, whereby schools send formal notices to parents when their children are exemplary. Overall, parents should be taught the material benefits of using positive reinforcement and affirmations.

Finally, the high number of African American males who are being raised in homes without fathers increases the need for policies to support parent cooperation programs. Family court judges who oversee child custody cases should encourage parents to use formal parental cooperation and agreement courses to increase opportunities for students to have harmonious contact with both parents.

Overall, we must open and expand our view of Black fathers to include those who are not physically in the home and who are not biologically related to the child they raise. We also must understand that fatherless children are everyone's responsibility, as it is easier to prepare a child than to repair an adult. Undeniably, the real promise of Black fatherhood cannot rest in the idle hands of socially able Black men, but must materialize through a united community that leaves no Black child without a father and no Black father without a safety net.

Reflective questions

1. What was/is the impact of the War on Drugs on Black fathers and thus the Black community? Was the effort purposeful? Does that matter?
2. Discuss "Talk to the Kids" section. Why is this activity so important?
3. What is "fatherlessness?" What is the more important research question that must be asked in generating data about Black dads?
4. What impact does a college-educated father have on his son's education? His daughter's?

References

Bruck, C. (1997, July 7). The takedown of Tupac. *The New Yorker*, p. 46.

Churchill, W., & Vander, J. (2002). *The COINTELPRO papers: Documents from the FBI's secret wars against dissent in the United States*. Boston: South End Press.

Shakur, T. (1995). Dear Mama. On *Me Against the World* [CD]. Santa Monica: Interscope.

Theohris, A. G. (2004). *The FBI and American democracy: A brief critical history*. Lawrence: University Press of Kansas.

Toldson, I. A. (2004). *Black sheep: When the American dream becomes a Black man's nightmare*. Baton Rouge, LA: House of Songhay Commission for Positive Education.

Toldson, I. A. (2008). *Breaking barriers: Plotting the path to academic success for school-age African-American males*. Washington, DC: Congressional Black Caucus Foundation.

Toldson, I. A., Braithwaite, R. L., & Rentie, R. (2009). Promoting college aspirations among school-age Black American males. In H. T. Frierson, W. Pearson, & J. H. Wyche (Eds.), *Black American males in higher education: Participation and parity*. Bingley, UK: Emerald Group Publishing.

Toldson, I. A., & Toldson, I. L. (2007). A father's call: Father-son relationship survival of critical life transitions. *The Black Scholar, 37*(2), 26–31.

U.S. Department of Health and Human Services, National Institutes of Health, & National Institute of Child Health and Human Development. (2001). *Health Behavior in School-aged Children Survey, 1997-98* [Computer file]. Calverton, MD: ORC Macro.

U.S. Department of Health and Human Services, Substance Abuse and Mental Health Services Administration, & Office of Applied Studies (2007). *National Survey on Drug Use and Health, 2006* [Computer file]. ICPSR21240-v3.

chapter ten

Black fatherhood
Reflections, challenges,
and lessons learned

Kevin Cokley
University of Texas at Austin
Austin, Texas

When Barack Obama was installed as the 43rd President of the United States in January 2009, a wave of emotion swept across this nation, and especially in Black America. Tired of the constant negative messages about absentee Black fathers and single-parent homes in the African American community, the Obama family represented what many African Americans have known all along: that there are responsible and present fathers in the African American community. The impact of fathers should not be underestimated. Fathers play an important role in the cognitive and emotional development of children, including language development and emotional regulation (Cabrera, Shannon, & Tamis-LeMonda, 2007). The absence of fathers can negatively impact children in terms of locus of control, social sensitivity, and self-worth (Balcom, 1998; Fry, 1983). A recent national survey found that the absence of fathers is associated with reduced well-being, worse health, and lower academic achievement (DeBell, 2008). This survey also found that a disproportionate number of African American children in Grades K through 12 were living without their fathers (69%) compared to Hispanic students (39%) and White students (28%).

However, recent empirical research on fatherhood tells a different story about Black fathers. In one study, African American fathers were more involved with their children in terms of monitoring and supervising their activities compared to White fathers (Toth & Xu, 1999). In another study, African American fathers were more likely to report participating in cognitive activities and social skills activities with their children than were European American fathers (Shears, 2007). In a complete defying of stereotypes, Cabrera, Ryan, Mitchell, Shannon, and Tamis-LeMonda (2008) found that nonresident African American fathers were more involved with their children than nonresident White fathers. It is against this backdrop of conflicting accounts of Black fatherhood where my story begins.

On September 23, 2008, my son, Asa Akil Awad Cokley, was born. Words cannot describe the wave of emotion that swept over me, and for a couple of minutes I wept uncontrollably as the weight of that moment fully hit me. For months I had been preparing to be a father, and I wondered what kind of father I would be. There were classes on caring for a newborn baby, but there were no classes on fatherhood (at least none that I was aware of). Like many people in this country, I had been exposed to the dominant media discourse of the absentee Black father. I was painfully aware of the often cited statistics that over 50% of Black children live in fatherless homes. I knew that a number of Black men either did not know their fathers or had damaged relationships with them. Even Senator Obama, in his 2008 Father's Day address to a Black church in Chicago, strongly rebuked absent Black fathers. Discourse on Black fathers is dominated by a deficit perspective; however, recent scholarship on Black fathers has challenged this deficit narrative (Bright & Williams, 1996; Coles, 2009; Connor & White, 2006; Franklin, 2009). Scholarship that takes a strengths-based approach rather than a deficit-based approach is more reflective of my experience because the proverbial absent Black father was not my reality. I grew up in a two-parent household with a loving mother and father. Virtually everything that I know about being a Black father I learned from my own father. In fact, I've learned more from my father than I probably would ever share with him. For my father, Black culture, manhood, and fatherhood were not ideas that were consciously passed down as much as they just were lived by him. As I start this new phase of Black fatherhood, it is important to reflect on the many lessons that I learned from my father, both intended and unintended, and to recall those critical junctures in our relationship that left lasting impressions with me.

On gender and masculinity

To understand my father, one needs to understand my father's father. While growing up, I was not privy to the dynamics of their relationship. I don't know explicitly what kind of relationship they had. What is important to note is that my grandfather was present and a father to my father. In the Cokley family, there was not the cliché of missing Black fathers. My grandfather had a temper and a huge personality that commanded attention and respect wherever he went. He was a deacon in the church and was known for delivering very long prayers both in the church and at family gatherings. He had very strong ideas about what it meant to be a Cokley man, and his words and deeds communicated this. He would shower a disproportionate amount of his attention and affection on his grandsons, often taking the boys out to flea markets and giving us money. My grandfather was fond of saying that only the boys were true Cokleys, presumably because we would carry the family name. His ideas and behaviors were clearly sexist, but probably not unlike the majority of men in his generation. He was very traditional in his beliefs about male and female gender roles. He was the primary breadwinner, and while eating dinner he would always expect my grandmother or mother to fix his plate and to serve him. I sensed that my father had a tremendous amount of respect for his father. My father eventually became a deacon in the church and was the primary (though not sole) breadwinner in our family. Like my grandfather, my father also expected my mother to serve him. Interestingly, as I grew older I became less and less comfortable watching my mother have to fix my father's plate and serve him, especially after she had worked all day. I can recall many times my father being in the living room and yelling my mom's name to bring him something to eat or drink. He would leave his shoes on the floor in the living room, and my mother would have to pick them up and put them away. He would also leave his dirty dishes for my mother to wash. I felt bad for my mother and would often wonder why he didn't just get up and do these things himself. This unintended lesson taught me that I wanted to be more egalitarian in my relationships with women. I never wanted to feel that there were strict prescribed gender roles that I had to follow, especially if they seemed unfair to me. It wasn't until I was much older that I realized that my mother had a lot more power than I perceived her to have. I figured out that whatever power my father had, my mother had given to him willingly and with full awareness. I'm not sure that my father ever knew this (maybe he did and was playing his role as expected), but it became increasingly obvious to me that my mother was not to be pitied and would have never wanted anyone's sympathy. She was a strong Black woman who balanced the demands of her family with the demands of her job. My father was acting out the gender role that had been prescribed to him by his father.

One of the earliest memories that I have of my father are comments he made to me regarding my fondness for taking a pocket mirror to school with me. As a young boy I was always preoccupied with my appearance, and I spent a lot of time making sure that my shirt was neatly tucked in, belt buckle was properly aligned, and hair combed just right. I kept a mirror in my pocket at all times so that I could make sure that I was always looking my best. One day my father discovered that I brought a mirror with me everywhere, and he told me very bluntly to stop doing it. Although I don't remember his exact words, he asked me something to the effect of "Are you a sissy?" These words burned me like nothing else he could have said. As the oldest child, I very much wanted my father's approval. I was a good student, and I knew that was important to my parents. I also wanted to be the best athlete that I could be, in part because I knew that was something my father would be proud of. For my father to ask me if I was a sissy was the ultimate embarrassment for me. It was not something that I could easily shake. There were other incidents that occurred which escape my memory, but they all contributed to my feeling emotionally distant from my father. I felt that I was a disappointment to him. Finally, I felt that I could not take it anymore. I made the decision to run away from home. My goal was to ride my bicycle to Mississippi and to live with my maternal grandmother. I wrote a note expressing my feelings, got on my bicycle, and left my house. As I rode my bike, streams of tears ran down my face as I thought about the implications of my actions. While I was on the road, my great-uncle saw me, picked me up, and took me to his house. I told my great-aunt everything, and she called my parents to tell them that I was there. My parents came to pick me up, and we had a quiet ride back home. Once home, I went to my parents' bedroom and my mom started talking about how upset they were. My father sat silently, but it was the first time that I can recall seeing him almost in tears. For a few moments I began to have hope that my father finally understood how I felt, and that our relationship would change for the better. However, reality quickly settled in after my father said something to the effect of if I pulled something like that again, I would not be coming back to the house. Looking back I can see that my father struggled to express his emotions to me. He clearly was hurt that I felt the need to run away from home because of him, but he did not know how to communicate this to me. Instead, I believe he needed to reestablish his parental authority and regain control of the situation. However, this was a turning point because from that point on, our relationship greatly improved. I never felt the need to run away again. In retrospect, it is hard to imagine that I really believed that I could ride my bike from North Carolina to Mississippi. It clearly was my cry for attention to have a better relationship with my father.

How to treat my mother

One of the most important observations that I made about my father was how he treated my mother. He took great pride in making sure that my mother had nice things. Every Christmas and for her birthday, my father would buy my mother expensive perfume, jewelry, and beautiful clothes. I would look in admiration every year as my father would give my mother these expensive gifts. These gifts were my father's way of showing his love and treating my mother like a queen. Like many men, my father expressed his love through material things. My father knew that his sons were watching him closely. He once told us that it didn't matter whether he had nice clothes or nice things, as long as my mom had nice things. My father believed if my mom ever dressed shabbily that it would be a reflection of him. This is a lesson I would never forget and that I carry with me to this day. Additionally, my father never raised his voice at my mother in front of me, and never used demeaning or degrading language to refer to her. In fact, he never used any disrespectful language to refer to women, and was always respectful of all women. Although he never talked explicitly to me about how to treat women, I learned more from his example than anything he ever could have said. Being in situations where some Black men have disrespected Black women and use sexist and degrading language, I never consciously thought about the reasons why I was never comfortable engaging in this behavior. It is so easy for Black men to get caught up in this culture of misogyny and objectification of Black women, yet my father in his own subtle way taught me some of the most valuable lessons I would ever learn about how to treat Black women.

Ironically, another critical juncture in our relationship involved my treatment of my mother. At one point during my high school years, I had gotten upset with my mother. I do not recall the details, but I remember that I did not speak to my mother for almost a week. My mother apparently told my father, who proceeded to call me upstairs to give me "the talk." It was one of the angriest times my father had been with me. He chastised me in a way that he never done before, with the message being that if I could not respect my mother then I would not be living in the house.

Importance of religion and faith

Another important lesson that I learned from my father was the importance of religion and faith in our family. Consistent with many Black families, religion and going to church was a central part of our lives (Taylor, Chatters, & Levin, 2004). In many Black families it is the mother who is responsible for making sure that the family regularly attends church. Furthermore, it is well known that Black women make up the majority of Black church congregations. In fact, it has been noted that many Black men do not attend church (Kunjufu, 1994). However, in my family, my father took just as active a role in the spiritual well-being of our family as my mother. It was my father who, in his role as patriarch, would bless the food every Sunday. It has always been my father who has said the prayers for the family during times of sickness and bereavement. For as long as I can remember, my father was always a very active member of the church. He has been a Sunday school teacher, Vacation Bible School teacher, choir member, and deacon, among other church roles. During good times and bad times, my father's faith guided him and was instrumental in his ability to be a provider for the family. Ironically, it was also through the church that I witnessed my father express emotion (other than anger) that we rarely saw at home. As he became more involved in the church, particularly as a deacon, he began to testify more. His testimonies revealed an emotional sensitivity and even vulnerability that I did not know existed. This was a far different image of my father than the image I had of him as a young boy. This is the one lesson that I continue to struggle with, because it is not easy for me to reveal any vulnerability. Although my father modeled through his example that showing vulnerability in church is part of what faith requires you to do, some lessons can only be learned when the learner is open to, and ready for, learning.

Being a provider

While growing up, I remember being proud of my father being the primary breadwinner. While I did not know exactly how much money he made until I was completing financial aid forms for college, I always believed that he made a lot of money. My mother would often comment about how much money my father made, and her apparent pride contributed to me feeling proud. Considering that there were five children in the household, I thought we lived relatively well. We didn't always have the most expensive things, but we weren't living in poverty either. My father always seemed to be able to pay for things, which reinforced to me that a father needs to be able to provide for his family. As I prepared to go to an expensive private college (Wake Forest University), I did not think very much about the stress of having to pay for college. During Christmas break of my freshman year, my siblings disclosed to me that my parents were worried about how they were going to come up with the money for my tuition for the second semester. I had no idea how close I was to not being able to return to school because of money. I found out much later from my mother that my father sold his stock in the company he worked for, and did whatever else he needed to do to come up with the money to keep me (and, later, my other siblings) in school. This is just one of the many examples of sacrifice exhibited by my father. The sad thing for me is that I will never know how many sacrifices he made for all of us. The lesson for me was a profoundly simple yet powerful one: Provide for your family by any means necessary. No amount of sacrifice is too much when it involves providing for your family.

Health, well-being, and emotional expression

As I grew older and became a man, my relationship with my father changed and I began to see him in a much more humanizing manner. Specifically, I began to see more of his vulnerabilities along with his strengths. The biggest scare came during my late 20s when my father became extremely sick and had to be hospitalized. He was diagnosed with prostate cancer, a disease that disproportionately impacts Black men. I remember visiting him in the hospital room and, for the first time in my life, being scared that I might actually lose him. I had never seen him look so frail and helpless before. My father is the type of person who never wants people to worry about him, so he downplayed the seriousness of his condition and did his best to try and make our family feel OK. What was especially memorable for me was how he treated me. As the oldest child, I think that my father felt that I was the strongest and most able to deal with the possibility that he could die. He talked to me very candidly about this, and I did my best to live up to his view of me. This was the start of many more occasions where I would see the vulnerabilities of my father, which I think drew us closer and made me appreciate him even more. My father began to have a series of health challenges, many of which could be directly linked to his diet and lifestyle. I grew increasingly frustrated with my father because of his failure to stick consistently to a healthy diet. My father has truly struggled with his diet, to the point where it seems that he has no will-power over food. It finally got to the point where the doctor told him that if he did not make some permanent changes in his diet, he would die. This message got the attention of our entire family, and my mother began changing the way she cooked for him and closely monitoring his diet. To his credit, my father has tried his best to eat healthily, but his upbringing and immersion in Southern Black church culture and constant exposure to Southern cooking have made it extremely difficult to stay on the path of healthy eating. I have tried to appeal to my father that he needs to take better care of himself and eat healthy so that he can be around for a long time for his family, but nothing seems to result in a permanent change in behavior. I don't think that my father was necessarily trying to "eat himself to death"; however, I think his eating was indicative of a deeper psychological issue and was a coping mechanism related to his changing status from the primary breadwinner to secondary breadwinner.

Between 2003 and 2005, R. J. Reynolds, the tobacco company my father worked for, began cutting a number of manufacturing jobs. R. J. Reynolds was considered a very good job at that time, because it paid well and had provided great benefits. My father had worked there for over 20 years, and he became concerned as the proverbial handwriting was on the wall about the downsizing that was to take place. When he finally received the news, he outwardly expressed relief and joy that he would no longer have to work. He was going to receive a severance package, and he looked forward to not having to work third-shift hours anymore. However, I think what he underestimated, or perhaps didn't think about, were his feelings regarding what that would exactly mean for the family. Specifically, I don't think my father thought very much about the strain this would put on my mother, who suddenly became the primary breadwinner. Their household income had been dramatically reduced, but their bills and expenses were the same. My father was in an unfamiliar role for which he was not emotionally equipped to handle. This is what I think triggered my father into becoming more of an emotional eater than he had ever been before. He did not express his emotions verbally, so in a sense eating became his therapy.

The most emotions that I ever saw from my father came as a result of his parents' death. My grandmother had been battling cancer, and after the cancer returned from remission we knew it was only a matter of time before it would claim her life. When I received the call in May 1995, I had already started to emotionally prepare to hear that my grandmother had passed. My father had made the call, which was somewhat out of the ordinary because he rarely called me. However, I was totally unprepared for what he said next. He told me that my grandfather had also passed on the same day. I was in total shock and disbelief. As I started the drive from Atlanta to North Carolina to be with my family, I had to pull aside as I became overwhelmed with grief. When I arrived home, my siblings were there and everyone appeared to still be in shock. My father was remarkably calm and I wondered how he was able to keep his emotions in check. Later I remember sitting in the kitchen and suddenly hearing loud sobbing come from my parents' bedroom. My siblings and I ran to the room and found my father lying on his bed curled up and crying uncontrollably. I immediately embraced him while struggling to manage my own emotions. Never had I seen such raw emotion expressed by my father. At that moment I felt that our roles were reversed, and it was time for the son to be a source of strength for his father.

Lessons learned

There have been several lessons that I've learned from my father that inform my role as a father. My first lesson is to constantly work on being comfortable expressing emotions toward my son and maintaining positive communication with him. My father's hard work and sacrifice undoubtedly demonstrated his love toward me and my siblings. During the few times when we had personal difficulties, it would have also meant so much to me to hear the words "I love you, son" or any expression of his feelings toward me. Unfortunately, that was not the way my father was raised or socialized. His love was manifested in being the provider and avid supporter of my athletic accomplishments. I have learned from this experience, and I never want my son to long for an outward expression of my feelings for him. As a result, I frequently tell my toddler son that I love him while showering him with kisses and affection. To be clear, this is not an indictment of my father. Instead, it is an affirmation of my love for him and of wanting to make sure that my son knows how much I love him because of my relationship with my father. Regarding positive communication, I learned from my father the tremendous power his words held over me. I want to be vigilant about not saying anything to my son that would cause him unnecessary emotional distress. Of course, I say this now with the best of intentions, while recognizing that I cannot predict the future. I can only promise to do my best to be sensitive to the power that my words will have with my son.

My second lesson is to make sure that the messages I communicate to my son regarding the treatment of women are egalitarian, are nonsexist, and reflect a genuine love and respect for all women. There is no more powerful example that I can provide my son about the treatment of women than the relationship I have with my wife. I will teach him through my actions in our home that his mother is loved, valued, and respected and that his actions should reflect the same. I want my son to see that household responsibilities are divided equitably between his mother and father. Even in those instances when the household responsibilities are based on traditional gender roles (e.g., my wife doing the cooking while I mow the yard and take out the trash), my son will also observe his parents taking on nontraditional gender roles (e.g., I do much of the dishwashing and kitchen cleaning while my wife is good at solving mechanical problems and following instructions to put things together). The point is that I do not want my son to ever think that his mother is being treated unfairly. I do not want him to adhere to rigidly defined gender roles that are oppressive to women and restrict men to narrow and ultimately unhealthy definitions of manhood. Instead, I want him to have flexible gender roles that are guided by his respect for women. Having said that, I would be less than honest if I did not admit that I do want my son to evince a certain "healthy" and nonhegemonic masculinity that I hope I model in our home. That is, I want him to ultimately be able to provide a sense of safety and security to whomever he ends up marrying. Additionally, I hope that my son never feels the need to use words that demean and denigrate women. I never use these to refer to my wife, mother, or sister, and I try my best to never use these words to refer to any women. This is what I observed and learned from my father, and this is what I hope to teach my son.

The third lesson I learned from my father is the importance of working hard and doing everything in my power to provide for my family. I am somewhat of a workaholic, and I have never been one to be idle. I cannot go for any long periods of time without doing something related to my career, and in fact much of the motivation that I've used to be successful in my career is rooted in my desire to be the best academic that I can be so that ultimately I can have job security to be able to always provide for my family. The biggest difference between me and my father in this regard is that I love my career and feel that I am fulfilling a higher purpose, which makes it easier for me to be a workaholic. In contrast, my father worked for over 20 years in a job that I don't think he was passionate about in order to provide for his family. Moreover, he worked the third shift, and research has shown that working the night shift has a negative impact on health outcomes, including poorer quality and quantity of sleep, chronic fatigue, anxiety and depression, increased cardiovascular morbidity and mortality, and gastrointestinal disease (Costa, 1999; Harrington, 1994). From that vantage point, what my father did was much harder and more sacrificial than what I'm doing, and this makes me appreciate him even more. However, there is also a downside of this lesson, which are the consequences of being a workaholic. Being an academic at a major research university, there is the constant pressure to publish, especially when you're not tenured. This pressure caused me to develop an approach to work in which I was always thinking about research and the next article that I needed to write. Work was not confined to my office, but in my home and when I visited my family over the holidays. I was always writing, and I did not take time to vacation or engage in self-care. Conference traveling was constant, with my traveling to as many as five conferences a year. However, I need to be vigilant in not letting work and my career prevent me from giving my son the quality time he needs. Nothing is so important about work that makes it acceptable to choose work over my son. I never want my son to see me as an absentee father even though I physically live in the house. Fortunately, my wife will never let this happen. As an academic, she understands very well the demands of the academy; however, she values a healthy functioning family over career success. She keeps me accountable as a father by constantly making sure that I am involved in my son's life. She has made it clear that staying long hours in my office is no longer acceptable, and that my son needs me to be actively involved in his life. I want Asa to learn the difference between working hard and being a workaholic, and that nothing is more important than spending quality time with family.

Conclusion

Writing this chapter has been, in many ways, cathartic and eye-opening for me. I had never taken the time to really think about my relationship with my father and all the lessons (intended and unintended) that I have learned from him. Now that I am a father, I realize that I have a much deeper well of my father's wisdom, knowledge, and experience to draw from than I had previously imagined. I learned as much from my father's struggles related to traditional gender roles as I did from his many successes as a father. Based on my reflections of my father, an important intervention strategy is to develop programs for Black fathers designed to facilitate the exploration of emotional inexpressiveness. While research on the emotional behavior of men has increased, most theories and models (and thus interventions) are based on White men in the United States (Good & Sherrod, 2001). Black men have the pressures shared by most men as well as the pressures from dealing with a racist society. In many instances, Black fathers learn to cope with racism by restraining their emotions, and they also model emotional inexpressiveness to their sons that they learned from their fathers. Interventions should be developed that help Black fathers improve their communication and express their emotions in constructive ways.

In conclusion, I thank my father for the lessons I have learned about Black manhood and fatherhood. I will pass these many lessons, intended and unintended, on to my son with the hope of making him the best man and father that he can be.

Reflective questions

1. In what ways does internalization of traditional gender roles both help and harm Black fathers?
2. A recent *New York Times* article claims that fathers are not really necessary, citing as evidence research that shows single fathers are less involved, communicate more poorly, and feel less close to children than single moms. The article also states that the trend is similar in a traditional man–woman family when compared to lesbian parents. If the research is true, can it be concluded that Black fathers are not as important to Black families as Black mothers?
3. How can Black fathers still feel needed in Black families when they aren't, or are no longer, the primary breadwinner?

References

Balcom, D. (1998). Absent fathers: Effects on abandoned sons. *Journal of Men's Studies, 6*(3), 283–296.

Bright, J., & Williams, C. (1996). Child rearing and education in urban environments: Black fathers' perspectives. *Urban Education, 31*(3), 245–260.

Cabrera, N., Ryan, R., Mitchell, S., Shannon, J., & Tamis-LeMonda, C. (2008). Low-income, nonresident father involvement with their toddlers: Variation by fathers' race and ethnicity. *Journal of Family Psychology, 22*(4), 643–647.

Cabrera, N., Shannon, J., & Tamis-LeMonda, C. (2007). Fathers' influence on their children's cognitive and emotional development: From toddlers to pre-K. *Applied Developmental Science, 11*(4), 208–213.

Coles, R. (2009). *The best kept secret: Single Black fathers*. Lanham, MD: Rowman & Littlefield.

Connor, M., & White, J. (2006). *Black fathers: An invisible presence in America*. Mahwah, NJ: Erlbaum.

Costa, G. (1999). The impact of shift and night work on health. *Applied Ergonomics, 27*, 9–16.

DeBell, M. (2008). Children living without their fathers: Population estimates and indicators of educational well-being. *Social Indicators Research, 87*(3), 427–443.

Franklin, A. (2009). Another side of invisibility: Present and responsible Black fathers. In *Counseling fathers* (pp. 121–140). New York: Routledge.

Fry, P. S. (1983). Father absence and deficits in children's social-cognitive development: Implications for intervention and training. *Journal of Psychiatric Treatment and Education, 5*(2–3), 113–120.

Good, G. E., & Sherrod, N. B. (2001). Men's problems and effective treatment. In G. R. Brooks & G. E. Good (Eds.), *The new handbook of psychotherapy and counseling with men* (pp. 22–40). San Francisco: Jossey-Bass.

Harrington, J. M. (1994). Shift work and health: A critical review of the literature on working hours. *Annals of the Academy of Medicine, Singapore, 23*(5), 699–705.

Kunjufu, J. (1994). *Adam! Where are you? Why most Black men don't go to church*. Chicago: African American Images.

Shears, J. (2007). Understanding differences in fathering activities across race and ethnicity. *Journal of Early Childhood Research, 5*(3), 245–261.

Taylor, R. J., Chatters, L. M., & Levin, J. (2004). *Religion in the lives of African Americans: Social, psychological, and health perspectives*. Thousand Oaks, CA: Sage.

Toth, J., & Xu, X. (1999). Ethnic and cultural diversity in fathers' involvement: A racial/ethnic comparison of African American, Hispanic, and White fathers. *Youth & Society, 31*(1), 76–99.

chapter eleven

Black man defined
A boy with a purpose becomes a man when the purpose is fulfilled

J. Phillip Rosier, Jr.
Kente Circle
Minneapolis, Minnesota

According to Hare and Hare (1989), Black manhood

> is a quiet strength. The positioning of oneself so that observation comes before reaction, where study is preferred to night life, where emotion is not seen as a weakness. Love for self, family, children, and extensions of self are beyond the verbal. Black manhood. Making your life accessible to children in meaningful ways, able to recognize the war we are in. Doing anything to take care of family so long as it doesn't harm or negatively affect other Black people. Willing to share resources to the maximum. Willing to struggle unrelentingly against the evils of this world especially evils that directly threaten the race. Black manhood. To seek and be that which is just, good and correct. Properly positioning oneself in the context of our people. A listener. A student. Historian. One who develops leadership qualities and demands the same qualities of those who have been chosen to lead. See material rewards as means towards an end and not an end in themselves. Clean—mentally and physically. Protector of Black weak. One who respects Black elders. Practical idealist. Questioner of the world. Spiritually in tune with the best of the world. Black manhood. Direction giver. Husband. Sensitive to Black women's needs

> and aspirations. Realizing that it is not necessary for
> them to completely absorb themselves into us but
> that nothing separates the communication between
> us. A seeker of truth. A worker of the first order.
> Teacher. Example of what is to be. Fighter. A builder
> with vision. Connects land to liberation. A student
> of peace and war. Warrior and statesman. (p. 41)

In this definition of Black manhood, there are some ambitious ideas and goals for boys aspiring to be men. Directly and indirectly, a sense of purpose is articulated in the definition. There is a clear road map of acceptable actions and beliefs. This quote was chosen as a definition because it acknowledges the many roles and responsibilities that come with manhood. Perhaps one of the most influential roles is making your life accessible to children in meaningful ways. This role addresses an expectation of fatherhood. What should be the purpose of Black fathers? It is clear in the definition that a Black man must be a father. Also, the role of father does not limit one to just the responsibility of one's biological offspring. The previous definition hints at a collective responsibility for guiding children to adulthood.

The idea of guiding children dates back to traditional rites of passage. Men use rites of passage to communicate the purpose of manhood. In traditional rites of passage initiations, it takes 4 years to communicate the purpose. Therefore, to attempt to communicate the purpose of manhood in one chapter may be overly ambitious. Instead the chapter will focus on Black fathers and the importance of forming an agreed-upon purpose to ensure the survival and optimal functioning of the African American family. It is important to note that a purpose or lack thereof will be shared with Black boys either with or without the assistance of Black men. At times, Black men have influence over the development of Black boys. However, it is unclear that Black men communicate a shared purpose that ensures the survival of Black boys. The goal of this chapter is to expose the influence of institutions and social fathers on the development of purpose for Black boys and to propose a unified purpose for Black boys to assist them in their transition into fatherhood.

Many Black fathers, like others, struggle with role definitions. As a volunteer teacher with a rites of passage program in Tallahassee, Florida, my exposure to the roles and responsibilities of African American manhood was understood. A teacher in this rites of passage program began his "Who Am I" or introduction to the rites group as "I am a father, son, brother, friend, Black man, student, husband, cousin, uncle, counselor." This list initiated thoughts about the many roles Black men manage as human beings. However, the role of Black father is a distinct role shared only by Black men and it denotes responsibility to the community. The experience of being Black adds a unique social dynamic to all the roles my fellow teacher recited in his introduction. This implies that Black men share the responsibility to protect and enhance our community.

Black fathers share a common goal of managing the misinformation and outright distortions and lies perpetrated by wider society. They also have the goal of defining what it means to be Black and what it means to be a responsible, engaged man and father. A commonly agreed-upon definition allows the community to hold men accountable for their actions, deeds, responsibilities, and activities.

Regarding the question, "Who Am I?" one cannot respond without recognizing and considering one's actions, deeds, and contributions. The inquiry forces one to think about what is meaningful, what are one's core beliefs and values, and what is one's purpose in life. In absence of a purpose, the motivation for completing meaningful activity dwindles; motivation is lost and the activity becomes a waste of time. This is analogous to the challenge that Black men face in defining their roles as fathers. Black fathers face many barriers, and one of the most serious can be the absence of purpose. Black fathers who take on the responsibility of raising children share a common purpose. Those who are not responsible for their children do not share this common purpose. They are often distracted by barriers such as the relationship with their children's mothers, financial limitations, illegal behaviors, the impact of limited educations, and difficulty with emotion regulation.

It is important to recognize that these barriers are influenced by many factors, including the economic impact of poverty and racism, as well as individual problems in the form of unresolved or unidentified mental illness. These issues have the potential to steer Black men away from their purpose. However, if there is an awareness of how these factors impede fathers from sharing and carrying out a common purpose (i.e., reaching the goal of providing for their children), and the determination to confront and overcome obstacles, the barriers can be triumphed over.

The current institutions that are defining our purpose

African societies were organized around the "nation" or "tribe," clan, family, household (Mbiti, 1990). Nations or tribes (sometimes consisting of several clans) ranged from thousands to millions of people who were distinguished by a unique history in which they traced their origins to God, first ancestors, a national leader, and a common culture distinguished by a distinctive language, geographical area, and social, political, and economic organization (Dixon, 2007, p. 2). In traditional African societies, manhood was often defined through rituals known as "rites of passage." Raphael (1988) writes that the use of structured initiation rites helps guide youth through their development. Elders would teach boys to become men through trials and tasks aimed at helping them understand manhood through experiences in controlled environments, apart from the women of the tribe. Their definition of manhood addressed kinship, responsibilities, obligation to elders, how to treat and interact with women, and how to protect and serve their specific village. What made this process work was the involvement of the men in the community, their agreement about what needed to be taught to the boys (i.e., *purpose*), and the trust that the community had in the process. Upon their return, the community changed its treatment of these boys, as it now considered them to be men and thus assigned adult responsibilities to them.

In contemporary American society, several institutions have assumed primary responsibility for teaching African American boys about responsibility, manhood, and survival. Although many Black boys "complete" high school, college, military, or jail with specific ideas about these concepts, unfortunately, the institutions listed often have different values, ideas, and definitions regarding manhood, fatherhood, or what it means to be African American. What is more unfortunate is that African Americans have little control over these institutions or their definitions. For example, Black folk are often not at the table when important decisions regarding the school curriculum are made, rendering them invisible within educational institutions. Carter G. Woodson (2000) writes, in *The Mis-education of the Negro,* "The thought of the inferiority of the Negro is drilled into him in almost every class he enters and almost every book he studies" (p. 2).

A likely exception occurs at Historical Black Colleges and Universities (HBCUs), some charter, and Afrocentric-based schools. Although HBCUs have generic mandates that they follow for accreditation, they may have some autonomy to execute their own values and beliefs. Thus, it is no surprise that African American boys who enter HBCUs often are exposed to values and purposes that prepare them to contribute to the community. The genius of African Americans can also prevail in White institutions. In these situations, many come together in fraternities, Black student unions, cultural specific clubs, and churches on or near campus, which offer African American men the opportunity to support Black children and give back to the Black community. Almost intuitively, African American men seem to know the importance of creating their own definitions of manhood and fatherhood. Some Black college students participate in organizations that mentor Black boys, organizations led by African Americans who share the commitment of community service. Black men attending colleges and universities can take advantage of these opportunities where their voluntary contributions can give them a greater sense of purpose as it pertains to their education.

Because the military values the objectives of the United States, African Americans who join the armed forces learn to value the United States over their communities. The military can also help to instill values that are useful to the Black community. One goal is survival under adverse conditions (war); another involves providing training or being trained. Support and reinforcement are offered by rewarding men who adhere to the agreed-upon purposes. Validation comes in the form of hiring and promoting practices, increased social interaction from citizens, and housing and financing benefits.

The military contains some aspects of traditional rites of passage. As such, the benefits of the military can be compared with the initiatory aspects of rites of passage programs. They are remarkably similar. For example, boys are sent away from home for an extensive time where men attempt to instill values that will aid in their survival. They are given tasks and opportunities to develop new skills. Thus, the military can be perceived as a modern-day attempt at implementing rites of passage. However, one of the major differences between traditional rites of passage programs and the military is the lack of agreement between the men in the institution.

For many, there is a definite sense of respect that comes with joining the military. For example, my father, who is a Vietnam veteran, often boasted about how "the Marines made a man out of him." He talked about the discipline, confidence, and maturity it developed in him, qualities that are useful in today's communities.

Prisons may or may not have an agreed-upon purpose, but "informal" mentors are also there to teach manhood and responsibility from perspectives ranging from local street gangs to the Black Muslims. Within the prison walls, African American men volunteer time to teach values to younger men they encounter. However, upon returning to the community, African American men may receive a mixed response. The career criminals may give the kids a stamp of approval whereas other community members lose respect and withhold trust for those returning from the penal system. The "rites of passage" programs that take place in the penal system are usually incomplete due to the lack of a common purpose between the prison, the community, and society at large. This can leave these men more confused, concerned, and frustrated about manhood.

A major disadvantage regarding contemporary institutions is that they do not directly address the role of the father. This lesson, if taught, is taught by the immediate family and the men who sacrifice their time in the community. Where does one learn how to be a father? In the previous edition of this book, Connor and White (2006) addressed the concept of social fathers. Social fathers are men who assume some or all the roles fathers are expected to perform in a child's life whether or not they are biological fathers (Coley, 2001). As a more inclusive term, *social fatherhood* encompasses biological fathers and extends to men who are not biological fathers but who provide a significant nurturance, moral-ethical guidance, companionship, emotional support, and financial responsibility in the lives of children. These men contribute time, knowledge, and resources to helping boys become men. They seem to share a consciousness about the importance of committing time and effort to raising young boys. Most have been taught from their own families, military, college, and social organizations to value the commitment of teaching young boys how to reach manhood and prepare themselves for fatherhood.

What social fathers do

In my life, there are many men who were social fathers, including my father (who is a former law enforcement officer); the local martial arts instructor, who taught boys and girls for free; an advisor, who taught a youth leadership development program; and, an adjunct professor, who organized a rites of passage program for young boys and inspired college men to commit their time and energy to youth. Although there were many models in the community, they all shared the commitment of teaching boys what they need to become successful fathers.

My father is a military veteran and a former deputy sheriff, who made the commitment to devote time and resources to assist me in becoming a man. He provided discipline for me, as he understood that discipline is a vehicle to achieve goals; he understood the importance of protecting children and encouraged me to accept responsibilities; he was committed to my success and the success of my peers. Through his actions, I developed trust in our father–son relationship, which provided a model for how to be a father.

My martial arts instructor made a commitment to teach African American children in a local community center. In addition to sharing his genius with us, he taught us pride in being Black. The uniforms were red, black, and green, which symbolizes the continent of Africa, and he made sure we worked to our potential. By instilling a work ethic, our teacher (master) shared Eastern philosophical concepts that were applicable to life. The teacher did not ask for monetary payments; rather, his request was that we make a commitment to learning. This social father readily gave his time, expertise, and experience to many African American boys in the community. Some of the students learned to apply the same work ethic and values to other aspects of life.

One of my college professors also demonstrated social fathering. He helped define purposes for the students in his class and for their participation in a rites of passage program. His objective was centered on the survival of the individual, family, and race, and he provided an opportunity for Black students to experience a rite of passage. The professor gave of his time voluntarily. He made sure we could all articulate the purpose in order to share it with others in the program. He made sure the community validated the efforts of the boys by celebrating those who graduated from the program. The community was instructed to expand their expectations of the boys and to provide more freedom to them.

In traditional African societies, the developmental life cycle for males consisted of birth, childhood, rites of passage, marriage, fatherhood, becoming an elder, and transition to the world of the ancestors. These milestones were shared by the men in the community and were highly valued. Expectations about how to excel in these roles were communicated to the men of the tribe. In the tribe, the council of elders was revered as counselors and problem solvers. They set the standard for how people interacted and what was acceptable behavior. In today's society, there are both social and biological fathers who take on the responsibility of teaching the youth. However, as noted previously, there is lack of consensus regarding definitions of manhood and/or fatherhood. Although many fathers teach their values, they may be teaching different values, which creates confusion for impressionable boys. Therefore, it is important to have consistent values through role models to provide boys with a clear purpose.

The purpose

Practically, there should be some framework to help Black men discover purpose. What follows is a framework that provides an opportunity for clarifying that purpose. A Rites of Passage purpose was to provide a sense of purpose to manhood. The tribe would celebrate the completion of this process. In observing mental, physical, and spiritual needs of African American men, the following four declarations for building a framework for one's purpose may be useful.

Commit to know one's self and the discovery of one's genius

A commitment to know oneself and the discovery of genius is a lifelong purpose that is rooted in the love for oneself. The phrase "man know thyself" is a powerful phrase that validates the importance of self-inquiry. It encourages insight into actions. This is essential in therapy. Insights into behavior help a client to gain control over behavior. Control over behavior is needed to carry out the purpose. As a result of insights, one's genius can be recognized. As a father, decisions can be made in the best interest of children as opposed to the unresolved needs of the father.

Contribute to the advancement of humanity

When Black fathers contribute to humanity, it reinforces a sense of belonging to the human race. Black fathers have a responsibility to the advancement of the human race. Historically, Black men have been placed under inhumane conditions. Efforts to contribute to humanity remind them that they are human and must not accept these conditions. Their struggle can be considered the contribution to humanity. Therefore, the response to that struggle to be treated with dignity and respect brings value to humanity. It encourages the respect of our children. Recently, the President of the United States was awarded the Nobel Peace Prize. The Nobel Peace Prize symbolizes a contribution to humanity. Many Black boys observed the struggle that Barack Obama and other Black men endured over time and were inspired by his actions. His election inspired a sense of connection to the human race.

Commit to the survival of the African American community

The African American community needs men and women to contribute. Black men should be measured by their ability to assist in the survival of the community. This purpose is similar to the rites of passage. Black men are servants of the African American community and will be measured by the community.

Match one's unique genius to the needs of the African American community

Many Black men have gained specific knowledge and skills that are often used in areas outside of the African American community. Directors and leaders of major companies, computer programmers, scientists, lawyers, and many other professionals are consumed with providing their services in places where they will receive the most monetary gain. This can be seen as a draining of resources from the African American community.

This purpose aims at encouraging Black men to share their genius with their community.

Conclusion

This chapter calls for the development of a new sense of purpose for the African American father. This definition encompasses the group survival mentality of the past. Black men's existence is truly dependent on each other and is systemic in nature. Black ancestors understood this concept. This definition also takes into account a person's individual talents and gifts. However, those talents and gifts should be used to serve the collective.

Providing young Black men with a sense of purpose helps to provide a meaning to life, a reason to live life to the fullest, and a purpose that will enhance motivation for engaging life challenges. Now that there is a proposal for the purpose of manhood and fatherhood, we have the task of spreading the collective purpose to community programs and organizations that share the definition of manhood/fatherhood.

Currently, values are shared through our churches, recreational sports, clubs and social networks, fraternities, secret societies, schools, military, jails, gangs, and so on. All of these institutions and organizations continue to honor separate values for each other. Spreading of the purpose goes counter to the free world thinking of our society. Inherent in accepting a purpose is the reality of conforming to that purpose. We value our freedom of thought. Therefore, the idea of a shared purpose or road map seems limiting. This is the dilemma of standardizing a common purpose. What remains is a number of boys, with different purposes validated by different institutions and family values, who work diligently to fulfill their purpose. The commitment to fulfilling one's purpose opens the door to fatherhood.

Reflective questions

1. Is there a common purpose of Black fathers? Should there be?
2. Does the community recognize a common purpose of Black fathers?
3. In what ways do African American men initiate Black boys into fatherhood? Can more be done? Should it?

References

Coley, R. (2001). Invisible men: Emerging research on low-income, unmarried and minority fathers. *American Psychologist, 56*(9), 743–753.

Connor, M., & White, J. (2006). *Black fathers: An invisible presence in America.* Mahwah, NJ: Erlbaum.

Dixon, P. (2007). *African American relationships, marriages, and families*. New York: Taylor & Francis.

Hare, J., & Hare, N. (1989). *Crisis in Black sexual politics*. San Francisco: Black Think Tank.

Mbiti, J. S. (1990). *African religions and philosophies*. Oxford, UK: Heinemann.

Raphael, R. (1988). *The men from the boys*. Lincoln: University of Nebraska Press.

Woodson, C. (2000). *The mis-education of the Negro*. Chicago: African American Images.

chapter twelve

Making room for Black men to father and mentor

Larry G. Tucker
Kente Circle
Minneapolis, Minnesota

Introduction

African American[*] males hold significant roles within their families and communities, as leaders, mentors, and role models that show up in their relationships as uncles, sons, brothers, nephews, cousins, and social fathers. These males have always been present in their families and the communities where they live, but their presence and positions within their families go unnoticed (Tucker, 2000). It is also important to acknowledge and validate the various ways that African American males are involved in mentoring and childrearing. This chapter seeks to explore the diversity in how African American men and boys see themselves and insert themselves in the lives of those around them.

It is a stereotype that African American men as a group are not having a positive impact on children, due to divorce, joblessness, incarceration, and so on. According to White and Cones (1999) "North and South, America was saturated with images of clowning, cunning, lazy, ignorant, pleasure-seeking, childlike Black men who needed to be supervised and controlled by powerful, competent, responsible White males" (p. 35). That imagery served as a powerful tool that shaped how the public feels and thinks about Black males. For the purpose of this chapter, the reader is invited to consider this issue from several other perspectives. Whereas there are some Black men who are irresponsible and not present in their

[*] For the purpose of this chapter, African American and Black will be used interchangeably. The author realizes that there are numerous ways in which people identify themselves that are rooted in germane history, culture, and life experiences. He does not mean to diminish how anyone defines who he or she is. Grace is humbly requested.

children's lives, there are many others who are present, and often there are significant social, cultural, economic, and class components that are rarely considered or respectfully acknowledged (Staples, 1982).

The author will use examples, experiences, and stories of boys and men who grew up in African American families and communities to demonstrate scenarios of how Black men are present in the lives of children. To provide context and to demonstrate how Black men are present in the lives of children, the chapter will explore the following areas: historical background, cultural implications, barriers to relationships, and myths.

Historical background

Historically, many Black women have been left standing to bear the role of single parents. According to Boyd-Franklin (1989), there has been a "startling increase in Black female-headed families within the last decade [which] parallels a similar trend in all American families. Since 1970, the number of single parent households in the United States has more than doubled. These single-parent households include a diversity of family structures (e.g., single never-married, single divorced or separated, and single widowed)" (p. 191). It is exciting to see Black men starting to be honored and recognized for how they too are shouldering the responsibility of parenting. We are seeing this being done in more public ways. "Either/or" thinking has infested the American culture's thought process in many ways. Here too, it feels like Black men and Black women are in hierarchical competition, relative to parenting roles and family positions.

Apparently, some families adapt an ideology that puts either a man or a woman in charge of the family, placing an unbalanced amount of authority in one person's possession. In some cases, women (i.e., mothers, grandmothers, aunts, sisters, and other females) come together as a unit to raise children to replace the male and female household structure altogether (McGoldrick, Giordano, & Pearce, 1996). This seems to go against the old proverb, "It takes a village to raise a child." Within every family, each member has strengths that benefit the whole. When we buy into a destructive, individualistic mind-set, we are not living in harmony with values that embrace that proverb. This mind-set has affected Black men and women's ability to compromise and co-parent.

The media rarely models the necessity of Black two-parent households (Staples, 1982). Growing up, the author recalls experiencing Black women modeling behaviors suggesting that they did not need Black men. They appeared to navigate life's challenges routinely with an understanding of their social position and authority. Black women's social status did not fluctuate or vary on the basis of their marital status. The assumption was that the spirit of these interactions was not done intentionally to emasculate Black men, but that appears to be the outcome in some respects.

Again, Black men and women live within a system that has placed strains on their relationships. Black men are vilified and feared in American culture. Presenting Black men in this light directly impacts how men are able to be present and provide for their families. Furthermore, when Black men make mistakes in desperation, they find themselves being held to standards that are not equal to their White counterparts. An example of this is seen in how often Black men are charged with felonies as compared to Whites or any other ethnic group. As they find themselves in these situations, learning from their mistakes often seems daunting and, for some, impossible. It becomes harder for Black men to discover who they are when they become renamed and labeled as a result of a poor choice.

There are numerous other reasons African American men may not "show up" in some of the traditional ways that we think of fathers and men being present in the lives of children. One of the primary barriers is that society, and in some cases Black families, cannot conceptualize Black men being present and available to their children. The fact is that "the Black community" does not look the way it did in the 1970s and 1980s. Older Blacks tell stories of their experiences of growing up in a Black community that was drastically different from Black communities today. Many of these Blacks grew up in communities that were predominately Black. Their foundation was grounded by a shared sense of community that was dictated or shaped by religion and the arts, among other guiding forces. Church and organized religion were a huge aspect of the Black community. Many families spent several days a week attending prayer, Bible studies, choir practice, board meetings, Sunday school, and Sunday church services. Men were involved at this time, and entire families participated in these activities. Moreover, communities were organized around values and principles that were derived from such regular routines. In reference to the arts, music has always significantly influenced boys, men, and African American culture as a whole. Artists such as Marvin Gaye and James Brown told stories in the music that they sang. Their music asked thought-provoking questions. Examples of this can be heard in some of Marvin Gaye's music, such as "What's Going On," "What's Happening Brother," and "Inner City Blues." The words in those songs touched our consciousness. For example, Marvin Gaye's "Save the Children" (Cleveland, Gaye, & Benson, 1971) poses:

> You see, let's save the children
> Let's save all the children
> Save the babies, save the babies
> If you wanna love, you got to save the babies

The listeners could relate to the heartfelt messages that served as inspiration and accountability. Marvin's message suggests that he realized that he was a member of a larger community; this level of awareness of one's connectedness is invaluable. For so many others it was a common experience of what it meant to be Black, which is often articulated differently depending on with whom you are speaking. When you listen closely to the music that is popular today, you will hear a different message. The message embedded in today's music is a reflection, to some extent, of what this culture values. Minimally, the music is influencing American culture like it did in the past.

Cultural implications

In today's culture, some have argued that the Black community is so diverse, widespread geographically, religiously, economically, and culturally, that it is too difficult to define (Boyd-Franklin, 1989; White & Cones, 1999). It might be impossible to construct a definition that satisfies all who consider themselves African American. What about those individuals who make a distinction between being Black, African American, or a person of color? How one self-identifies has become a major area of contention for some African Americans. This struggle is a result of what is happening in American culture surrounding race and ethnicity. The media bombards society with misinformed ideas about what it means to be an African American man and father. The media's impressions rarely leave room for multiple ways for a person or community to choose how they would identify themselves. In addition, there has never been a balance between the positive information and the maladaptive behavior of a few that is depicted in the mainstream culture.

Americans have historically wrestled with the issue of identity. Therefore, it is not surprising that African Americans have also struggled with this issue. For example, within the African American community, there is ongoing contentious discussion and dissension pertaining to variations of skin color. Conflicts between light-skinned or dark-skinned Blacks and the positive and negative stigma attributed to each are debated, discussed, and lived. Historically, the media depicts White as good and Black as bad.

A major problem that dates back to slavery is Black men being seen as objects (Morrow, 2003). This is evidenced by how they were sold as goods and used as sexual objects to turn a profit. At that time, Black men, and in some cases boys, were forced to have sex with females for the sole purpose of procreating more goods in the form of children. Historically, there was no expectation to raise those children, as the owners of the slaves trained the children and told them who they were. There are examples that this practice has continued today. One might compare the identity crisis that some Black men experience when they have children and abandon them as a residual of slavery. During the era of slavery, this practice was widely practiced and it was a "part" of some Black men's identity that was forced on them. Furthermore, stress can cause people to regress to previous ways of coping and surviving that are not healthy. It seems logical that if Black men found identity in "sexually performing," then some might do this as a way of coping with stress. It is well documented that the legacy of slavery and oppression has impacted the way Black males are perceived (Franklin, 1988; Gary, 1981; Grier & Cobbs, 1968; Staples, 1982; White & Cones, 1999).

We live in a culture that has always been economically driven, and there is always going to be a need for "cheap" labor. Unfortunately, when you do not know who you are or what you stand for, some people may be prone to fall for others' ideas or definitions of who you are. Black men must resist accepting how external forces seek to impose identities on them that do not fit with how they see themselves. Black men are more than procreators of cheap labor. Although Blacks are no longer sold into slavery, many have lost their identity as a result of oppression that continues to exist (Tucker, 2000).

Barriers to relationships

Some of the challenges that impact our involvement in our children's lives have evolved over the years and are not as simple as "good men" or "strong Black men" forgetting who they are and where they come from. There appears to be strong feelings by some African American women that Black men are abandoning their post. In addition, there is a sense that Black men are going off to college, getting educated, and bettering themselves in general and not looking back to offer further support in childrearing. This perception does not tell the whole story. Black men are present and engaged with raising their children; in fact they are also offering their education and experience up as mentors to students on college campuses and community schools where they live (Connor & White, 2006; White & Cones, 1999).

Many African American men are no longer physically located in the same region where they grew up. For some, jobs, college, loved ones, hopes, and dreams have carried them to different communities. These hopes and dreams are some of their own, their parents, grandparents, and inspired by their ancestors. The other side of answering the call of pursuing dreams is the unpaved and, at times, uncharted territory that many African American men find themselves in. As an African American father, who now has children of his own, the author finds himself asking where to find parental allies in a community that is predominately Caucasian with different values from those of his childhood. Parenting today feels like being on an island surrounded by shark-infested waters. It isn't about the people around us as much as it is parenting in isolation. The author grew up in the inner city of Milwaukee, Wisconsin, which came with its unique challenges and disadvantages at times. However, when my parents were not available or lacked skills in certain areas, I had other family and there was a community who stepped up.

Marriage stability is another issue to consider in that the rate of divorce has skyrocketed (Johnson & Staples, 1993; White & Cones, 1999), and many children find themselves being raised by one parent, or two parents living in separate households, if they are able to work out their differences for the sake of the children. Many relationships that bear children do not evolve into a marital or co-parenting situation. The result of these relationship choices, pre- and postdivorce, often come with financial and time challenges, both of which can limit children and families getting their needs met. These issues have shaped how African American fathers are able to participate in their children's lives and have limited their access to being able to pass down some of their values that help shape cultural understanding. This has left the impression that Black fathers are uncaring, when in truth communities are stuck in patterns and ways of being that stifle growth and prevent fathers from engaging in adequate ways.

The myth

There is a widespread myth that African American fathers and men, in general, are absent and unavailable to the children in their communities (Staples, 1982). Positive African American males are all around us. Somehow it appears as though "the Black community" has veered away from valuing or being able to see the essence of all its men. It feels like a dominant cultural virtue to only value men with certain features or attributes. Historically, all men held valuable roles and positions in the family and community. In the past, to be a blue-collar worker had value. It meant that you were a hard worker and someone who could provide for your family. White and Cones (1999) called this group the "quiet heroes." These folks are not "celebrated by the media, popular culture, or social science research like upscale super athletes or sensationalized like the street Brothers" (p. 79). Today, Black men who are not lawyers, doctors, or local heroes are somehow seen as less than those who are. It feels like positions outside the scope of those mentioned are no longer held in as high esteem as in the past. The concern is that such a mind-set fails to see the value or skills that every person owns that is unique to him or her. Such a limited scope is likely to stifle our ability to see Black men, in all their variation, as resources.

Author's experience

As a child growing up, I had many father figures and male role models in my life. Some of the African American men who were in my life were a bus driver, laborers, coaches, a mail carrier, janitors, carpenters, small engine assembly workers, an accountant, business owners, and pastors. However, the mentors who made some of the biggest impacts were those who most people would not want to consider as positive. These people were unemployed, homeless, broke, drug dealers, drug users, high school dropouts, gang members, and people with criminal records. It goes without saying that what these individuals were involved in was illegal and unhealthy, and some of them knew it. Others were aware of how their choices seem to collude with principles of genocide, but they appeared powerless to do anything about it. Yet, I was encouraged by these same individuals to stay away from the vices that had chokeholds on them. What sets these men apart from some of my other mentors and social fathers is that they were available to me. They had time and knowledge that most of them knew I needed. I was taught very important life lessons, which embodied remnants of values and tools that I still use today. One of these wise men taught me to "give a hundred and ten percent to whatever you do." Another said, "Always surround yourself with people you can trust" and "You are smart, but you have to believe in yourself or no one else will." Many of my mentors modeled how to stay calm and "cool" in stressful situations. This is a skill that I use on a daily basis. These men also modeled and taught me the importance of honor, loyalty, and trust. It is in honor of their relationship with me that I teach my children what was lovingly given to me.

It is unfortunate that these men's genius is overlooked and often unnoticed. Each of their genius is what makes them unique and special. They each possess gifts that set them apart from others. Yet, often in American society, being unique does not appear to be valued or seen as a talent when it comes to these men. As a result, their uniqueness is overlooked. People are comfortable with what is familiar to them. This is a daunting idea, given that the United States is likely the most ethnically diverse country in the world with immigrants from all over the globe. One of the United States of America's greatest assets is the diversity of its people. Americans do not seem to value this diversity in its citizens. This is a loss to the individual and to the country in the form of missed opportunities and wasted talent. African American men embody resources and skills that are underutilized and undervalued, which is a loss for everyone, especially African American children who look to them for tutelage.

Rejected role models

Jack's story

One of my African American clients, we will call him Jack, came for therapy to address struggles with identity issues. He was a young professional in his late 20s. When asked what he was hoping to get out of therapy, he responded, "I am not sure, but I don't like who I am becoming and I have two little ones." He was able to articulate that he was sad and unhappy most days. He also gradually (with some caution and reluctance) revealed that he was self-medicating with regular cannabis use, late nights out at the club, and sexual rendezvous with ladies who helped him to momentarily escape his unhappiness. At some point during our journey together, he decided to divorce the mother of his children. This was not an easy decision. Jack describes his children as the joy of his life and that one of his primary goals in life is to be a positive role model for them. He expressed feeling like a failure in his inability to do what he knew was right. After mapping out his family history, it became clear to both of us why he had been struggling with self-medicating and promiscuity. It was how most of the people in his family lived their lives and coped with their problems.

He also discovered that, along the way, he had developed some unhealthy ideas about relationships and what it means to be a man. Looking at his genogram (family tree or family map), he began to recall many lessons and values learned from those around him. One of the most damaging lessons Jack learned was "the more women you have, the more of a man you are." He found it very confusing the more he thought about the fact that "everyone knew what was going on," referring to the men cheating on the women. Jack was mentored and fathered (socially) by his biological brothers and "older guys" from the neighborhood. He recalled holding these men in high regard. Jack wanted his peers and social fathers to respect him. Because they were his models for what it means to be a man, he took on their values. When he was a child, his father was often not present. One of the things Jack shared about his father was that he had another family and that his mother was "the other woman." In all of our sessions, over the course of several years, Jack never spoke ill of his father.

Jack recalls that there was another social father, who made a lasting impression on him. This person motivated him to make positive choices, such as finishing high school, going to college, and entering his current career. Jack was describing a local high school teacher as a "positive Black

man who cared a lot about kids" and as one of a few people who was helping kids at that time. He was someone doing positive things with his life
and the kind of person who Jack felt like he could look up to. However, Jack
vividly recalls that people in the school and community "suspected" that
his teacher was "gay." Jack expressed feeling sad about how his mentor
was treated. Jack believes that people's suspicions caused his mentor to
not help more kids. In this situation, I wonder how rumors and specula-
tion clouded this relationship with Jack and his mentor. It is foreseeable
that it minimally caused the relationship to be diminished by fear and
misguided assumptions.

This is a story of an African American man stepping up and mentoring a young man who was in need of a positive mentor. However, in
this scenario, the teacher did not live up to the community's preconceived
ideas of who/what a role model is. There are several things that are dis-
concerting about this story. One, a man decides to help a child in need
and this selfless act is not met with support and appreciation. Rather his
character is questioned and defamed. Jack stated that no one ever knew
for sure if his mentor was gay or not; "they just assumed he was." Jack's
mentor is an example of a professional African American man who had
the desire and experience as an adult male, yet he was still rejected as a
positive influence.

This scenario tells a story that appears to be an injustice perpetrated
by one or two individuals, but the community is also culpable. The injustice is that early in American history, Black males were identified as sexual objects and today we are still fighting to break free of those chains.
It appears that Jack's questions about identity had been impacted by the
conflicting messages and ideas he experienced in the context of his relationships at school and in the neighborhood where he was growing up.

In his therapy, Jack struggled with having "soft feelings and thoughts."
He has reported having feelings of guilt and shame for cheating on his
wife but thought he was weak for having those feelings. Jack grew up
in an environment where the norm was to have multiple partners. This
was one of the characteristics or attributes he saw in some of his social
fathers growing up. Like most children, Jack aspired to be like his father.
Jack is able to clearly articulate that it is wrong to cheat and that this idea
goes against who he desires to be. However, the values learned as a child
have been his primary way of coping with life. It seems apparent that Jack
believes that his teacher has been a positive force in his life. Jack considers
all of his experiences when he makes choices, and this is likely why he
experiences stress and symptoms of depression.

The preceding scenario also demonstrates the false conclusions that
often result from one-dimensional concepts of people: Why would a man
want to spend time with a child unless he desired them in some sexual

manner? These ideas inaccurately depict men as emotionless, sexual predators with one-track minds and negative motives. The concern here is that this is an example of a double bind that can be placed on individuals who decide to mentor children. This triggers a series of questions, including: Has society become comfortable with not having mentors for Black children? Other questions for consideration are listed below.

Conclusion

The purpose of this chapter was to show how African American men are present in the lives of Black children by exploring how those relationships are impacted by history, cultural factors, different barriers to relationships, and stereotypes or myths. The author discussed how the issue of Black men being involved in children's lives as leaders, mentors, role models, uncles, sons, brothers, nephew, cousins, and social fathers is complicated. However, society at times oversimplifies the issue and reduces African American males to their mistakes and rarely acknowledges them for their successes. It is the author's hope that the reader's understanding and scope of viewing African American men has been expanded with a greater awareness of the importance of looking at African American men in the context of their culture.

President Barack Obama's words stood out, at the July 12, 2007, NAACP forum, when he stated, "We have more work to do when more young Black men languish in prison than attend colleges and universities across America." The sentiment of this message says that we are in need of a paradigm shift. As a society, we are also in prisons that have restricted our vision and how we allow ourselves to see the value and genius of Black men. As a result, there are gaps and holes that go unfilled. The hope is that we will realize that perfection does not exist in humanity. If we are able to have this realization, it will create more opportunities for healing to occur, and it will also likely create space where there once was none.

Reflective questions

1. Does your perception of African American men encourage or discourage them from getting involved in the lives of children?
2. What are ways that you support the media's representation of Black men?
3. How can you make room in your children's lives for them to experience Black men whose genius might go unnoticed by the majority culture?
4. How do you include your children when making decisions about who their mentors are going to be?

References

Boyd-Franklin, N. (1989). *Black families in therapy: A multisystems approach.* New York: Guilford Press.

Cleveland, A., Gaye, M., & Benson, R. (1971). Save the Babies [M. Gaye]. On *What's Going On* [LP]. Detroit: Tamla Records.

Connor, M., & White, J. L. (2006). *Black fathers: An invisible presence in America.* Mahwah, NJ: Erlbaum.

Franklin, A. J. (1988). *Therapeutic support groups for Black men.* Paper presented at the conference of the American Group Psychotherapy Association, New York.

Gary, L. (Ed.). (1981). *Black men.* Beverly Hills, CA: Sage.

Grier, W., & Cobbs, P. (1968). *Black rage.* New York: Basic Books.

Johnson, L. B., & Staples, R. (1993). *Black families at the crossroads: Challenges and prospects.* San Francisco: Jossey-Bass.

McGoldrick, M., Giordano, J., & Pearce, J. (1996). *Ethnicity & family therapy* (2nd ed.). New York: Guilford Press.

Morrow, A. (2003). *Breaking the curse of Willie Lynch: The science of slave psychology.* St. Louis, MO: Rising Sun Publications.

Staples, R. (1982). *Black masculinity: The Black male's role in American society.* San Francisco: Black Scholar Press.

Tucker, L. (2000). *The role of African American males in the family.* Research paper, Menominee: University of Wisconsin-Stout.

White, J. L., & Cones, J. H., III. (1999). *Black man emerging: Facing the past and seizing a future in America.* New York: W. H. Freeman.

section three

Thoughts and reflections

chapter thirteen

Fatherhood love

Gerald Green
Husband/Father/Cancer Survivor
Oakland, California

In the 1950s Mother and I lived with her parents because Dad often travelled in the navy. My grandparents Charlie and Cornelia Patillo migrated
from Norlina, North Carolina, and they watched over my youthful play
within the boundaries of Chesapeake Gardens, one of Norfolk's colored
communities. They shepherded me through the intricacies of a separate and unequal society, typical of the segregated South. Mother was
the youngest of five daughters, and she loved taking me to her grandfather's two-story white farmhouse surrounded by green crops and red
soil. My mother's grandparents and five other families purchased land
in 1879 and built Chapel on the Hill Baptist Church about a mile from
their house. Those founding families instituted homecoming on the third
Sunday in July, and over time, the small church grew. Many families that
had migrated north returned to their agrarian roots for homecoming
and made large annual donations to support church projects. As a young
boy, I would sit still on pews in sweltering heat next to my great-aunts
fanning their perspiration-dotted faces. Watching their arms move back
and forth reminded me of times when they whipped sweet potatoes into
smooth pie fillings. I listened to the choir and preacher, rocking my head
in cadence with the spirit, until time to feast on home-grown fried chicken
and smoked ham, fresh greens from the garden, rice and gravy, and of
course, sweet homemade pies with cake on the side—the type of cuisine
Dr. Gavin's Health Guide for African Americans (Gavin & Landrum, 2004)
recommends that people eat in moderation.

Granddaddy owned a janitorial company, and I helped him clean
White people's churches. "Does we pray to the same God?" I asked.
Charlie's majestic Black face smiled. "Yes." This strong proud Black man
taught me humility and showed me how to line up chairs in rows. My
grandmother on the other hand tempered my defiance with fresh green
switches. We lived for a better future by day and at night filled our lungs
with sentinel spirits from Norlina's red clay. Granddaddy died when he

was 68 and returned to the red-clay plot at the Chapel on the Hill. His spirit still helps me in my time of need.

Kids at the "colored" elementary school pushed in their noses while looking at me and shouted "snub-nosed .38," and others laughed when I stammered, "Uh ... uh ... sqr ... eet," for the word *street*. Some called me Gappy Hayes because of the gap between my front teeth. My immediate family called me Jerry, and other relatives called me Cousin Jerry. This youthful preteen banter lowered my self-esteem, before I started high school in Lexington Park, Maryland, where White students called me "nigger."

On cold Maryland nights, Dad taught me the strategic sacrificial role of pawns in chess, a similar role a disproportionate number of African Americans soldiers played in the Vietnam War. In the spring of 1966 when the war was escalating, we relocated to San Diego. The name-calling taunts didn't stop. I was late for class one day when a Black high school student shouted, "Look at that nigga walking like a tinman." Some students imitated my knock-kneed walk while others called each other names like Zit-face, Monkey-man, and Foe-head. Foe-head's real name was Paul. He was my best friend and he had a big smile, overshadowed by his Rock of Gibraltar-sized forehead, crowned with black kinky hair combed into a pompadour. Foe-head started calling me Tin-head because I would drink more than my share of liquor when the bottle was passed around in the car en route to parties. Foe-head was drafted and died in Vietnam a few years after graduating from high school.

Although I had good college prep grades, my test scores were weak—except on the civil service exam. Immediately after high school, I went to Mesa Community College in San Diego to evade the draft. I partied more than I studied data processing and wrecked my white convertible returning home late one night. Many times my father had told me, "As long as you live in my house, you will obey my rules. And I don't care how late you stay out, you're going to church." I struggled getting up in time for church and felt like a hypocrite sitting in the pew with a hangover. When Dad returned from 6 months at sea, he sought solace on the golf course—no more chess games. His absences caused marital tension and emotionally wounded me and my brothers, pain I thought moving out would help heal.

I was determined not to become a pawn in the Vietnam War after graduating from high school in 1967; however, I dropped out of college and accepted a civil service job where my strong math skills helped me learn two jobs in less time than most people took to learn one. I worked in a production control unit that managed repairs and overhauls on airplanes from aircraft carriers deployed in Vietnam. In the summer of 1969, I moved to the Bay Area to attend a dental technology school, not knowing at the time the Bay Area harbored cancer clusters in some of its heavy industrial communities.

By that fall, many college students had protested the Vietnam War. Shortly thereafter, the government made everyone's chance of being drafted equal by using birthdays instead of local draft boards; the lower one's number was the greater the probability was that one would be drafted. My number was 363 out of 366, which assured me that I would never be drafted. I dropped out of school, started partying more and slipped into the Bay Area's blissful subculture. I introduced myself as Tinman because that persona wasn't afraid of rejection and was immune to those hurtful words that made Jerry and Gerald feel inadequate. I eventually lost my job. I slept on a friend's floor, where rat traps snapped continuously, and I foraged for burned meaty dog scraps my friend brought home from local barbeque joints. Things improved when I started working for Chevron, but I soon discovered that I worked long odds hours, compared to those with a college education. So I returned to college in 1975 when I was 25, and 7 years later I graduated with a degree in mechanical engineering—cancer wasn't in my lexicon.

I was a newly hired design engineer at PG&E (Pacific Gas and Electric Company) in the fall of 1982, and I had the great fortune of meeting Mr. Owen Davis. I'm 6'2" and he towered over me, and corporate cuisine challenged both of our waistlines. His intense work load didn't stop his regal smile or hinder him from sharing friendly words of encouragement. He was a big supporter of employees volunteering on company time to serve community-based organizations. He once said, "Everybody wants a problem solver on their team," and he became PG&E's first African American vice president. Mayor Diane Feinstein appointed him police commissioner, and everyone was shocked when this Renaissance man died from pancreatic cancer.

PG&E allowed me to volunteer at the San Francisco African American Cultural Society (SFAACS), while on probation for my first 6 months of employment. I arrived early for a meeting and surprised Monica Scott, the executive director. I stammered, "Hello, my name is Gerald, isn't there a meeting here?" "Yes," she hesitantly answered. She then cracked the door open a little, exposing her bright smile. My eyes ventured beyond her radiant face, before reuniting with hers. "I'm Monica, please come in." The butterflies in my stomach fluttered, when she welcomed me into her apartment with its expansive view of Lake Merritt and Oakland's downtown skyline. I enjoyed playful flirting with her that spring when I volunteered at the SFAACS. We completed a book, *Contemporary African American Scientists and Inventors From 1920 to the Present*, in late October, and PG&E published it in time for Black History Month (February 1984). And in time, I became more than a volunteer in Monica's life.

My pneumatic gas well control design set the stage for a promotion to a gas engineer in the spring of 1984. I developed and managed projects to drill gas storage wells, became PG&E's expert on subsurface safety valves, and played a key role in converting analog well controls into digital. I often travelled to southern California to test equipment in Ventura, where a very large confederate flag at a truck stop reminded me of the old segregated South. Sometimes while testing, a White inspector would attempt to tell me jokes about "colored people." When I returned to northern California, I supervised the removal and installation of safety valves on work-over rigs that employed predominantly White crews. Many had never worked with a Black engineer and their questions suggested a distrust in my ability, and their demeanor brought back memories of my Maryland high school classmates who called me "nigger."

In 1978, PG&E had a Blow Off Prevention Equipment failure. It was similar to BP's 2010 experience in the Gulf of Mexico, except PG&E's gas wells are on land. A major fire resulted and burned for weeks before a relief well was drilled to kill it. Afterward, safety became the number one priority on the rig. It was shut down for repairs when equipment failed, and many times operations took longer because a procedure failed a test. Consequently, I spent many cold nights sleeping in the back of a station wagon, waiting to remove or install subsurface safety valves. Thoughts of Monica kept me warm.

We were married in October 1991, and at our reception her father, Mr. Scott, tapped rhythms as he sauntered and danced to the Calvin Keys Trio. He had that big father-of-the-bride smile, waving his white table napkin above his head in traditional New Orleans steps called the second line: a partying dance step congregations did during burial rituals in New Orleans. The trio recognized his gesture and started playing "When the Saints Go Marching In." Mr. Scott had started playing drums in elementary school and had learned New Orleans-style music, which was influenced by African slaves' drumbeats and guttural chants from the Crescent City's past—the blue note tones. Monica's mother joined in and everyone danced the second line around tables in La Casa de la Vista, located on Treasure Island in the middle of the San Francisco Bay.

Four years later, my life changed during a routine dental visit to see Dr. Curtis Perry. Dr. Perry became a dentist like his father and uncle, and he loved electronic devices. He offered me special glasses to watch him work on my teeth. I declined the offer and listened to music instead. Dr. Perry told me how he had started a jazz band called Schedule II, which is the script name for state-controlled drugs. He played the bass guitar and had a weakness for chocolate. I, on the other hand, loved playing the phantom bass with Jimi Hendrix. Music stitched our fabric together. He discovered a lesion on my tongue that I thought was a simple tongue bite, and he recommended a follow-up visit with Dr. William R. Murphy, a specialist in oral and maxillofacial surgery. Dr. Perry had used Dr. Murphy's services before. He specialized in sedating patients to pull difficult teeth, and his office was walking distance from Dr. Perry's office. After a couple of visits to see Dr. Murphy, he requested permission to conduct a biopsy.

I tried to imagine a dentist cutting out a portion of my tongue, but the thought of cold hard steel against my tongue ignited my fear. How could I allow a medical inquisition into my most intimate muscle, designed from birth to nurture my body and articulate thoughts from my soul? Later that week, Monica and I celebrated Charles's first birthday. Charles crawled, smiled, and laughed as he played with other children. I enjoyed watching them. His antics helped me release suppressed thoughts of those unpleasant visits to Dr. Murphy. I ate Monica's delicious spaghetti dinner. My tongue cramped with spasms, but I was determined nothing would interfere with Charles's birthday, not even my slipping partials.

One week after Charles's birthday, Monica went on a business trip to Washington, D.C. She returned through New Orleans to check on her mother, who was recuperating from a heart attack. I called and talked about everything but never mentioned my growing anguish. The last thing she needed was more melancholy news. That night I tried to ignore the syncopated throbbing, which became more frequent and intense. My original decision to delay the biopsy haunted me. I surrendered to pain's grip and called Dr. Murphy the next morning for an appointment. It was time for a biopsy; time to confirm what these two men of medicine believed was going on inside me.

"Relax your tongue," he said. He waited. It seemed like an eternity. He then eased a long needle into my gum, reloaded his elixir, and injected various nerves throughout my tongue and mouth. Those injections didn't numb me, so he repeated and we waited. Ten minutes later, I lost all sensation and feeling. I closed my eyes as Dr. Murphy began snipping at my tongue. I could hear him cutting, and my mind told me it should hurt, but I felt no pain. Dr. Murphy scooped and gouged my tongue, and my mind felt like a fish with the hook torn from its mouth, while I listened to the soothing sound of Grover Washington blowing "Winelight" on his tenor saxophone in the background. Periodically, Dr. Murphy interrupted the melody with the clicking sound of his instrument cutting and stitching as he sewed my bleeding tongue, *click, click, click, click.*

Dr. Murphy warned me not to eat anything until the anesthesia wore off because I could mistakenly bite my tongue and not know it. His staff provided me some gauze and a prescription for some painkillers. I drove past Lake Merritt on the way home and thought about the first time I met Monica, which pushed aside my pain and hunger. Twelve years earlier, I had ridden a bus from San Francisco to the Lake Merritt area and met with members from various organizations to develop a book about the contributions of African American scientists and inventors. No thoughts of cancer then.

"Good morning, Mr. and Mrs. Green, please be seated," Dr. Murphy said. He was a slight man with a polite smile, not like some of those champion Walmart greeters. We sat in front of his desk flanked by family pictures of fishing trips and other vacations. Seeing those pictures brought back glum memories of Dad and me baking in the sun, fishing from a rowboat— we seldom caught anything. I felt trapped and hid suspicion of bad news from Monica. She relaxed in her chair, and we engaged Dr. Murphy in conversation. Our eyes were drawn to a manila folder. He picked it up from a pile, and the room became quiet.

"Mr. Green, I have your pathology report," he said. Our nervous energy warmed the room. We held hands and peered at the messenger. "Mr. Green, I'm sorry to tell you, but your report showed malignant cells. You have squamous cell carcinoma, cancer of the tongue."

Our hands broke apart. I choked, then gasped for air, and moisture escaped my mouth. I looked at Monica crying and wanted to say something comforting but sat speechless. Dr. Murphy's words—*cancer of the tongue*—continued to reverberate. Monica's face pleaded for help, and I did nothing. Her tears spilled to the floor, and her gut-wrenching sobs echoed in my ears. I wanted to hold her tight but didn't and retreated to my youthful safe harbor; and when I opened my eyes, I saw strained, uncomforting lines on Dr. Murphy's face.

He stood and pointed to the restroom. Monica didn't see my quivering hand. She ran into the restroom. I felt lost. The walls swallowed me. Cancer digested my energy. My soul sang, *Gerald, you must live, live for your son, live for your wife, live for yourself, just live!* I licked my lips and sang quietly to myself until Monica returned. "Baby, don't cry, we'll make it through this," I said. We hugged. Her crying slowed, but she still hadn't said a word. Silence heightened my anxieties, and my fears grew worse.

Similar to my grandparents, my core health providers were African American, but unlike them I had a choice. I was fortunate to live in a medical community where sons followed in their dad's footsteps, like my personal physician Dr. Geoffrey Watson. He inherited his father's good looks, taste for expensive shirts, and bedside manner, although he was a decade my junior. His father was one of three African American physicians who founded the Arlington Medical Group in 1956 in North Oakland and provided the predominantly African American community excellent medical services for over 30 years. He grew up in Norfolk, Virginia, and graduated, as my mother and her sisters did, from segregated Booker T. Washington High School.

Dr. Geoffrey Watson helped me navigate through numerous treatment decisions necessary to survive tongue cancer and, later, neck and prostate cancer. I trusted him because he had invested years in helping me understand what caused my health to change. He regularly prescribed diagnostic tests while treating my hypertension. He believed African Americans are more receptive to hypertension, because during the middle passage, slaves' bodies had to learn how to retain water in order to survive. Now that water retention serves as a potential source of hypertension.

My team of oncologists recommended two forms of radiation treatment for my tongue cancer in the summer of 1995. First, I had implant therapy, where my tongue was sewed to the floor of my mouth and 35 catheters were inserted through my cheek and circled the tumor in my tongue. A radioactive isotope was positioned in the catheters at various locations for short periods of time for eight separate treatments. Second, I had external beam therapy, where I was exposed to a gamma ray source for weeks at a time. Each treatment was painless; however, over time my neck and face were burned and blackened. It became painful to swallow water and food, and I lost all taste and most of my strength. I dropped from 235 pounds to 185, and spent many hours reading while in bed. Colin Powell's book, *My American Journey* (1995), lifted my spirits. It brought me some comfort to learn that he, too, thought that the deaths of many poor and less educated men drafted during the Vietnam War was unfortunate. An expendable "economic cannon fodder" considered by some policy makers.

Dr. Watson threatened me with an intravenous feeding tube if I continued to lose weight. I increased my consumption of Ensure Plus® from two cans a day to four. They wanted me to drink six. My strength slowly returned after I started adding ice cream to it. I started walking a few minutes a day on the treadmill, and thoughts about helping Monica raise Charles gave me hope for another day's breath. I gained enough strength to walk in the neighborhood where visions of Charles attending school motivated me to walk further and those thoughts helped me heal. Sometimes I prayed.

> Oh, God, please help me through this crisis. Charles needs me. Give me time in his early years of life to nurture his soul with love and prevent self-hatred. God, let me extend my hand to him, as my grandfather did when I was a little boy in need of guidance during my parents' temporary separation. Please allow me time with Monica to help Charles through his rites of passage and introduce him to African rituals and Kwanzaa celebrations so he may become a positive contributor and not dream of ways to escape responsibilities. Please make me whole, Lord, and allow me the privilege of growing older and wiser so I may share fatherhood life experiences with my loves, Monica and Charles.

Charles was born on June 6, 1994, and he was abandoned by his biological father. His mother decided she couldn't raise a baby alone. Her faith that Monica and I would give her newborn a better home led us to become first-time parents even though we were both in our mid-40s. His preschool teachers and other parents thought we were grandparents. That age differential forced us to exercise daily. We walked in open space within an eyeshot from our backyard, and occasionally, an off-leash dog startled Charles. One evening, we sat with him in front of the fireplace, and the red glow reflected off Monica's smile as she read aloud a children's book about adoption. His big brown eyes wandered before his attention focused on the fire. He didn't seem to care about the animal characters in the story. Monica gave me a perplexed look and then told him that just like Fuzzy Bear, he was adopted.

"I would have carried that secret to my grave," my mother told me later. Her forceful voice reminded me of arguments she had with Dad when he returned home after 6 months at sea. He eventually replaced us with golf, and my relationship with him all but ended after he deserted Mother and had two sons by his mistress in the Philippines. He later retired from the navy, moved back to Oklahoma all alone, and married a woman not much older than me. Hesitantly, I called him after I became ill, but neither of us shared the small talk gene. Our words got lost over the telephone line, and cramps rolled up my neck. My hands sweated, and I stammered, "I was diagnosed with cancer." Our conversation continued. I told him we adopted Charles. That was the longest we had talked in years, without me getting upset about something—until …

"Jerry, I adopted you," he said. I dropped the phone. "You did?" "I thought your mother told you," he said, and my wounded heart quickened. Silent tears tumbled into a world I once knew.

Mother and I had an awkward conversation the summer before she took Monica, Charles, and me to visit my deceased biological father's sister. I was told that he had been in poor health before he died. I was in my mid-50s and I felt angry and cheated when I carefully examined a picture of his face. I wondered what traits I had inherited from him. Was one of them desertion? Mother died 5 days before Christmas that year. She almost achieved her goal of taking her secret to her grave. My discovery helps me understand Charles's pain when he asks questions about why his biological parents gave him up for adoption.

In the spring of 1996, fifteen pairs of hands took turns feeling my tongue at the tumor board, where Dr. Michael Kaplan was the lead oncologist. Unlike the other doctors, he didn't believe my cancer had metastasized. But in his matter-of-fact tone, he explained that if it was cancer, his surgical team would have to reconstruct my jawbone, using a small bone from my lower leg, and remove a portion of my tongue before they woke me from the biopsy procedure.

"You're lucky; it's just radiation necrosis. Your pain comes from internal scarring, a by-product of radiation therapy," Dr. Kaplan said after the procedure. Happy tears rolled down the right side of my burned-black face. A smile larger than his small frame illuminated the room, and from that moment on, Monica and I looked forward to his medical counsel. I would later receive 4 weeks of 90 minutes per day of hyperbaric oxygen therapy sessions for pain relief.

At my first treatment for pain, a technician greeted me with a Southern drawl. "Howdy. Are you ready?" he asked. His voice reminded me of the not-so-good old boys from my 1950s childhood. My anxiety soared when he opened what looked like a blue-frame iron lung with a submarine hatch-like cover.

"Here, take this. It'll relax you," he said in his gatekeeper's voice. "You should feel your ears ... tightening." The pressure increased, and the glass walls hugged me tight like slaves packed in the hull of a ship. My eyes flickered. I looked up at the television through the convex glass, and the background music slowly relaxed me. I fell asleep and recalled one of my favorite childhood memories of skipping down gravel-covered Workwood Road in Chesapeake Gardens with cousins to Grandmother's house. It was when I felt most secure—kicking stones in one of Norfolk's 1950s segregated communities. I remembered looking up at them as they teased me while we walked. They constantly tried to avoid swarms of gnats that I simply walked under. I wanted to keep up with them, but their legs were almost as long as I was tall. They would run off and leave me alone to skip to Grandmother's house. Sometimes, when the weak part of my shoes hit sharp-edged stones not worn down by cars, I jumped because those sharp hot stones cut my foot. I felt relieved upon arriving at Grandmother's house because she had a smooth concrete walkway from the street to her front door, flanked on both sides by roses, which I saw from their bottoms. Usually, I ran up to the porch, next to those thorny sweet-smelling giant roses abuzz with big black bumblebees. Best of all was opening the storm door with the capital *P*, which stood for Patillo, before entering a little kid's paradise. Grandmother's living room had three tables with lots of whatnot figurines for a kid to play with, although her rule was, "Don't touch." All the grandkids played with the brightly painted opaque figurines, and Grandmother spanked those she caught. Playing with them was fun, and what I remembered most about those whatnots was licking their sour-tasting bottoms; it must have been the lead—a taste I hope Charles never experiences.

Charles and I would, years later, return to Workwood Road on the Fourth of July to celebrate colored people's 50th anniversary of home ownership in Chesapeake Gardens' enclave protection from White Southern brutality. My old haven, the woods and marsh, had been replaced with highways and sound walls that failed to keep the neighborhood quiet. Many houses still boasted green front yards full of roses and bumblebees; however, 860 Workwood Road no longer had a capital *P*. Mother and her sisters had sold the house. And like rhythmic singing cicadas rising from the ground to feed, we sampled cuisines in front yards. I later saw Charles sitting with a group of children on the grass listening attentively in a crisscross applesauce position that he hated in kindergarten. An elder called out names of the founding families of Workwood Road from a quilt. Tears and sweat clung to my cheeks as she read, "Charlie and Cornelia Patillo." I heard them whisper, "Present." In time, many families ventured from this safe harbor in pursuit of the American dream, only to live through decades of turbulent transition. Some have returned.

I emerged from the blue chamber with Monica in my heart. I wore thin light blue static-proof clothing with matching booties to reduce the potential of a spark and fire while I was inside the chamber's oxygen environment. The technician helped me stand on weak knees, and I meandered across the cold floor into the changing room. My tongue's pain ebbed at the end of my first treatment. Monica drove home. As I sat in the passenger seat, the lingering effect of the blue chamber continued to bring back old memories. I recalled how love had compromised our resolve not to socialize at the SFAACS while we worked and how we spent our honeymoon on Paradise Island in the Bahamas.

I had surgery in December 1997 to remove a tumor on the right side of my neck. A tendon was cut. Now my right arm droops, which makes my weak jump shot even weaker. I can't raise my arm above my head in one continuous move, and I have constant neck pain. But joy continues in simple pleasures like tasting good food and talking to family and friends. I'm privileged with breath and life's experiences that I may offer to those caught in cancer's grip. I'm living proof that time heals emotional and physical scars.

My first scar is hidden within my tongue, where external gamma-beam treatment killed the tumor but left scar tissue where it had once thrived. This invisible scar sapped my life's pleasure. Two years after tongue cancer, I washed my face and smiled in the mirror at the new scar on my neck, a constant reminder of my second cancer surgery. It is the source of great pleasure and sometimes throbs. I get joy looking at it and thinking how fortunate I am it was discovered before it metastasized. What's a little daily pain in exchange for years of life? I've been told an amputee has phantom pains. Who am I to complain about background soreness on a body part that still functions?

Between the two scars, which one would I trade in? Neither. I have grown with these pains; they are a part of who I am. To trade them in would be to deny me—a survivor—cancer free and ready for life.

> A life filled of joy and love of family,
> A life that gives back to my community,
> A life struggling to be the best father,
> A life with love,
> A life with Monica,
> A life with dancing memories,
> A life with scars, the scars that blessed me with another day.

Another day to observe a predawn duckling swimming alone on placid Lake Merritt with his breast leaning forward in the thick brackish water, where a V-shaped pattern trails. A group of ducks flies above in the same pattern. Their innate ability to travel in such patterns strengthens their survival during migration. Monica and I toiled to introduce Charles to his "V" survival pattern. We decided to ground him in the seven principles of Kwanzaa *nguzo saba*, as we prepared him for his flight in a turbulent world that sees little Black boys as an ugly gateway to manhood, not worthy of freedom. We pumped him full of *nia* (purpose) and *imani* (faith), in hopes a shield of Teflon would protect him from constant assault by a society blind to his humanity. We clothed him in *kujihagulia* (self-determination) as we pushed him further out on branches of his decisions until his wings either spread like the giant raptor that catches a gust of wind and carries him away on prosperity's breeze or like a homing pigeon that returns him home to surrogate parents, who would in turn pray that he accomplishes *ujima* (collective work and responsibility). We prayed that he would return to Workwood Road in time to celebrate its 100th anniversary. Maybe by then, it will reflect America's hue, and God will have touched homes with his blessings of *umoja* (unity) of faith, family, and friends.

I tried to hide my illness from Charles, but as he grew, my neck scar became a constant reminder. He didn't understand that he was one of the lucky ones. At least he had a father who loved him daily. I prayed that Charles wouldn't become an absentee father. Let him exercise *kuumba* (creativity) and improve our community's quality of life while practicing *ujamaa* (cooperative economics).

Monica and I prayed that our love coupled with the seven principles of Kwanzaa, Charles's "V" pattern, would guide him, but that didn't stop him from acting out in kindergarten. He began hitting little girls. A child psychologist encouraged us to enroll him in a martial arts class to curb his aggression. He seemed so excited when he took tests for his belts, and watching him perform gave my heart joy. In the third grade, Charles started taking Djembe (an African drum) lessons. He joined a chess club while in the fourth grade, which met in a local pizza shop on Fridays. When I played chess with him, it was hard for him to focus on the various moves, and he complained the pace was too slow. Monica and I played other board games with Charles, but he was impatient and hated losing. We took turns ferrying him to his different activities. I loved interacting with the other parents. They helped me smile. I wasn't surprised when Charles told us he didn't want to continue with the chess club. I guess the pizza lost its attraction.

However, he continued practicing his drumming, and his drum troop had the privilege of representing South Africa in a parade at the 2006 Beijing International Cultural Tourism Festival. They accompanied thousands of other representatives from around the world. They played at cultural events and at a school where all of the children in the auditorium spoke some English. I tried to help Charles understand that he was competing with kids not only in America but around the world. We were treated like dignitaries and toured the Great Wall of China, the Forbidden City, and other cultural sites. Charles currently plays his Djembe for the church choir and he plays behind me at public readings from my book *Life Constricted* (Green, 2010).

Monica and I were disappointed when he quit martial arts while studying for his black belt. He said it was because of a verbal disagreement with his Sifu (martial arts instructor). His teenage testosterone levels were rising and he repeatedly challenged authority. He had become more rebellious—nothing wrong was his fault. "That's not fair," Charles constantly says, and he is right. Life isn't fair, but as parents, we must teach our children fairness and—to our boys especially—that no means no. My grandfather and my son's namesake, Mr. Charles Patillo, a generation removed from slavery and an entrepreneur from North Carolina, overcame racism and taught me fairness, humility, and self-reliance in segregated Virginia. I hope to pass on his wisdom to Charles in post–civil rights America, while surviving cancer. Unfortunately, today's teenagers are digitally connected, and their peer pressure is ubiquitous. It challenges our skill set rooted in an analog world, although Monica and I are early adapters.

Charles constantly tells me how he isn't interested in boring school and how he doesn't want to be like me. I understand him not wanting to be like me. At his age, I didn't want to be like my dad either, but I'm concerned about his academic performance. We have tried numerous incentive-based systems to help improve his academics and behavior with minimum success. We told him if he improved his grades, we would consider getting him a puppy. His last marking period was his best to date in high school. Charles wanted to name his puppy "Catfish" after the name his cousins called him in New Orleans, the Crescent City. We suggested he consider another name. He searched the Internet and found a 7-week-old black and white cocker spaniel and settled on the name "Crescent."

Crescent, Charles, and I all share a common trait: We don't know our biological fathers' medical histories, and that ignorance could potentially be fatal. Crescent's unexpected bathroom slips are teaching Charles what it means to raise a child. He is learning it requires a mountain of patience and an ocean of love to motivate and encourage a youngster to behave and learn new social skills. Monica and I have given Charles our core values to help him cross the threshold to manhood, but that's not enough. We have asked our community of elders to help guide him on his journey to achieve self-truth so he may be responsible for his children and community. Hopefully, he and future fathers can build communities where our youth stop becoming "economic cannon fodder" in the local killing fields we call home.

I discovered a few weeks before our 2008 summer vacation that my prostate-specific antigen (PSA) score had jumped from 2.2 to 3.15. A PSA test is a common way to screen for prostate cancer. Although it was within the lab report's good reference range from 0.0 to 4.0, two things stuck in my mind. First, my previous PSA scores had moved up in small increments, and this one was up almost an entire point. And second, my neighbor who has survived prostate cancer for over 9 years had told me many times when a Black man's PSA score goes over 2.5, he should be concerned. Well, I was, but not enough to have a biopsy before my vacation.

We arrived in Raleigh, North Carolina, two days before the reunion. Charles, now 14, spent most of the time with his teenage cousins playing video games, and Monica and I settled into a quiet routine of morning walks. On Friday, the first day of the reunion, I greeted family members arriving for check-in. Relatives from all five Patillo sisters came, and two of the three surviving sisters were present. Charles and his cousins splashed in the swimming pool while adults sipped refreshing drinks. We looked at old pictures and videos from previous reunions that sparked intense dialogue about who remembered what. Everyone enjoyed the home-cooked and catered cuisine on Saturday, and we played bid whist, dominoes, and other board games. Budding family poets read on Sunday, the last day of the reunion, and we said blessings for the deceased. Everyone clung to precious memories, and I remembered how Mother thought my brothers and I were sick if we didn't eat seconds at dinner. And now we struggle against mid-ridge bulge.

As we drove away from the reunion, sheets of rain flushed away views of trees' green canopies, and darkening clouds hid daylight. The car hydroplaned, and lightning lit up the sky, but that didn't faze Charles. He stayed glued to his electronic game's flashing screen. Monica's voice crackled, and I pulled off the road. Unlike our first trip, we had no grapes to share as rain pelted the car. Our breath fogged the windows, and a crescendo of thunderclaps finally scared Charles. He dropped his electronic device.

Eventually, the sun came out and bake-dried sides of trees whose inner growth rings had witnessed runaway slaves escaping through the thicket. Unfortunately, some were trapped, returned, and hanged from local branches. My great-grandfather survived that American tragedy and pooled his resources with several families to purchase land, after the Civil War, on which they built the Chapel on the Hill Baptist Church. He and his descendants, and members of those other families, are buried adjacent to the building, and my mother rests a few rows down a gentle slope from them, a stone's throw from creeks that once nourished crops. Charles, Monica, and I held hands, bowed our heads, and said a prayer at her grave, and fond childhood memories visited me.

Every summer, Mother would bring me to a big white house, surrounded by corn and tobacco, where her father grew up with his 10 brothers and sisters, about a mile down a dusty road from the church. The elders would get up before dawn, eat a big breakfast, and go to work, many in the fields. I shared breakfast with them, but instead of working, I chased chickens and ran through the fields' red soil. Mother's thin lips would smile at me while we swung in the porch swing on those cool evenings drinking fresh lemonade.

None of the circuitous, mazelike dirt roads had names then, but Mother navigated them with ease. Now they are paved, and many carry her relatives' last names, and during a recent visit, we saw my 92-year-old great-aunt. My grand-daddy's sister outlived all of her siblings and unlike them she never moved from Norlina. While visiting, one of Mother's cousins saw the resemblance in my face. "That's Rotelia's boy," she said. Those words made me feel loved. I want that kind of love for Charles too.

Déjà vu, I heard *click, click*.

The doctor removed his staple gun-like instrument from my hemorrhaging rectum. I whimpered like a wounded ani-mal, and my muffled cries escaped from the tiny room. He carefully placed the sample on the tray before reloading a fresh needle and reinserting. *Click, click,* he snatched another piece of my prostate. At 60, I have survived tongue and neck cancer for 14 years with no guarantees, just daily opportunities to share love. Now prostate cancer has provided yet another thread to weave into my life's fabric and binds me with 192,000 American men who were diagnosed with prostate cancer in 2009.

Prostate cancer affects more African American men than men of other races. The legacy of segregation may play a part in the mistrust that hampers many Black men from going in for early screening; consequently twice as many Black men die from prostate cancer when compared to White men. A study published by the National Cancer Institute in 2000 sug-gests that environmental and nutritional factors may play an important role. Blacks in Africa do not have the same high rate of prostate cancer and mortality as Blacks in the United States. A genetic difference and lower levels of vitamin D may contribute to the higher rates of prostate cancer in African American men. It also states that less access to health care, including lack of insurance, may mean that African American men don't always get the preventive care they need. And that distrust or negative attitudes toward screening tests and health care may mean that prostate cancer is diagnosed when it is more advanced in African American men.

Because of my previous experiences with cancer, I aggres-sively pursue personal health matters. For example, even though my digital rectal exam was inconclusive and my PSA score of 3.15 was considered within the norm, I chose to get a biopsy. It revealed cancerous cells in the right apex of my pros-tate with benign results in all other sampled areas. My Gleason score was 6, where a score of 7 through 10 usually indicate a more serious prognosis. Again, I agreed with an aggressive treatment recommendation of a radical prostatectomy (removal of the prostate) by my urologist and Dr. Watson.

My brother-in-law had been diagnosed with prostate cancer a few years earlier and opted for brachytherapy, where radioactive seeds are planted in the prostate. A close family friend opted for external beam treatment. Both radiation therapies had acceptable long-term outcomes but not as good as a radical prostatectomy. I selected the robotic-assisted laparoscopic prostatectomy, where the surgeon sits at the console of the da Vinci® Surgical System. He or she views 3-D images and the system translates their hand, wrist, and finger movements into precise, real-time movements of surgical instruments inside the patient. I spent less time in the hospital, experienced less bleeding, and endured fewer days with a catheter in my penis, when compared to traditional surgery. I had surgery on a Friday morning and I was released the next day before noon. I started walking in my neighborhood that Monday, with my catheter and waste bag strapped to my leg.

Unfortunately, while writing this chapter, I learned that a family member died from advanced prostate cancer. Early detection and treatment could have potentially saved this 61-year-old father's life and spared his family and community a tragic loss.

New cars come with a manual, with a list of instructions for the owner to follow. Charles's pediatrician gave us such a manual in the form of an infant and child care handbook. It contained an infant care schedule through young adulthood. It started at Week 1, with the collection of medical history; regrettably we could not offer any information about Charles's biological parents, and the appointment concluded with a physical examination. The schedule progressed to Week 2, then Month 1 through 18 and then each year thereafter until age 20. All visits included a physical examination, a basic requirement for good health, and this is especially true for men with incomplete family medical records.

Our bodies and automobiles are similar in that they work, consume fuel, and require maintenance. The car was originally designed to transport passengers from point A to point B; however, over time they have morphed into something else—a fashion statement for some who adorn them with 26-inch rims and treat them like kings. Some drivers (fathers) take their cars in for maintenance checkups, but fail to get annual physical exams. It's a matter of priority. Which is king—the car or the driver (father)?

I remember when a gallon of gas cost less than 25 cents. Then American cars came equipped with big engines and few were concerned about gas mileage. The American diet for cars changed when gas prices climbed above 50 cents a gallon. Fuel-efficient imports stole the lion's share of purchases, and Japan replaced Detroit as auto king. The American auto failure isn't lost on the food industry. Now corn is king, and its pervasive calories invade our meals and drinks, accompanied by meat growth hormones. Our children's waistlines have ballooned and their health has plummeted. In *Dr. Gavin's Health Guide for African Americans* (Gavin & Landrum, 2004), he says if a man's waist exceeds 40 inches and if a woman's waist exceeds 35 inches then they have what is referred to as central obesity. They are at risk for heart attack, heart disease, diabetes, and death, because their vital organs and insulin could fail to function properly.

Fathers, get on your job and get a physical exam and learn your blood pressure, glucose, and cholesterol numbers! Understanding those three vital statistics could save your life. Start treating yourselves like kings instead of pawns—potential casualties of war (foreign and/or domestic). Your family and community need your wisdom to guide new generations.

> Are you ready for Fatherhood Love?
> Your children are.
> Don't disappoint them,
> Or, your family, and community.
> Get a check up,
> Don't check out!
> We need you, Dad
> Alive!!

Conclusion

I'm living proof that early medical intervention works; however, it's my loving family's strength that sustains me. And the challenge was learning how to reciprocate their love, because I didn't know how to love myself. I had bought into years of a false manhood doctrine— be a strong and courageous individual; real men don't cry or show weakness—a belief system that's incongruent with making sound medical decisions. Before I could break out of my cocoon of medical ignorance, I had to peel back years of loneliness, those selfish bachelor years before I developed a loving and understanding relationship with my wife, Monica. And then, I had to learn how to accept her love and acknowledge her needs, including the need for my unconditional love. She needed me to help her raise our son, Charles. Monica helped facilitate my transformation, and that change prepared me for my destiny, to become a multiple cancer survivor. We were shepherded by caring medical professionals and graced with excellent medical coverage that didn't bankrupt us.

My transition to fatherhood love requires men to answer the following questions:

1. What will cause me to love myself so that I will make good health care decisions?
2. How can I overcome societal distractions that prevent me from seeking early medical attention?
3. What will stop me from practicing emergency room medicine and take myself and my children in for routine and regular checkups?
4. How do I go about establishing a healthy medical baseline that includes knowing my blood pressure, glucose, and cholesterol levels and PSA score?

Our wives and families deserve answers to these questions, which support our sons' decisions to build strong healthy communities—a legacy of longevity.

Reflective questions

1. Many African American males are hesitant to seek medical advice in their youth, particularly as relates to prostate health. What issues are involved and what can be done to correct the situation?
2. A major area of concern and support is that offered by one's mate. What is reflected in the author's story about this issue?
3. Adoption is a topic of concern. What should children be told and when? What are the cultural issues?

References

Gavin, J., & Landrum, S. (2004). *Dr. Gavin's health guide for African Americans.* Alexandria, VA: Small Step.

Green, G. (2010). *Life constricted: To love, hugs and laughter.* N.p.: Xlibris.

Green, G., & Scott, M. (1984). *Contemporary African American scientists and inventors 1920-present.* San Francisco: Unpublished manuscript.

Powell, C. (1995). *My American journey.* New York: Random House.

chapter fourteen

Strategies for therapeutic success with African American males

William D. Allen
Healing Bonds
Minneapolis, Minnesota

J. Phillip Rosier, Jr., and Larry G. Tucker
Kente Circle
Minneapolis, Minnesota

Introduction

In this chapter, the authors discuss strategies and resources available to clinicians seeking to improve their effectiveness when working with African American males across the life span. Throughout their lives, African American males interact with others in relationships that range from casual to intimate, and whose duration can span from minutes to decades. As is the case for males in other ethnic groups, these relationships are shaped by both internal and external factors. Examples of internal factors include these males' psychological and physical health, as well as their intelligence, skills, and resiliency. External factors include material resources (e.g., wealth), social influences (e.g., institutional racism or the local economy), and environmental influences (e.g., neighborhood health or weather). When these factors cause Black men and boys to struggle in their relationships, counseling or psychotherapy can help increase insight about problems and solutions, provide emotional relief from the distress the problems cause, and provide a path back to individual and relational well-being (Boyd-Franklin, 1989; Franklin, 1992).

Although this book is primarily focused on African American fathers, Black males who are not fathers are also important to consider when discussing effective therapeutic approaches. These youth and adults tend to be intimately involved with Black fathers and represent the pool from which Black fathers emerge (White & Cones, 1999). In their interactions with Black fathers (and other members of the African American community), these "social fathers" and "fathers-to-be" shape expectations about Black fatherhood and influence paternal behaviors. Clinicians seeking to work effectively with African American fathers must be prepared to address the therapeutic needs of African American males across the life span with an awareness of the experiential hurdles these males will likely face (Lee, 1999). Thus, the chapter seeks to improve the cultural competence of readers in the specific area of engaging African American males in improving their own mental wellness, the health of those they love, and the general well-being of the African American community.

The intended audiences for this chapter are mental health and medical practitioners whose clientele may include African American males. However, the authors hope it will also be useful to other social service providers, clergy and lay staff within communities of faith, counselors at academic institutions, and others who work with individuals, couples, and families in the African American community. Readers should gain a better understanding of the typical obstacles to therapeutic engagement. They should also learn how to identify familial and community supports for successful treatment of concerns that African American males and their families bring to the helping professions.

Theoretical foundations

The authors believe that a prerequisite for therapeutic success with African American males is awareness and acceptance of the reality that several factors affect these males' lives, including the following:

Psychological and emotional factors
Social factors
Environmental factors

This perspective encompasses an ecosystemic approach to understanding Black males and their environments (Bubolz & Sontag, 1993; Westney, Brabble, & Edwards, 1988). To be sure, much of this might also be said of males in other ethnic groups. However, the particular mix of the factors and their relative weighting in determining Black males' beliefs and behaviors is distinctly African American (Allen & Connor, 1997). This is due in part to the group's difficult immigration from Africa to the Americas, its history in what became the United States, and to the residual influences of African culture(s) (Billingsley, 1993; Staples & Johnson, 1993). It would take an entire book to adequately address all of the factors (common and unique) influencing the African American male experience, but the authors intend to highlight several factors they believe have an especially powerful impact on therapeutic success.

Powerful images shape the emergent self-identities of young Black men and influence how older men think of themselves as well (Hunter & Davis, 1994). Youth in particular are constantly choosing between numerous, often conflicting cultural models and role definitions of appropriate male behavior (e.g., Anderson, 1989; Majors & Billson, 1993). Some of these models are positive; others are negative. For example, images can portray responsible versus reckless, tender versus unapproachable, and self-respectful versus self-destructive attitudes and behaviors. The problem is that youth often do not have the life experience to know the difference between the positive and negative models. Many of these youth develop and cling to dysfunctional beliefs about themselves and the world, even when they produce behaviors that damage their lives and the relationships with the people they love. As African American males age, their actions and experiences continue to reflect the images and cultural models of Black manhood they encounter. But they also recursively influence the ongoing definition of the African American male experience. Thus, Black boys and men can both affect and be affected by the cultural models of what it means to be Black and male (and Black, male, and father).

Fatherhood is a pivotal aspect of the Black male experience for many men (McAdoo, 1993). A growing literature is documenting the diversity in the paternal experiences of African Americans and the ways in which fatherhood is both similar to and distinct from the paternal experiences of men in other ethnic groups (Connor & White, 2006; White & Cones, 1999). This and the literature describing clinical interventions with African American males (e.g., Davis, 1999) is documenting that external factors such as institutional racism can affect the quality and trajectory of Black males' lives (Bowman & Forman, 1997; Staples, 1982). These external factors can also reinforce negative models of Black men, including casting doubt on their potential as members of families and society. This, in turn, can have devastating effects on African American men's ability to meet their paternal aspirations and obligations.

Sociopolitical systems like capitalism and consumerism generate wants and desires in all segments of society. Advertising and the mass media constantly focus on what people want (or should want, or think what they should want) but spend little time helping people understand what they can actually afford or acquire in sustainable ways. To obtain the objects of material wants and desires, financial resources or skills are necessary. Thus, segments of society that have fewer resources or skills are at a disadvantage in a sociopolitical system that demands these resources and skills in exchange for the things folks want.

A disproportionately large number of African American males live at or below the poverty level (U.S. Bureau of the Census, 2008), and most of these also lack the skills to secure the resources to lift themselves out of poverty and to provide for their families. These males are at particular risk of becoming disenchanted with the very sociopolitical systems driving their frustrated desires because they typically lack the resources and skills needed to obtain and maintain material things (like electronic gear, cars, homes). This can lead to self-defeating thinking and behavior among disadvantaged subpopulations where there can be a divergence between *what people want* versus *what they can actually do to get what they want*. (For example, some young men have justified in their minds criminal behavior as doing whatever they have to do to get what they want. They may come to consider theft, assaulting others, and other criminal activity as legitimate forms of "work.")

Although some consider poor values or poor moral standards to be at the root of many problems affecting the African American community, even problematic rationalizations such as those mentioned earlier need to be understood in the larger context of values across social groups throughout the United States. Rampant individualism and unbridled capitalism are contributing factors in many of the maladaptive solutions that some young Black males develop in their search to satisfy their wants and desires. Examining these interrelated values and their potential for harm must be part of any effective therapy with African American males.

Social learning theory (Bandura, 1986) suggests that community expectations of Black males are typically transmitted through personal interactions with others. The most important of these are with other family members and extended family, but other significant influences may include neighbors and other community stakeholders. As is the case for other ethnic groups, African American culture (and to some extent, ethnic identity) is transmitted primarily through social interactions between community members (and, to a lesser extent, is affected by interactions with other ethnic groups). Community expectations of responsible Black male behavior are typically transmitted through personal interactions with family and extended family members, but other significant influences may include neighbors and other community stakeholders.*

---

* One of the authors (Rosier) presents the example of his wife's grandfather in their old neighborhood in Kansas City, Missouri. Whenever someone walking in his neighborhood littered the street or someone's lawn, this man would come out of his house and confront the offending party. By his behavior, the grandfather was defining community expectations of acceptable (or unacceptable) behavior. The interaction also provided a model for others witnessing it. Cultural expectations of how males should conduct themselves were transmitted to everybody in the neighborhood, not just the grandfather and the person he challenged. Anybody who witnessed the incident would likely interpret it as a demonstration of what men are expected to do in this community. The absence of confronting litterers also sends powerful messages about community tolerance of litter, or about fear of sanctioning wrongdoers. The collective absence of corrective messages supporting social order potentially lead to the perception (and reality) of community degeneration.

Changes in technology have facilitated fewer interpersonal interactions and increasingly more indirect transmissions of cultural images and values (e.g., mass media, Internet, etc.). The African American community (like other communities of color) struggles to maintain both its cultural identity and the ability to define itself in the face of larger societal forces seeking to define who African Americans are. When an increasing number of transmissions of cultural definitions and values occur over cable and the Internet (e.g., "reality TV" and videos) or through iPods (e.g., the lyrics of rap music) the African American community risks losing its capacity for self-definition and to develop indigenous cultural values. Young African American males may be at risk for failure if the strongest transmitters of cultural and community expectations of what Black manhood is and what Black fatherhood is (or should be) are images in the mass media. This is especially true when the images are created and promoted from entities that have little or no investment in the Black community.*

Unfortunately, this may already be happening, judging from the comments of some young Blacks we currently see in therapy. Many of these youth report that they are getting most of their ideas about identity and values from materials in their iPods or contacts in Facebook, rather from parents/fathers, extended family members, adult family friends, and neighbors. Some of this phenomenon is typical of most adolescents' preference for peer involvement over reliance on parental/paternal influence, but given these trends we believe the African American community is at particular risk of losing its ability to define role expectations for males.

Key principles

In this section, we present several key principles that guide our work with African American males. These are followed by some specific therapeutic strategies that have guided us in our effort to help the men and boys whom we have seen. We believe that these strategies will be helpful to others, as many of the problems these clients bring into therapy appear to be typical of those facing other African American males.

Systemic approach

A systemic view of the presenting problem(s) is the key to helping families that come to us for help with their life problems. A systemic conceptualization of the case starts with a comprehensive assessment that goes

---

* Unfortunately, some African Americans are also guilty of creating and promoting negative images of Black males. They do this under the guise of portraying reality, but more often they are operating under the same profit motives that drive non-Blacks.

beyond what the referring entity (e.g., a parent, guardian, school official, or law enforcement) reports as "the problem." These sources typically have critical information for clinicians but may also have vested interests in presenting certain aspects of the case while withholding others. Effective clinicians constantly reexamine the case conceptualization to ensure that they have enough data from enough sources to develop informed interventions. This often means evaluating the significance of one set of data in light of evidence (corroborative or contradictory) from another source.

Marriage and family therapists, as well as many other practitioners working with Black men and boys, have studied general systems theories and approach therapeutic work from a systemic perspective. Yet, even here clinicians may forget to keep a systemic conceptualization of their work, particularly when only one member of the family is in front of them, or designated as the "client." Even when working directly with only a single client, it is essential to keep in mind the contextual factors shaping both the problem and (potentially) the solutions to the problem.

Another important aspect of the systemic approach is to assess the perspective of the client (or clients) regarding what constitutes the presenting problem. This may include whether or not the client believes the "problem" is really a problem or not. For example, many youth are referred to therapy by school or justice officials for problems the youth themselves do not acknowledge. In some cases, they are unaware of negative consequences of the problem; at other times, they may be in denial or simply trying to "save face." In any case, there is no substitute for directly assessing the client's perception of why he has come to therapy even though this can sometimes be difficult.

Multiple sources of information

Identifying multiple sources of information to inform therapy can also be difficult. Clinicians may be tempted to build therapy on information from a single source or point of reference. There may be pressures from referral sources regarding time constraints or the need for prompt resolution of the problem. This can often cause practitioners to narrow their scope of analysis of both presenting problems and possible solutions to what the referral source provides. Although the perspectives of the referral sources are important, there may be contextual factors that contribute to the problem that referents are unaware of. These may represent potential therapeutic resources but only if clinicians take a wider view of the case(s).

For example, when clinicians approach therapy assuming that they can "fix" a child, based solely on a referring child welfare worker's description of the presenting problem, therapeutic failure is likely to be the result. Similarly, couples counselors who start marital or relational therapy based solely on the report of one partner (typically the female in heterosexual relationships) without gaining the perspective (and trust) of the other partner decrease the probability of successfully assisting the couple to co-construct and achieve their relational goals. Additionally, teachers and social workers often fail to contact and gather data from fathers, who may not reside in the home.

Client–clinician relationship

The quality of the therapeutic relationship between the client and clinician is the key to all successful psychotherapy, and this is even more the case in cross-cultural work. It is the therapeutic relationship that heals, not the various treatment techniques and theories that may come into and out of fashion. Although psychotherapy is often referred to as "the talking cure," it might more aptly be thought of as the "relational" cure when considering clinical work with Black men and boys. The client's perception of the relationship between himself and the clinician is the gate through which all therapeutic healing occurs. It is also the mediating process through which cross-cultural differences are evaluated. If African American boys and men perceive that the clinicians (regardless of ethnicity) understand them, respect them, and are dedicated to helping them, they are more open to engaging in the therapeutic process. Thus, it is surprising how little attention is paid in training or continuing education programs on the depth and quality of therapeutic relationships versus the latest treatment technique or "evidence-based practice." We have found that without the former, the effectiveness of the latter is always in doubt.

The idea that the relationship between the client and clinician is the primary component in healing may be problematic in a society that privileges independence, autonomy, and technology. Add to these a professional predisposition toward the illusion of clinical objectivity and it is easy to see why many clinicians believe that perfection of techniques is the key to successfully treating behavioral and relational problems. These approaches are particularly problematic when working with clients whose ethnic and familial background values communal ties over individualism. In the case of African American males, focus on technique rather than building a resilient, therapeutic relationship may be a risky strategy. This is because whatever potential benefit a particular technique or practice holds may be diminished by an inadequate relationship capable of supporting the therapy.

Significance of culture in the therapeutic relationship

In our work with African American males, we have found that it is not helpful to pretend that clinicians deliver services in a "value-less" vacuum. Each clinician brings a unique set of values and experiences to the therapeutic process (McGoldrick, Giardano, & Garcia-Petro, 2005; Sue & Sue, 2007). The notion that any clinician (regardless of his or her cultural backgrounds) enters the therapeutic encounter without bias has been seriously challenged in recent decades. Still, there are individual practitioners and organizations who continue to believe that adopting a "value-less" perspective is a prerequisite for accurate diagnosis and treatment. This approach is often evident in provider training and case staffings that emphasize problem identification, symptom definition, and diagnostic labeling while the influences of cultural contexts (such as those of either the clinician or the client) are typically absent or minimized. This is problematic for several reasons.

First, it assumes that our cultural backgrounds have little or no effect on our thinking and actions over time. It should be obvious that cultural contexts such as ethnicity, religious beliefs, national origin, and immigration status have direct effects on what we believe about ourselves as well as our place in the world. This is true whether we think consciously about these effects or not. Ignoring culture's significance in the therapeutic process increases the risk that the client's presenting problems will be either misidentified or misinterpreted. This is especially true if the client and clinician come from different cultural backgrounds.

Cultural contexts shape how we perceive others, but the converse is also true: They shape how others perceive us. Thus, another problem with the "value-less" perspective is that it assumes that clients are not affected by their cultural backgrounds. Even if clinicians could truly "free" themselves from the effects of their cultural background, they would still need to take into account the likelihood that their clients may bring culturally based values and perspectives into therapy. These in turn could moderate a client's ability to engage in the therapeutic process regardless of whatever the clinician does or doesn't do.

Cultural backgrounds and values

A final problem caused by the "myth of clinical objectivity" is the likelihood that clinicians may adopt their cultural backgrounds and values as the normative standard against which the backgrounds and values of others (including clients) must be compared. Cultural backgrounds and the values they shape can be compared to "lenses" through which individuals "see" the world. Most people become acclimated to the effect of wearing these lenses over time, assuming that how *they* perceive the world is how *others* perceive it, or should perceive it. When interacting with others who use different (cultural) "lenses," the natural tendency is to use one's own perspective as the norm, or basis for comparison.

However, this can also result in the conclusion that the "lenses" of the majority are more normative or "objective," and thus preferable to those of nonmajority members whose "lenses" are seen as "subjective" (or even abnormal). This can clearly have negative consequences for clinicians and clients from different cultural backgrounds unless it is accounted for. In our collective experience (and based on anecdotal reports from clients), many cross-cultural therapeutic efforts fail because clients and clinicians are unable (or unwilling) to reconcile their cultural perspectives in mutually respectful ways. One way to do this is to work from an approach that acknowledges that clinicians and clients operate from distinct cultural contexts that must be reconciled as part of the therapy. Rather than see therapy as a unidirectional process of healing (flowing from the clinician to the client), this approach assumes a bidirectional, co-construction of both the presenting problem(s) and potential solution(s). Thus, the clinician is responsible for incorporating his or her own cultural contexts and their potential impact on therapy, along with assessing the client's contexts and monitoring their impact.

Suggestions for clinicians

The authors have several suggestions for clinicians whose clientele include African American men and boys. These are based on our clinical experience and our knowledge of the growing literature on clinical work with this population. At the end of this section, we will present suggestions for additional research that might move the therapeutic field forward in its ability to help African American males and the people who depend on them.

We begin by noting that clinicians cannot treat clients they are afraid of, clients they do not know, or clients they do not respect. Much has been said about the fear that many popular images of Black males invokes in the mind of the public. Clinicians are not immune from this barrage and before accepting African American men and boys as clients, clinicians need to reflect on their views about Black males. Several pertinent questions include the following:

1. What do I think about when I picture a Black man, a Black father, or a Black adolescent?
2. What are my views about the underrepresentation of Black males/ fathers in higher education and employment?

3. What do I think about the overrepresentation of Black males/fathers in the juvenile and criminal justice systems?
4. Do I have thoughts about how these perceptions might affect my ability to work with African American men/fathers and boys in therapy? (If not, do I assume these larger, systemic realities will not affect therapy?)

The last question is important because when clinicians encounter difficulty working with African American males/fathers, the problems are often seen as failure on the client's part rather than the result of an insufficient (or absent) therapeutic bond. Thus, these therapeutic failures are often attributed to the client's inability to commit, to be insightful, or to otherwise be engaged in the therapeutic process. However, we suggest it is impossible to build a strong, resilient working relationship with an individual (or group) of whom one is afraid, much less one for whom there is little respect or knowledge. Our view is that many of the problems therapists encounter working with Black males are caused, or at least heavily influenced, by therapists' preconceptions about the Black male client's ability to benefit from psychotherapy.*

A major contributing factor in many of the presenting problems African American men, fathers, and boys bring to therapy is difficulty managing the emotional and psychological consequences of the stress they face in their lives. Although all people have to deal with daily stress, African American males typically encounter an added layer of stressors related directly to ethnic bias and indirectly to a variety of personal and social consequences of bias.† Effective therapy needs to help these males become comfortable with the range of emotions they experience. It must also facilitate management of emotions in ways that do not lead to neglect, abuse, cut-offs, or other destructive resolutions of interpersonal conflict. In essence we are describing *emotional maturity,* the result of continuing emotional development starting in childhood and continuing throughout life. We define emotional maturity as the ability to recognize one's feelings and live with them throughout a range of life events (good and bad).

In most places in the United States, males are socialized to suppress their emotions, or at least narrow the range of appropriate emotional responses to a select few as compared to females. For example, anger is

---

* Similar preconceptions on the part of clients can also inhibit therapy, as many Black males see therapy as an inappropriate medium for resolving their problems.
† An example of an indirect personal problem would be health, as African Americans are disproportionately affected by poorer health than their European American peers. This is at least partially the result of institutional racism, which affects access and treatment. Indirect social problems include various aspects of poverty and economic distress, such as chronic unemployment, malnutrition, and homelessness.

one of the few emotions many boys and men are comfortable expressing openly. This situation holds for African American males as well. However, given the increased levels of stress they face, Black men and boys may be at particular risk of behavioral and relational problems directly attributable to this narrowing of "socially sanctioned" emotional expression. Inability to recognize and manage emotions limits one's ability to express the range of human emotions experienced over the life span. It may also limit the capacity for emotional intelligence,[*] an important component of overall cognitive ability.

In particularly distressed segments of the African American community, there may be even less support for recognizing or expressing emotions. There is little or no value in expressing emotions if communicating them does not give you satisfaction or fulfill your needs. Development of emotional maturity may also be stifled when caregivers' ability to nurture their children is overwhelmed by daily struggles for essentials such as food and shelter, or the ability and opportunity to be present in their lives. Many of these African American families have a number of risk factors that threaten to break emotional bonds between caregivers and children. These include problems such as higher incarceration rates among African American males, higher incidence of involvement in systems such as juvenile justice and child welfare, higher rates of female-headed single-parent households, and disproportionately higher rates of mortality (across the life span) and poverty. These factors create barriers for African American boys to develop the emotional maturity that will serve them later in life. To enhance emotional maturity, the African American community and other stakeholders such as clinicians working with its men and boys need to address these risk factors.

Psychotherapy can provide an effective medium for fostering the development of emotional maturity in Black males. This is turn can provide the basis for developing effective relational skills and healthy relationships. Discussing emotions can be a difficult, even scary, proposition for many men and boys. Helping males overcome their fears about having emotions frees them to become fully human. They can expand their repertoire of feelings beyond anger to include the wider range of human emotional expression. This is a good thing not just for these males but for all others who are part of their public and private lives. Incorporating emotional growth into therapy prepares older men to foster the emotional growth of younger men and boys and thus facilitate the development of better relationship skills. In this way, therapy can also promote community

---

[*] *Emotional intelligence* is defined as "the ability to sense, understand, and effectively apply the power and acumen of emotions as a source of human energy, information, connection, and influence." (Cooper & Sawaf, 1997, p. xiii)

development, as clinicians can also help their clients define what community means to them.

The fear of being judged or misunderstood is a primary reason many African American men avoid seeking therapeutic help for individual and relationship problems. Most Black males are aware of how negatively they are typically portrayed in the American mass media. Clinicians working with this population need to be aware of this sensitivity and make extra efforts to display compassion and empathy toward these clients. They should also be able to demonstrate respect for these men's intelligence and dignity and an awareness of their historical backgrounds. Even African American therapists working with African American male clients must be willing to demonstrate that they can engage clients in a mutually respectful manner that facilitates the clients' trust. Clinical success hinges on the therapist's ability to be invited into the client's world and the capacity to validate the client's experience.

It is important that clinicians proactively work to mitigate the effects of institutional racism in the therapeutic process. Cross-cultural dynamics (such as institutional racism) affect not just how clinicians see their clients, but how clients see their clinicians. This is particularly true when the client is an African American male and the clinician is European American (or ethnicity other than Black). However, it can also be the case when both clinician and client are African American because of the wide diversity of views and experiences within ethnic groups. We believe that minimizing the deleterious effects of systemic bias in the therapeutic process should be a foundational topic in training programs. Yet, this has not been the case historically and judging from informal reports from colleagues around the country. Depending on the training program or specific counseling course, the issue of ethnic diversity and how it potentially affects psychotherapy is minimally covered if mentioned at all. The more typical foci of such training are specific therapeutic techniques and their theoretical underpinnings. We believe African American males/fathers and other members of the Black community would be better served by balancing the technical approaches with greater emphasis on the cultural contexts in which they will be applied.

In numerous practice settings, the authors have participated in case staffings of African American families, which too often begin with blanket dismissals of male familial involvement of African American adolescents or adults. Phrases such as "the dad is not involved" or "I haven't spoken directly with him; he seems kind of scary" are the typical starting point, whereas when referring to European American fathers in similar situations, the introductory phrase is more often "he has a very demanding job," or "the dad suffers from depression," or even "he doesn't say much." What is important here is the characterization of Black males as disengaged from or even harmful to families versus that of European American males as "engageable" and potentially helpful. The difference is partially the result of differential conceptualizations of the family and the potential role(s) that males play in family life across the life span. These conceptualizations affect both client and clinician, and potentially hold for many African Americans as well as European Americans. Thus, an important therapeutic objective in these cases is for the clinician (regardless of his or her ethnicity) to assess and (if needed) develop positive, engaged familial roles for his or her male clients.

Clinicians attempting to better understand the clinical needs of their African American clients should also try to balance their focus on the problems Black males/fathers present with identification of resources for addressing those problems. Clients bring both problems and the resources for their solution to therapy. Systems of care (including individual practitioners) are good at recognizing stereotypical patterns of poor relational skills, underinvolvement, chemical dependency, and even domestic violence in their Black male clients. They find it difficult to look beyond these for resilience, determination, optimism, and faith in these same youth and adults. We have found that the keys to successfully addressing many of the problems African American males/fathers bring to therapy lie in their personal and environmental resources. An example of a personal resource is the intelligence that Black males are born with and which they develop over the course of their lives. What they do with their intelligence, and how they use it to benefit themselves, their children, and others, is influenced by factors such as their circumstances as children, how they fare in social systems such as school and employment, and their perceptions of the life courses open to them.

When working with African American males/fathers, therapists must recognize their client's genius, which is defined here as the originality, creativity, or intelligence associated uniquely to one individual. Unfortunately, because of centuries of negative stereotypes, genius is not a word generally associated with Black males. The purpose of using the word *genius* is to help clinicians avoid getting stuck in problem-saturated ways of interpreting Black men's experiences. Clinicians must remember that clients seek therapy because they are stuck in thinking or behaviors that are unhealthy for their lives or the people they are in relationships with. They must also understand that each Black man has the potential for unique insight related to his gifts and talents that encompass who he is. Sometimes due to isolation and feeling misunderstood, African American men choose not to take advantage of help even when court ordered or with heavy consequences looming. But this should not diminish their human potential, their ability to be loving family members, or their ability to be productive members of communities.

In our clinical work, we have observed that the men who are "doing what they should be doing" for themselves, their children, and their communities are not always "stable" in the sense of being confident and fulfilled. This may be because there seems to be less social support for consistently doing the right thing as there is negative attention paid to those not measuring up to socially approved standards. A critical question for clinicians working with African American males is how to get males who aren't doing what they should to move over to "doing the right thing." There appear to be two major influences that help Black males stay on the right path throughout their lives.

1. Good social support networks
   • Healthy family relationships, involvement with own children
   • Community bonds and obligations (e.g., a job or other responsibilities)
   • Connections with others through faith or affiliation groups (e.g., church)
2. Being accountable to others
   • Own children
   • Family, friends, and neighbors, church guy, or even your ancestors
   • Openness to criticism and suggestions (i.e., nondefensive)
   • Acknowledging the support of others
   • Accepting one's obligation to others (e.g., those who came before you)

When we have successfully attended to all of these aspects of the therapeutic relationship, we have seen our African American male clients make better progress addressing the initial concerns that brought them to therapy. These clients and their families also report a greater sense of competence in their familial roles within the home and at various social locations (e.g., school, work).

A call for additional research

There is a need for more research on the spectrum of close relationships males enter into throughout their lives that promote (or possibly inhibit) their roles as fathers. The lion's share of the recent scholarship on Black males has focused on fatherhood and this is good, but there are a variety of relationships that boys, adolescents, and adults have that can either prepare them for fatherhood or help sustain them in their paternal roles. We would like to see an expansion of the research into the diversity of familial roles Black males have and more depth in our understanding of these roles. Research is also needed on how best to promote healthy familial involvement of adults who are not fathers but nonetheless are intimately involved in the lives of children (e.g., boyfriends, partners, grandfathers, etc., i.e., "social fathers"). For example, what relational skills do African Americans need to master as boys that promote better outcomes in their roles as fathers? Also, what therapeutic strategies can best facilitate emotional maturity and development of characteristics such as empathy? These questions need to be addressed from an Afrocentric perspective of how the skills and roles would most likely be experienced in African American families.

A great deal of clinical research is designed to find the best treatment approaches to problematic behaviors, but we suggest more research on how and why some African American boys and adults succeed in spite of the challenges they encounter. With ever-increasing numbers of Black boys being diagnosed with attention problems, how do others manage to stay on task in school? What keeps some youth from becoming early fathers when so many around them are becoming parents? How do some Black men support their families and stay involved when some of their siblings struggle with commitment to partners or children? This may initially appear as a misguided misallocation of precious research dollars allocated to finding therapeutic approaches to help the majority of patients who come into therapy or counseling seeking help. This is not our intention. *The problem with organizing all of our research and practice strategies around what isn't working is that it may simply produce more (albeit better understood) failure.*

Currently, there is a call in many quarters for so-called evidence-based practices. The stated rationale behind these is their ability to harness the power of generally accepted scientific methods, such as use of inferential statistics and randomized samples. These methods can help us discover effective treatments for many of the concerns discussed in this chapter, but they embody several major weaknesses. Inherent in the "evidence-based" approach is the "myth of objectivity" discussed earlier. The methodologies required to support these approaches also tend to favor issues of concern to the mainstream (European Americans) over those of African Americans. For example, although evidenced-based practices have been advanced that claim to optimally address specific clinical concerns (e.g., depression), few practices specifically address ethnic or class components of these concerns (e.g., how institutional racism may contribute to feelings of hopelessness that in turn exacerbate depressive symptoms in ethnic minorities). As many of the studies are conducted by academics in research settings, there can be a disconnect between what the clients we see need and what is feasible to study from a funding or methodological standpoint.

There is a need for more emphasis on "practice-based" evidence in the form of validation (or refutation) of what individuals and agencies are successfully doing with their African American male/father clients and their families. This may require exploration of solutions offered by nontraditional social service providers and other stakeholders that have interests in improving the health and well-being of Black men and boys. Examples of the latter might be successful faith-based groups and "rites of passage" programs, as well school-based, afterschool, and athletic programs. All of these settings may hold clues for more effective engagement of African American males in traditional therapeutic settings. However, further research is needed to understand why particular programs work better than others and which work best for specific subgroups within the population. We also must understand the processes that promote or hinder acquisition and maintenance of relational skills among African Americans at various stages across the life span.

There in a continuing need to broaden the socioeconomic sample base from which much of our knowledge of African Americans developed. We currently know more about young fathers and those encountering economic distress than we do about fathers in midlife or those who are relatively secure financially. There is also an imbalance in the type of data we have on various groups within the African American community. Our understanding of Black males' lives is enhanced by both *quantitative data* (based on statistical analysis, aggregate data, and trends) and *qualitative data* (based on thematic analysis and individual stories). There is relatively more qualitative data about the lives of African American males in difficult conditions (e.g., adolescent fathers in poverty) than there is about Black males encountering success (e.g., young adults successfully starting new families and careers). Again, we need both types of data on African American males in the full range of life circumstances they are likely to encounter to be helpful to those that end up seeking therapy.

Finally, there is a pressing need for research on the relational consequences for African American males of multiple fertility. This is an issue that affects men regardless of their socioeconomic status and has serious ramifications for Black women and (of course) children. Although the authors do not believe the practice of multiple fertility benefits either adults or children, it is a fact of life for a significant number of African American households. Males attempting to meet their paternal obligation in more than one household face a complex set of challenges that are poorly understood.* Moreover, therapeutic approaches to motivate

---

* There is a body of literature on so-called blended families and stepfamilies, but these typically assume (a) dissolution of a single nuclear family into two new households, and (b) a new marital bond in one or more of these new households. What we are describing are multiple households in which children are being raised by one or more caregivers who have never been married (to each other or anyone else), in which there is ambiguity about basic issues such as paternity, inclusion, and mutual obligation.

and support these men in their familial work need to be developed from cultural contexts that reflect their lived experiences. For example, it is not known what specific psychological attributes or relational skills are most important in assisting fathers in balancing their obligations to children and maternal partners in multiple households, especially when there may not have been marital bonds to stabilize these households. Similarly, we need more research on specific approaches clinicians working with boys and adolescents could employ to assist these youth in their efforts to enter and maintain stable, committed relationships.

As has proven to be the case in other social phenomena, many of the research issues outlined in this section that currently affect African Americans may demand greater urgency as they increasingly affect other communities in the mainstream of American culture. For example, the issue of multiple fertility and its effect(s) on paternal involvement may command greater research interest as increasingly more European American fathers begin to struggle with the complexity of managing paternal responsibilities in multiple households. Thus, successful research on these issues as they pertain to African American males can provide solutions for similar concerns in other segments of society.

Conclusion

This chapter explores key principles and strategies for successful clinical interventions with African American males/fathers. The authors suggest several principles that have shaped and continue to inform their work with Black men/fathers and boys. These principles include placing these males in the larger contexts of relationships with females in their lives (e.g., mothers, sisters, girlfriends, wives, daughters). They also take into account a variety of social roles these males would be called upon to play throughout their lives. The chapter also outlines strategies that promote the kind of engagement with African American males/fathers that will most likely result in successful therapeutic intervention. There are undoubtedly other principles and strategies that clinicians may find useful. As is pointed out here and elsewhere, the African American community is diverse; the men and boys of this community are equally diverse in the problems they bring to therapy and the resources they use to solve the problems. Success is often as dependent on keeping one's perspective of both the problems and resources as it is on being able to narrow in on the specific approach that will work best in a given situation.

As increasing numbers of African American men/fathers and boys enter counseling and psychotherapy, clinicians will need to continually learn about the cultural contexts in which these males conduct their lives. It is clear to the authors that Black males/fathers are not adequately served by the majority of mental health agencies in the United States, as evidenced by persistent health disparities across the nation. When these men have poor therapeutic experiences, it diminishes the probability that they will seek such help again. It also reduces the chance that they will support therapy as a solution to the problems of those they love. Thus, improving the access to effective therapy, coupled with improvement in the quality of therapeutic services, is essential if we hope to improve the general health and well-being of the entire African American community.

Reflective questions

1. What insights have you gained from this chapter that are most relevant to your work with African American males/fathers?
2. Have your impressions or assumptions about African American males/fathers as therapeutic clients changed as a result of reading this chapter? If so, how?
3. How might your approach to clinical work with African American males/fathers be different in the future?
4. What unanswered questions remain, and how might you go about finding answers to these questions?

References

Allen, W. D., & Connor, M. (1997). An African American perspective on generative fathering. In A. Hawkins & D. Dollahite (Eds.), *Generative fathering: Beyond deficit perspectives* (pp. 52–70). Thousand Oaks, CA: Sage.

Anderson, E. (1989). Sex codes and family life among poor inner-city youths. *Annals of the American Academy of Political and Social Science, 501,* 59–78.

Bandura, A. (1986). *Social foundations of thought and action: A social cognitive theory.* Englewood Cliffs, NJ: Prentice-Hall.

Billingsley, A. (1993). *Climbing Jacob's ladder.* New York: Simon & Schuster.

Bowman, P., & Forman, T. (1997). In R. Taylor, J. Jackson, & L. Chatters (Eds.), *Family life in Black America* (pp. 216–247). Thousand Oaks, CA: Sage.

Boyd-Franklin, N. (1989). *Black families in therapy: A multisystems approach.* New York: Guilford Press.

Bubolz, M., & Sontag, S. (1993). Human ecology theory. In P. Boss, W. J. Doherty, R. LaRossa, W. Schumm, & S. Steinmetz (Eds.), *Sourcebook of family theories and methods: A contextual approach* (pp. 419–447). New York: Plenum.

Connor, M., & White, J. (2006). *Black fathers: An invisible presence in America.* Mahwah, NJ: Erlbaum.

Cooper, R. K., & Sawaf, A. (1997). *Executive EQ: Emotional intelligence in leadership and organizations.* New York: Grosset/Putnam.

Davis, L. (1999). *Working with African American males: A guide to practice.* Thousand Oaks, CA: Sage.

Franklin, A. J. (1992). Therapy with African American men. *Families in Society, 73,* 350–355.

Hunter, A., & Davis. J. (1994). Hidden voices of Black men: The meaning, structure, and complexity of Black manhood. *Journal of Black Studies, 25*(1), 20–40.

Lee, C. C. (1999). Counseling African American men. In L. Davis (Ed.), *Working with African American males: A guide to practice* (pp. 39–53). Thousand Oaks, CA: Sage.

Majors, R., & Billson, J. (1993). *Cool pose: The dilemmas of Black manhood in America.* New York: Touchstone.

McAdoo, J. (1993). The roles of African American fathers: An ecological perspective. *Families in Society, 74,* 28–35.

McGoldrick, M., Giordano, J., & Garcia-Petro, N. (2005). *Ethnic & family therapy* (3rd ed.). New York: Guilford Press.

Staples, R. (1982). *Black masculinity: The Black male's role in American society.* San Francisco: Black Scholar Press.

Staples, R., & Johnson, L. (1993). *Black families at the crossroads.* San Francisco: Jossey-Bass.

Sue, D. W., & Sue D. (2007). *Counseling the culturally diverse: Theory and practice* (5th ed.). Hoboken, NJ: Wiley.

U.S. Bureau of the Census. (2008). *Income, poverty, and health insurance in the United States: Current Population Survey (CPS).* Washington, DC: U.S. Government Printing Office.

Westney, O., Brabble, E., & Edwards, C. (1988). Human ecology: Concepts and perspectives. In R. Borden & J. Jacobs (Eds.), *Human ecology—research and applications* (pp. 129–137). College Park, MD: Society for Human Ecology.

White, J., & Cones, J. (1999). *Black Man emerging: Facing the past and seizing a future in America.* New York: W. H. Freeman.

chapter fifteen

Afrikan-centered fathering and the Afrikan-centered paradigm

Hurumia Ahadi/Lionel Mandy
California State University
Long Beach, California

"... is what one learns worth what one forgets?"

C. H. Kane
1972, p. 34

Introduction

In 2007, I journeyed from my home in California to Rhodes University in Grahamstown-iRhini, Azania (South Africa), to deliver a paper at the First Congress of the African Sociological Association. My paper was titled "Afrikan Sociology: A View From the Diaspora." The thesis of my paper was that Afrikan[*] scholars should cull core sociological principles from traditional Afrikan cultures, and if a sociology was to be applied to Afrikan people, that it reflect their cultures, values, and beliefs. One would have thought I had blasphemed against the gods of these largely Afrikan scholars. In effect, that is what I had done. In arguing that Afrikan cultures and concepts should hold a central place in an Afrikan sociology, I was distancing myself from the intellectual gods of European sociology and centering my understanding of sociology in the order and organization of Afrikan families, clans, and nations. But I was not without my advocates. The strongest of these was a quiet elder, Professor Akinsola Akiwowo, a retired Nigerian professor of sociology. Baba[†] Akiwowo was the first to tell me that he agreed with me. I could see in his eyes and sense

[*] I follow the convention noted by many scholars, such as Haki Madhubuti (1990), of spelling *Afrika* with a *k* to signify first that *Africa* is a European name ascribed to a continent that others call Alkebu-lan (ben-Jochannan, 1971), and to represent an Afrikan-defined worldview.

[†] *Baba* is a term of respect used by people of Afrikan descent to refer to male elders. It honors their age, signifies their wisdom, and offers the respect due to them.

in his voice that I had spoken a deep truth in presenting my paper. He had left Nigeria in his youth to obtain a doctorate in sociology at a university in the United States. As he later told me, it was only in his later years that he began to rethink the Eurocentric sociological principles that he had been teaching and return to his roots in Yoruba culture. It was there that he rediscovered his center. I had affirmed his journey in my presentation at this congress.

I carry Baba Akiwowo's affirmation to this present effort. Just as the study of sociology, which is an invention of the West, is a compartmentalizing of knowledge into a discrete category, so too, are the topics of Afrikan American fathers and fathering. Elsewhere in this book, my colleagues have done a masterful job of deconstructing the pathology-ridden research and literature on the topics of Afrikan American fathers and fathering. My task is to suggest that we use a different, actually, an old, traditional theory, to discuss these topics. In so doing, I hope to unify and reunify fathers with their families at a theoretical level. This will create a pathway into a rediscovery of how Afrikan peoples successfully organized themselves and their families for millennia prior to incursions by cultures alien to the Afrikan continent and how we currently organize ourselves as well. To the extent that this effort is successful, the practice of assisting fathers of Afrikan descent on their journeys into and through manhood will be clarified, enhanced, and more successful.

What is the Afrikan-centered paradigm?

As I scrolled through hundreds of journal abstracts on Afrikan American fathers and fathering, I was struck by their sameness. Many of these articles spoke of broken men, broken children, and broken women in broken families as part of a broken Afrikan community. Many of these articles spoke of family and community disintegration, and of helplessness and hopelessness. Others spoke of adaptation, but only a few spoke of success and triumph. Even fewer spoke of culture, community, continuity, spiritual connection, or African manhood. These are elements of a paradigm* that is centered in Afrikan people. That paradigm has three components: centeredness, agency, and liberation.

---

* *Paradigm*, as the term is used here, refers to the affective, cognitive, conative, structural, and functional ways in which Afrikan peoples are understood and live their lives (Mazama, 2003, pp. 7–8). This analysis of Afrikan-centered fathering creates a model and offers examples for implementation, all as part of the paradigmatic process of restoring Afrikan consciousness to Afrikan peoples (Mazama, 2003, pp. 5, 30).

Centeredness

The concept of Afrikan-centeredness, which is also referred to as *Afrocentricity,* has been much debated and analyzed. Adeleke (2001) rightly teaches us that Afrocentricity gives definition to a phenomenon that has existed among Afrikan peoples for centuries, if not millennia. Its clearest definition is provided by Asante (2003), who writes that "Afrocentricity ... means, literally, placing African ideals at the center of any analysis that involves African culture and behavior" (p. 38). Carruthers (2010) refers to it as a "conversation among Afrikans based upon the interest of Africans." This definition is further explained by Mazama (2003), who clarifies the concept of *centering* in a theoretical sense. Understanding oneself through the lens of one's traditional Afrikan culture and behaving in consonance with that culture—its history and its biological underpinnings—is to be and act in an Afrikan-centered manner (Mazama, 2003). In practice, this would result, for example, in valuing braided or locked hair highly, as these are traditional forms of beautifying hair in Afrikan cultures. This centeredness does not reject other forms of hair any more than the Afrikan-centered paradigm rejects other forms of culture. Rather, it values Afrikan traditional forms first and foremost for Afrikan peoples.

Agency

Another way of describing and clarifying centeredness is to use the term *agency.* In general, used as a noun, agency refers to action or being in action (Adeleke, 2001). As concerns the Afrikan-centered paradigm, agency involves Afrikan people being "the subjects of history and culture" (Modupe, 2003, p. 65), rather than objects. In other words, Afrikan people who are reasoning and acting in Afrikan-centered ways view all within their purview from the lens of their cultural and historical perspectives as Afrikan people. They do not view all that is around them from the cultural perspective(s) of other cultures. Hence, if it is customary for Afrikan peoples to express joy by singing, shouting, and moving, then, from that cultural perspective, we would expect a group of persons from another culture to express joy in a similar fashion. If that group expressed joy in a quiet manner, we would learn that such is one way that those of that culture celebrate joy, but we would retain our preference for our own cultural form(s) of expression.

As applied to academic theory and practice, Afrikan-centered agency involves Afrikan peoples defining and deciding what is good and just for Afrikan people. It is also deciding how to interpret events and processes that have been interpreted differently by peoples and scholars from other cultural contexts, or other worldviews.* Schreiber (2000) concludes that the methods used to do research would be altered, depending on the world-view of the culture. Taking such a perspective results in research evolv-ing from the perspective or worldview of the culture, rather than from assumptions that lie outside that culture's realities.

Liberation

The Afrikan-centered paradigm redresses the historical appropriation of the Afrikan culture of ancient Egypt (hereinafter referred to as Kemet[†]) by Europe and rightly ascribes its creation to Afrikan people. Further, Afrikan-centeredness reconstructs Afrikan values and recreates self-worth, self-esteem, and social cohesion among Afrikan peoples (Schreiber, 2000). These two aspects free those who participate in Afrikan-centered research and implementation from being objects. They then become sub-jects of the research done by and about them.

Goals

It is this perspective that will be applied in the analysis of Afrikan-centered fathering that follows. The goal will be to look at research and analyses with which many are familiar from a new, different perspective or worldview. The result is a revival of the understanding of the posi-tive, communal roles of fathers of Afrikan descent in the United States in the early part of the 21st century.

Afrikan American fathers and fathering: From negativity to confusion

As Connor (1988) noted, what little research was done up to the late 1980s portrayed males of Afrikan descent negatively. According to Bryan (1997), absent fathers are a function of a culture in the United States that expects emotional distance from its men. In an early study by Schulz (1968), three types of fathers were discussed: monogamous, "discreetly free," and "indiscreet" (p. 658). The latter two categories were for those men who "cheated" on their families. Schulz describes monogamous (a term that

---

* *Worldview* (also written as *world view*) is a conceptual framework from which a racial group looks at, understands, and organizes its history, philosophy, and culture as part of its need to see itself as the center of life and the universe in order to survive as a people (Kambon, 1998, p. 533).

† *Kemet*, which means "land of the Blacks," is the name given to the culture and geo-political space now known as ancient Egypt by the people who lived there in ancient times (Kambon, 1998, p. 530).

ascribes a European standard that still, irrelevantly, holds sway when discussing Afrikan family structures) Afrikan American fathers as "an adequate model for respectable behavior" (p. 658). Early research done on Afrikan American fathers also often portrayed these fathers as either absent or uninvolved in the lives of their children (Mitchell & Cabrera, 2009). As was often the case in earlier studies of Afrikan American men and fathers, done almost exclusively by White researchers from a White worldview using White standards, "adequate" was the highest praise such a father could garner. Interestingly enough, more than 40 years later, little has changed. As White (2006) pointed out, many policy makers and media focus on what fathers of Afrikan descent *lack* rather than the positive qualities that they *possess*. Afrikan American women affirmed that fathers were the heads of families in an article on fatherhood in the Afrikan American community of Chicago (Neff, 2004). The stance taken by these women was racially correct, but the questioner exposed the White supremacist nature of research on Afrikan American fathers by asking only Afrikan American women who the head of household was. A researcher using an Afrikan-centered approach would not have asked that question in that way, and would have honored the communal nature of the topic by asking men, elders, and children in these families, and those in the immediate community around them as well.

Much has been written about the enduring effects of the Maafa* of enslavement of Afrikan peoples and its effects on descendents of Afrikan people who live in the United States (Elligan, 2000). The ways in which social and familial relationships functioned across the Afrikan continent were altered and/or destroyed for Afrikans in Afrika and in the United States through this process (Hare & Hare, 1985). One of the lessons to be gleaned from Alexander's (2010) essay, "The New Jim Crow," is that modern enslavement in the form of the massive incarceration of Afrikan American adults has resulted in fewer children being raised by both parents today than during the epoch of the Maafa. Franklin (2009) lists four factors that have impeded Afrikan American men from becoming successful fathers: "(1) slavery, (2) economic changes, (3) cultural change, and (4) public policy" (p. 83). All of these challenges are consequences of the Maafa. Their effects on Afrikan American families are still not fully clear.

Recent research and programmatic efforts have focused on "redefining" what it means for an Afrikan American man to be a husband and a father. Many of such studies and programs focus on what are termed "at risk" or "low-income" Afrikan American males (Aronson, Whitehead, & Baber, 2003). These programs seek to "redefine men's sense of self, their

---

* *Maafa* refers to what Karenga (2002, p. 134) calls the "holocaust of enslavement" of Afrikan peoples by Europeans. See also Kambon (1998, pp. 65–66).

relationships with others ... and their responsibilities to others ... or to enhance these factors" (Aronson et al., 2003, p. 732). This framework is an interesting twist on the deficit model. The model uses a set of norms of European middle-class origin to postulate that the challenges faced by Afrikan American men are not the result of issues external to them, such as individual and institutional racism and the ravages of a system of White supremacy, but rather they derive from weaknesses found in the victims themselves (Cochran, 1997). A study of young Afrikan American fathers named four aspects of a responsible father: "economic support, emotional support, caregiving, and assuming legal paternity" (Peart, Pungello, Campbell, & Richey, 2006, p. 71). Notice that the entire focus is on responsibility toward the children. There is no attention paid to responsibility toward the larger family, community, or nation. In narrowing the focus and locus of study, the richness of Afrikan culture and communality are sacrificed, and a fuller understanding of Afrikan American fathers is missed. In a comparative study of Afrikan American and Afrikan Jamaican men, Whitehead (as reported in Aronson et al., 2003) offers attributes of the concept of respectability that include being a strong economic provider, having a higher education, and owning property, all attributes that are largely determined by societal and cultural factors that are outside or beyond the grasp of most Afrikan American (and Afrikan Jamaican) men from poorer socioeconomic backgrounds. The Afrikan American men in the Aronson et al. study pointed clearly and directly to system-generated problems that obstructed their ability to be successful as fathers and as men.

This "redefinition" has more recently been brought into focus by the efforts of two Afrikan men: one a politician and the other an entertainer. For the past few years, comedian Bill Cosby has toured the country blaming men of Afrikan descent for the epidemic of fatherlessness in the country and for using racism as an excuse for not taking responsibility (Bosman, 2008). Similarly, (then) presidential candidate Barack Obama publicly addressed the need for Afrikan American fathers from lower-class backgrounds to take greater personal responsibility for the success of their families (Bosman, 2008). Both Cosby and Obama engage in reductive analyses that focus on what these men *are not* doing rather than what they, their families, and their communities *are* doing. Their comments contrast with conclusions reached in a study of low-income Afrikan American fathers by Dubowitz, Lane, Ross, and Vaughn (2004), whose participants proudly put time, emotional and financial support, role-modeling, protection, and discipline into their fathering roles. Obama's comments and Cosby's campaign no doubt play well in White and conservative circles. Neither proposes a solution beyond the oft-repeated individual lifting himself up by his bootstraps, which denies many realities and focuses only on chosen weaknesses rather than on the overall situations of these men, their families, and their communities.

Smith (2008) studied Afrikan American fatherhood as portrayed in three television series: *The Cosby Show, Run's House,* and *Snoop Dogg's Father Hood.* The author noted that none of the shows tackles systemic issues such as racism, focusing instead on family success and harmony according to a White, middle-class standard. Smith asserts that *The Cosby Show* actually contributed to the continuance of racism in the United States by convincing many that racism was no longer an issue and that any failures by Afrikan American men was due to their shortcomings (the same analysis Obama and Cosby use in their public speaking efforts). In this analysis, Snoop Dogg is credited with staying true to his culture for visiting the neighborhood of his youth and eating soul food (Smith, 2008). Such a reductive analysis does nothing to explain fathering or Afrikan culture. Anointing Snoop Dogg as a successful Afrikan American father for not forsaking his roots and his culture is laudable as far as it goes, but the analysis does not offer any standards or guidelines for responsible Afrikan American men to follow in fathering their own children.

An interesting comparison to the Cosby and Obama perspectives is provided in an article in the popular Afrikan American magazine, *Ebony.* In the article, titled "Are You a Dead Man Walking?" the author, Kevin Chappell (2004), notices himself being reflected in a comedy routine by the Afrikan American comedian, Chris Rock. Chappell concludes that becoming a father means becoming a "responsible adult." In the process, he misses the point that Afrikan males should become responsible long before they become fathers. He is one of many "analysts" who utilize a worldview replete with mainstream European standards and goals, which were not constructed to affirm people of Afrikan descent. These analyses are sharply contrasted in an unusual article by Robert Cochran (2004), whose thesis is that Joel Chandler Harris, the author of the *Uncle Remus* stories, actually subverted the racism and White supremacist sentiments of his era in his creation. In the process, Cochran notes that the character of Uncle Remus is a father who not only takes his responsibilities seriously, but also acts as an elder, passing his deep wisdom on to younger generations through his stories. Uncle Remus, depicted as an elder slave, becomes the keeper of Afrikan American traditions and a focal point for cultural transmission through the folktales he tells. Hoem (2000) discusses how the Afrikan American author John Edgar Wideman understood the Afrikan American writer Charles Chestnut's use of signifying language not only to allow his characters to get around an oppressive cultural code without the knowledge of the master, who was attempting to impose the oppression, but also to get around the European editors and publishers who published Chestnut's work. In similar fashion, men of Afrikan descent in America find ways around the laws, rules, and cultural impositions of a White supremacist system to fulfill as many aspects of the multifaceted roles of fathering as they can. Theirs is not signifying language; rather, it is signifying *action*.

In a review of the literature on Afrikan American men from the 1980s to the 1990s, D. L. Cochran (1997) found five theoretical frameworks were used to study these men. Two of these models, the aforementioned deficit model and the matriarchy model (which asserts that Afrikan American women head so many households because Afrikan American men have failed to fulfill their roles), are both negatively focused on men of Afrikan descent and are the two most popular models used to analyze Afrikan American fathers and fathering. The other three frameworks, the Afrocentric, ecological, and choice or exchange models, are more positive in their perspectives, taking into account a wider range of factors and contexts (Cochran, 1997). Yet all of these models are deficient if not defective from the Afrikan-centered worldview.

Coles (2001) did a qualitative analysis of 10 Afrikan American fathers. Her conclusion was that being a father had positive effects for the fathers as well as for their spouses, partners, and children. This conclusion offers some contrast to the theories that presume that Afrikan American fathers avoid and reject their roles as fathers. An example of the latter position is often found in the literature. Peterson (2006) studied the impact of Afrikan American fathers on sexual risk-taking by their daughters. Three types of fathers emerged from this study: directive, insightful, and absent/ avoidant. Left out of the analysis are systemic and cultural frameworks from which to view this issue, as well as the family and community contexts in which young women are guided, not just by their fathers but by all people in the Afrikan American community. Elligan (2000) points out how funding for governmental programs, such as the welfare system, as well as for studies, is phrased in ways that focus on the needs of Afrikan American women and children at the expense of Afrikan American fathers. Such systems create an institutional disadvantage for Afrikan American fathers and for those who wish to explore Afrikan American fathers in new and nontraditional ways. One way in which this occurs is that instruments used to conduct research on Afrikan American men are not relevant for Afrikan American fathers, in general, or for those fathers who do not live with their families, in particular (Julion, Gross, Barclay-McLaughlin, & Fogg, 2007).

White (2006) did a study of Afrikan American feminist* fathers, whom she defined as equally sharing parental duties with their spouses (p. 48). Her findings are primarily focused on the parents and children within

---

* See Hudson-Weems (2003, pp. 153–163) for a discussion of the distinction between Black feminism and Africana womanism.

individual family units, thus largely ignoring input from extended family, the larger community, and the larger Afrikan American culture. An exception to this is found in the area of politically conscious parenting (White, 2006), where the fathers modeled shared responsibility in all aspects of parenting, including ongoing discussions with their partners and their children about the effects that the parents' and the children's behavior have on other community members. This focus is communal, though limited in scope to the (nuclear) family unit. Even the more positive Afrikan American fathering studies, such as that of White, use the same mainstream European worldview as the deficit and matriarchal models, with modifications, from which to view these men. In the meantime, Afrikan American men are involved with Afrikan American children in a variety of roles, all of which are vital to the prosperity of the Afrikan American community in America (Connor & White, 2006).

Afrikan-centered fathers and fathering: From theory to theory

A search of the literature to discern what has been written specifically on Afrikan-centered fathers and fathering leads to a surprising result: Almost no such literature exists!* This is partially due to the recent formal enunciation of Afrikan-centeredness as a theory. It also results from the natural process of moving from theory to application. It results from the amnesia of the Afrikan community regarding how Afrikan peoples traditionally lived their lives, viewed from the lens of their understanding of the world and themselves. It results from not understanding how Afrikan peoples in present-day Afrikan cultures live their lives. And it results from the difference in perspective between how mainstream European society views men, fathers, and fathering, and how one sees these things from an Afrikan-centered framework.

Afrikan-centeredness and the role of Afrikan American men

As I have elsewhere written (Ahadi/Mandy, 2007), the worldview that one uses to understand Afrikan Americans is determinative of all understanding that comes from that perspective. The mainstream European worldview sees, studies, and analyzes Afrikan American men separately from their spouses, families, and communities.† Studies of Afrikan American

---

* In fact, the only writing done in this area was by the present author (see Ahadi/Mandy, 2007, pp. 9–13).
† While it is not the focus of this chapter, Afrikan American women are similarly studied in isolation, as are Afrikan American elders and children.

men include how their class status affects their chances for success on any number of levels, how they relate with and care for women, and how they relate with and care for children. In each case, Afrikan American men are viewed as *individuals* and *in isolation*. This perspective is in sharp contrast to the Afrikan-centered worldview, where an Afrikan American man is understood from a variety of perspectives.

First and foremost, this man is a member of a continuum of community that encompasses ancestors and those yet to be born, as well as children, adults, and elders. Afrikan-centered men are simultaneously fathers and sons, brothers and uncles, grandfathers and husbands (and Afrikan-centered women are mothers and daughters, sisters and aunts, grandmothers and wives). Each has roles and responsibilities as members of a family, as members of a community, and as members of the nation of Afrikan-centered peoples. Fatherhood is both a learned role (Canada, 1998) and a role ascribed to any man that assumes the responsibilities of a father in a family. In traditional Afrikan societies, orphans and adoptions were unknown concepts (Asante, 1990). Furthermore, it is popularly believed by Afrikan people that Afrikan American families function better when fathers have a significant role to play in them (Allers, 2009).

Some recent literature on Afrikan American fathers has attempted to resurrect their roles and successes. One way in which to clarify the difference in these roles is by viewing persons of Afrikan descent as "extended" selves, where the individual derives his or her identity from membership and place in the group (Nobles, 1972, p. 29). One way that this has been addressed is by including men who act as fathers, such as "peripheral fathers" and "father figures" (Rentie, 2006, p. 1) in the discussion of fathers. Another method involves recognition that fathering roles in Afrikan American communities are less clearly defined and more fluid than among other cultural groups and that "'social'" fathers, who are men that may not be biologically related to the children that they father, play roles in these children's lives (Letiecq, 2007). Further clarification of the roles of Afrikan American men is discussed later.

The communal roles of Afrikan-centered people

Afrikan-centered peoples are *communal*. *Communal* refers to the collective nature, the shared nature of these persons. In a communal setting, community is the primary focus for the group, and the individual finds his or her clearest expression of himself or herself in the group (Harris, 2003). Kambon (1998) uses this concept of communality when he discusses a core tenet of Afrikan-centered people, which he calls Afrikan "survival thrust" (p. 120). This survival thrust is the core desire by any group of people to ensure that they survive, that they continue to exist, and that they continue to grow and thrive. Kambon asserts that this survival thrust is a drive innate to all people of Afrikan descent. For people of Afrikan descent, the survival and continuation of Afrikan peoples are their primary concern, the primary focus. From this worldview, behaviors that enhance the survival of the nation are normal, and those that threaten the group's survival are abnormal (Akbar, 2003).

In the United States, Afrikan communities are the primary focus of Afrikan-centered men and women. Collectively, these Afrikan-centered communities make up the Afrikan-centered nation, a nation within the United States. The core structure within these Afrikan-centered communities is the Afrikan-centered family. McAdoo (1993), author of the ecological and choice or exchange theories used to explain Afrikan American families, created these theories to show how these families are structured to foster the survival of Afrikan American families in a racist society. His research concludes that Afrikan American fathers share roles with their spouses and rely on extended family and kinship networks to facilitate the survival and prosperity of the family. White (2006) acknowledges a study by Dowd (2000) that lauded Afrikan American fathers' use of multiple generational kinship, racial consciousness, and spiritual beliefs in support of their fathering roles. These conscious and communal forms of family have fostered the survival of Afrikan American families in often hostile environments in the United States.

Afrikan-centered families

Baruti (2002), Ani (1994), Clarke (1975), and other Afrikan-centered scholars agree that the Afrikan family is the core of the Afrikan community. In fact, Baruti (2002) asserts that in traditional Afrikan societies, individuals do not marry individuals; rather, families marry families. From an Afrikan-centered worldview, families operate in a cooperative, extended fashion, where all relatives are responsible for the survival and success of the members of the family (Hyman, 1999). Its members do what is necessary to ensure the survival of the family and its members. To ensure survival of the family, its members act in complementary ways (Ani, 1994). Ani describes this complementarity as "appositional," where cooperation to ensure the survival of the group is the goal (p. 243). In a complementary framework, roles and responsibilities are adaptations to circumstances faced by the family, with females and males operating in partnership on a basis of equality (Asante, 2005). So if a male parent is away at work, an uncle, a brother, or a grandfather may take his place. Equally as true, if a male parent is away, a mother, aunt, sister, or grandmother may take his place. In other words, whatever is needed to ensure the survival and continued functioning and prosperity of the family is taken up and done

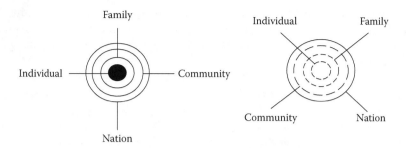

Figure 15.1 Left: Mainstream. Right: Afrikan-centered family structure.

by whoever is available to do it. No adult is of greater or lesser importance than any other adult; all work is done to ensure the prosperity of the children, who are the central focus of all Afrikan-centered families (Baruti, 2002). In a collective context, anything that benefits the family, community, or group also benefits the individual within the group. This framework is a sharp contrast to what is understood to take place in a mainstream American family.

Mainstream European-descended American families focus on the roles of the individuals rather than on the centrality of the family. The roles of each member are clearly defined, and sharp boundaries exist between each role. Hence, a "father" possesses certain roles, such as provider, that cannot be easily taken over by another. That leads to some of the identity confusion in current mainstream research on women's roles in female-headed households, which is itself a mainstream conceptualization. Since the terms *head of household* and *provider* are synonymous, the role of a man is diminished if he is not present in such a household. Terms such as *absent father* or *social father*, which are found in mainstream European research on fathers, imply a role of less than full commitment to the household. Not only are the roles of mothers and fathers discrete when viewed from the mainstream European worldview, but the individual rather than the group becomes the focus or locus of attention. It is the differences in the Afrikan-centered and mainstream perspectives that are depicted in Figure 15.1.

Afrikan-centered fathers and fathering: Worldview

The role of a father from an Afrikan-centered worldview is both defined and flexible. Fathers are providers in traditional Afrikan societies and mothers are nurturers. Asante (2005) states it succinctly: "All African moral teaching is derived from classical sources and rooted in a strong belief that a man should provide for his family and that a woman should raise the children.

There is nothing like the abandonment of the family because the family is central to the African concept of being" (p. 188). All members of the family are bearers of culture. Where circumstances require that an uncle assume the role of father, he does that to ensure the prosperity of the family. Such adjustments are made so that the goal of liberation that results in or reclaims the self-esteem, self-worth, and self-definition of the members of Afrikan American families is attained. It is with these theoretical understandings in mind that we look again at recent and current research on Afrikan and Afrikan American fathers, seeking insight and understanding.

de Latour (1994) offers a glimpse into an Afrikan concept of fathering in a present-day traditional society: the Bamileke of Cameroon. This society recognizes three fathers: the real or actual father, the mother's father, and the ancestral father. When a woman becomes a bride, all three fathers have a role to play in the process. Fouts (2008) studied fathering in two traditional societies in the Congo. She concluded that in these societies, fathers were involved with their children, sharing tasks with their wives in an egalitarian way that is enhanced by the cultural schema or worldview in which these societies operate. These analyses of traditional Afrikan societies provide present-day examples of the tenets held by Afrikan-centered theorists and practitioners.

Parham (2009) infuses these traditional values into his understanding of Afrikan American fathers. He includes such values as honor and respect, appreciation and spiritual connection, support and nurturance, and particularly cooperation rather than competition with others, both within and beyond the family. Baruti (2004) adds that Afrikan males become men when they master internal self-control based on Afrikan cultural precepts, rather than learning discipline from external sources. He adds a sense of inner strength and racial and cultural consciousness to this portrait. Madhubuti (1990) reminds us that Afrikan fathers traditionally taught their skills to their sons, and that elders trained men to be warriors that provided for and protected their families, communities, and nations. And so it is and should be today.

Afrikan American fathers and fathering: Solutions

Baruti (2002) states that "childhood is clearly a permanent condition in Western society" (p. 210), meaning that few males or females become men or women. It is in this milieu that Afrikan American fathers must operate, constructing and reconstructing family, communities, and a national cultural presence that provides protection and prosperity for all of its members. One of the goals of Afrikan-centeredness is to assist marginalized Afrikan people in freeing themselves from oppression (Schreiber, 2000). It is from this perspective that we can appreciate Abímbólá's (2006) approach to cultural identity, which is a combination of communal and individual beliefs and practices that provide direction for day-to-day living.

But one must be precise in defining such cultural identity. For to assert that Afrikan American fathers be seen through the lenses of cultural values in Afrikan American families and communities, as Cochran (1997) does, without defining those values and the worldview from which the definitions spring, could result in furthering the current confusion. Davies and colleagues (2004) recognized that behaviors can most effectively be changed if the individual receives support from their family and community, as well as other aspects of the larger social environment. The Afrikan church in America is often offered as the organizational framework to assist in the resurrection of those Afrikan American fathers who are portrayed in negative fashion. However, in so doing, one must heed Franklin's (2009) point that churches and religious institutions in the Afrikan American community and their leaders have to reflect on and adjust their own values to reflect the needs of the larger Afrikan American community.

At a more fundamental level, Afrikan-centered theorists and activists look to culturally conscious Afrikan Americans to engage in the reclamation and liberation of the Afrikan American community, liberating Afrikan American fathers in the process. Such a stance becomes clearer when analyzing such pronouncements as "Turning the Corner on Father Absence in America" (Clayton, Mincy, & Blankenhorn, 1999). This document offers 10 solutions to father absence in the Afrikan American community. Five of those solutions involve federal and state governmental agencies, which historically have shown little or no allegiance to the Afrikan American community. Conspicuously absent from these recommendations are traditional cultural rites and rituals. Without an Afrikan-centered worldview, this result is not unexpected.

Fathering in the Afrikan community is a communalist enterprise in which the family is the basic component. Individuals in such a community derive their understanding of themselves from their roles in the group. To move Afrikan American males to manhood, those who lack a communal, collective Afrikan consciousness must belong to a communally centered community in a way that leaves behind a childish self-centeredness (Baruti, 2004). Madhubuti (1990) offers further guidelines for Afrikan-centered fathers within the framework of the Afrikan family structure. He writes that Afrikan men must take responsibility for the creation and operation of Afrikan American culture. Within that cultural design, Afrikan men must model correct behavior for those aspiring to be men. Cultural groups must be created to re-create Afrikan-centered fathers. And aspiring Afrikan-centered fathers need to stop complaining and take responsibility for what needs to be done and do it (Madhubuti, 1990).

Conclusion

The ascension of Afrikan American fathers is part of a larger cultural enterprise: the liberation of Afrikan American people. That enterprise is part of the larger task of liberating Afrikan people around the world. Discussing Afrikan American fathers has presented a challenge common to Afrikan-centered theory. Removing Afrikan American fathers from their families, communities, and nations in order to discuss them is part and parcel of the Eurocentric enterprise of making individual components of Afrikan communal structures, which include families and communities, Afrikan cultures, and worldview constructs. One hopes that this effort will better inform those who truly wish to be of service to Afrikan people, and that the four aspects of Afrikan-centered relationships enunciated by Asante (1980), "sacrifice, inspiration, vision, and victory" (p. 59), become realities for Afrikan peoples worldwide.

Reflective questions

1. Can Afrikan-centered fathering principles be added to current programs that serve Afrikan American fathers? If yes, how? If no, why not?
2. How can the roles of Afrikan American fathers be studied in a communal context?
3. What other organizations and structures, other than Afrikan American religious institutions, can assist in the building of Afrikan-centered families in which Afrikan American fathers can assume a significant role?
4. Which mainstream European institutions, if any, can be recruited to assist with funding and directing research on Afrikan-centered families?

References

Abímbólá, K. (2006). *Yorùbá culture: A philosophical account*. Birmingham, UK: Iroko Academic.

Adeleke, T. (2001). Will the real father of Afrocentricity please stand? *Western Journal of Black Studies, 25*(1), 21–29.

Ahadi, H./Mandy, L. (2007). Fathering and the Afrikan-centered worldview/paradigm. *The Black Scholar: Journal of Black Studies and Research, 37*(2), 9–13.

Akbar, N. (2003). Afrocentric social sciences for human liberation. In A. Mazama (Ed.), *The Afrocentric paradigm* (pp. 131–143). Trenton, NJ: Africa World Press.

Alexander, M. (2010, March 8). The new Jim Crow: How the war on drugs gave birth to a permanent American undercaste. *Mother Jones.* Retrieved March 21, 2010, from http://motherjones.com/politics/2010/03/new-jim-crow-war-on-drugs

Allers, K. S. (2009). His turn: Black men embrace and redefine fatherhood. *New York Amsterdam News, 100*(19), S7.

Ani, M. (1994). *Yurugu: An African-centered critique of European cultural thought and behavior.* Trenton, NJ: Africa World Press.

Aronson, R. E., Whitehead, T. L., & Baber, W. L. (2003). Challenges to masculine transformation among urban low-income African American males. *American Journal of Public Health, 93*(5), 732–741.

Asante, M. K. (1980). *Afrocentricity: The theory of social change.* Buffalo, NY: Amulefi.

Asante, M. K. (1990). *Kemet, Afrocentricity and knowledge.* Trenton, NJ: Africa World Press.

Asante, M. K. (2003). The Afrocentric idea. In A. Mazama (Ed.), *The Afrocentric paradigm* (pp. 37–53). Trenton, NJ: Africa World Press.

Asante, M. K. (2005). *Race, rhetoric, and identity: The architecton of soul.* Amherst, NY: Humanity Books.

Baruti, M. K. B. (2002). *The sex imperative.* Atlanta, GA: Akoben House.

Baruti, M. K. B. (2004). *Asafo: A warrior's guide to manhood.* Atlanta, GA: Akoben House.

ben-Jochannan, Y. A. A. (1971). *Africa: Mother of Western civilization.* New York: Alkebulan Books.

Bosman, J. (2008, June 16). Obama calls for more responsibility from Black fathers. *New York Times,* p. A15.

Bryan, M. (1997). *The prodigal father: Reuniting fathers with their children.* New York: Three Rivers Press.

Canada, G. (1998). *Reaching up for manhood: Transforming the lives of boys in America.* Boston: Beacon Press.

Carruthers, J. H. (2010). *Reflections on the revision of the African centered paradigm.* Retrieved on April 2, 2010, from http://www.africawithin.com/carruthers/reflections.htm

Chappell, K. (2004). Are you a dead man walking? *Ebony, 59*(8), 40.

Clarke, J. H. (1975). The Black family in historical perspective. *Journal of Afro-American Issues, 3/4,* 336–342.

Clayton, O., Mincy, R., & Blankenhorn, D. (1999). *Turning the corner on father absence in Black America.* Atlanta, GA: Morehouse Research Institute & Institute for American Values.

Cochran, D. L. (1997). African American fathers: A decade review of the literature. *Families in Society: Journal of Contemporary Human Services, 78*(4), 340–350.

Cochran, R. (2004). Black father: The subversive achievement of Joel Chandler Harris. *African American Review, 38*(1), 21–34.

Coles, R. (2001). African American single full-time fathers: How are they doing? *Journal of African American Men, 6*(2), 63–82.

Connor, M. E. (1988). Teenage fatherhood: Issues confronting young Black males. In J. T. Gibbs (Ed.), *Young, Black, and male in America: An endangered species* (pp. 188–218). New York: Auburn House.

Connor, M. E., & White, J. L. (2006). Fatherhood in contemporary Black America: Invisible but present. In M. E. Connor & J. L. White (Eds.), *Black fathers: An invisible presence in America* (pp. 3–16). Mahwah, NJ: Erlbaum.

Davies, S. L., Dix, E. S., Rhodes, S. D., Harrington, K. F., Frison, S., & Willis, L. (2004). Attitudes of young African American fathers toward early childbearing. *American Journal of Health Behavior, 28*(5), 418–425.

de Latour, C.-H. P. (1994). Marriage payments, debt and fatherhood among the Bangoua: A Lacanian analysis of a kinship system. *Africa, 64*(1), 21–33.

Dowd, N. E. (2000). *Redefining fatherhood.* New York: New York University Press.

Dubowitz, H., Lane, W., Ross, K., & Vaughan, D. (2004). The involvement of low-income African American fathers in their children's lives, and the barriers they face. *Ambulatory Pediatrics, 4*(6), 505–508.

Elligan, D. (2000). Proceedings of the Father Friendly Initiative Conference. *Journal of African American Men, 5*(1), 63–68.

Fouts, H. N. (2008). Father involvement with young children among the Aka and Bofi foragers. *Cross-Cultural Research, 42*(3), 290–312.

Franklin, R. M. (2009). The future of fatherhood and families in African American communities. *Harvard Journal of African American Public Policy, 15*, 75–90.

Hare, N., & Hare, J. (1985). *Bringing the Black boy to manhood: The passage.* San Francisco: Black Think Tank.

Harris, N. (2003) A philosophical basis for an Afrocentric orientation. In A. Mazama (Ed.), *The Afrocentric paradigm* (pp. 111–119). Trenton, NJ: Africa World Press.

Hoem, S. I. (2000). Recontextualizing fathers: Wideman, Foucault and African American genealogy. *Textual Practice, 14*(2), 235–251.

Hudson-Weems, C. (2003). Africana womanism. In A. Mazama (Ed.), *The Afrocentric paradigm* (pp. 153–163). Trenton, NJ: Africa World Press.

Hyman, M. (1999). *Blacks before America.* Trenton, NJ: Africa World Press.

Julion, W., Gross, D., Barclay-McLaughlin, G. B., & Fogg, L. (2007). "It's not just about MOMMAS": African-American non-resident fathers' views of paternal involvement. *Research in Nursing & Health, 30*, 595–610.

Kambon, K. K. K. (1998). *African/Black psychology in the American context: An African-centered approach.* Tallahassee, FL: Nubian Nation.

Kane, C. H. (1963). *Ambiguous adventure.* London: Heinemann.

Karenga, M. (2002). *Introduction to Black studies* (3rd ed.). Los Angeles: University of Sankore Press.

Letiecq, B. L. (2007). African American fathering in violent neighborhoods: What role does spirituality play? *Fathering, 5*(2), 111–116, 118–120, 123–128.

Madhubuti, H. R. (1990). *Black men: Obsolete, single, dangerous? The Afrikan American family in transition: Essays in discovery, solution, and hope.* Chicago: Third World Press.

Mazama, A. (2003). The Afrocentric paradigm. In A. Mazama (Ed.), *The Afrocentric paradigm* (pp. 3–34). Trenton, NJ: Africa World Press.

McAdoo, J. L. (1993). The roles of African American fathers: An ecological perspective. *Families in Society: Journal of Contemporary Human Services, 74*(1), 28–35.

Mitchell, S. J., & Cabrera, N. J. (2009). An exploratory study of fathers' parenting stress and toddlers' social development in low-income African American families. *Fathering, 7*(3), 201–225.

Modupe, D. S. (2003). The Afrocentric philosophical perspective: A narrative outline. In A. Mazama (Ed.), *The Afrocentric paradigm* (pp. 55–72). Trenton, NJ: Africa World Press.

Neff, D. (2004, August). Creating husbands and fathers: The discussion of gender roles moves beyond "proof-text poker." *Christianity Today, 48*(8), 55–56.

Nobles, W. W. (1972). African philosophy: Foundations for Black psychology. In R. L. Jones (Ed.), *Black psychology* (pp. 18–32). New York: Harper & Row.

Parham, T. (2009, November). *The challenges of African centered maleness.* Presentation at the 30th Black Consciousness Conference, California State University, Long Beach.

Peart, N. A., Pungello, E. P., Campbell, F. A., & Richey, T. G. (2006). Faces of fatherhood: African American young adults view the paternal role. *Families in Society, 87*(1), 71–83.

Peterson, S. H. (2006). The importance of fathers: Contextualizing sexual risk taking in "low risk" African American adolescent girls. *Journal of Human Behavior in the Social Environment, 13*(3), 67–83.

Rentie, R. J. (2006). *The impact of father involvement on African American women pertaining to risky sexual behavior.* Unpublished master's thesis, California State University, Long Beach.

Schreiber, L. (2000). Overcoming methodological elitism: Afrocentrism as a prototypical paradigm for intercultural research. *International Journal of Intercultural Relations, 24*, 651–671.

Schulz, D. A. (1968). Variations in the father role in complete families of the Negro lower class. *Social Science Quarterly, 49*(3), 651–659.

Smith, D. C. (2008). Critiquing reality-based televisual Black fatherhood: A critical analysis of *Run's House* and *Snoop Dogg's Father Hood. Critical Studies in Media Communication, 25*(4), 393–412.

White, A. M. (2006). African American feminist fathers' narratives of parenting. *Journal of Black Psychology, 32*(1), 43–71.

chapter sixteen

Where from here?—Answers are in the community

Michael E. Connor
Alliant International University
San Francisco, California

The contributors to this volume share some poignant stories about the impact of African American fathers' presence and absence in the daily lives of children. They discuss paternal involvement in spite of odds against it, the impact of that involvement, and the struggle to maintain it. The contributors speak of some models of engagement that have worked and others that are struggling to work. There is no doubt that males who father children must be responsible to and for those children. They must support them in numerous ways, including providing for their children's material and emotional needs over many years and often providing for the needs of children who are not biologically their own. Ideally, African American males should be well on their way to becoming healthy, capable men before becoming fathers.

In the past two decades, there have been several efforts mounted to assist African American youth in their journey from childhood dependence to adult self-sufficiency and, potentially, responsible fatherhood. A major problem with many of the efforts in place to serve these youth is the lack of support and funding for long-term programs. Given the costs of local, state, and federal incarceration, the impact of incarceration on families in those communities, and the fact that incarceration alone does not deter crime, perhaps the time is ripe to explore (and implement) alternative strategies. Diverting funds used to jail Black men for petty crimes and redirecting such funds to prosocial training, education, and preventative programs could finance these efforts. Thus, long-term funding will not require additional expenditure of public money.

The available information suggests that, given the sordid history of treatment of Black men in the United States and the state of current affairs, it is doubtful that a "one size fits all" or similar approaches to training will be either effective or helpful. Successful approaches need to be flexible and innovative. Regardless of the specifics presented, certain general intervention topics are warranted. First, both long- and short-term strategies are needed. While the short-term solutions (commonly the 3- to 4-year funding cycles) may work for some recipients of services, they are likely to be inappropriate for many young Black males, including those who are already fathers. This primarily is because problems that have developed over generations are unlikely to be resolved in 3- to 4-year cycles. The mismatch between availability of services and the needs of recipients often results in the latter being left frustrated and their needs unfulfilled. Thus, long-term commitment and funding for research and treatment are needed if the goal is to truly make a difference.

Additionally, service models must reflect African/Afrikan philosophies that focus on collective versus individual values, and respect for generational authority and wisdom. In the African tradition, it is not chronological age that determines manhood, but rather the possession of knowledge and the ability to demonstrate competent behaviors and skills acquired through exposure over time. Often, these skill sets are shared, discussed, modeled, and reinforced by others who have mastered them in the past. Thus, becoming a man is a process involving the mastery of certain facts, experiences, behaviors, cultural concepts, and values over time rather than a specific event marked at a specific moment in time such as one's birthday.

Program overview

The author suggests that the commencement of the learning and mastery period in an African American male's life marks the end of childhood and the beginning of manhood, and this learning is ongoing and lifelong. Therefore, there is a need for formalized preparation or "Manhood Training" before fatherhood if these males are to become successfully involved fathers, effective family members, and productive resources in their communities. The purpose of Manhood Training is to provide a set of lessons and experiences to African American male youth. The author believes all African American youth could potentially benefit from the training and proposes it be customized to accommodate the specific needs of the various circumstances in which our youth and their families find themselves. The goal is for all African American young males to reach their potential as loving, committed family members and particularly as beneficially involved fathers.

The Manhood Training activities and lessons are designed to enable youth to move toward meaningful and responsible manhood. The focus is on creating and sharing positive life and career choices, which can make a difference in the lives of our youth. In so doing, we can help the young men develop their character and be in the position to make a difference in the lives of others (e.g., their children) and in the future of their communities.

To reach the goals, several interrelated components are required; each is dependent on the other to achieve success. The components include the following:

1. A motivated youth who wants to learn and engage (including those who may not yet recognize they are motivated to learn and participate);
2. An involved and committed family and extended family who will support the youth's learning;
3. Adults who function as teachers and/or mentors who commit to giving time, energy, direction, and effort to master the training material and then share it with the youth; and
4. A culturally sensitive curriculum designed to impart specific expectations, knowledge, principles, concepts, behaviors, experiences, and activities to allow the males to progress toward meaningful manhood. At a certain point in the training, the focus will be on becoming a father and fatherhood. The curriculum will reflect and engage an interactive teaching philosophy, which will endeavor to routinely include all participants. It is collective rather than individualistic.

Mentees/participants

Participants in the Manhood Training program may come from a variety of sources. Some youth may choose to voluntarily enter and recruit their peers. Others may be referred to the program by adults in their lives such as teachers, counselors, coaches, ministers, community elders, parents, family members, and guardians. Youth may also be directed to the program by various social service providers (e.g., mental health workers) or by agents of the juvenile legal systems as a result of their own involvement in the system, or that of other family members. Anyone who has knowledge of the young male, who sees his potential, who is invested in the community, and who has an interest in making a positive change in youth may refer an African American youth. The program will encourage those who make referrals to follow up with the program to ascertain what the adolescent is doing, how he is doing it, what his level of successful involvement is, and how they might assist in his development.

Once referred, the youth will be screened to determine program suitability and interest. An assessment of the participant's strengths and needs will form the basis for tailoring the training toward maximizing skills that already exist. An intake worker–counselor will explain the goals of the project, what is expected of the participant, and what the participant can expect of the Manhood Training program. Additionally, program "ground rules" will be explained (e.g., the need for being respectful of others, committing to sharing and listening to others, attending on a regular basis, completing all assignments to the best of one's abilities, respecting confidentiality boundaries, and generally respecting others). The interaction/orientation will also include an explanation of the expected time commitment, the likely advantages of participation, and the required level of involvement for success.

This assessment should help determine the participating youth's level of cognitive skill development (including reading comprehension, critical thinking, mathematical and computational skills, oral expressive skills, and social interaction skills). The assessment will take place prior to the start of training to determine where to place the student, and after training so that we might evaluate the effectiveness and impact of the training. It will include markers of both academic and social progress (grades, attendance, behavioral difficulties, etc.) along with several objective measures (i.e., the Comprehensive Adolescent Severity Index). Post-training assessment will be administered after participants have completed the training to help gauge both their progress and the effectiveness of the Manhood Training as an intervention. Through this assessment, the youth will be directed to the appropriate peer group for training.

Additionally, participants' general health and well-being will need to be assessed, including history or current involvement with chemical use. If a youngster is "using," he will be referred to a substance abuse program to get clean. After completion of that program, he is welcome to return to the Manhood Training. (Project staff will follow and monitor any referrals so that the teen can feel assured he is not being dumped and is in fact welcome to return for training.) Thus, the Manhood Training program will identify and work closely with those who service the target population in differing ways, including educational programs, athletic programs, mental health programs, the legal system, social service organizations, and faith-based community organizations, among others.

The author's work with young African American males over the years suggests that the population can be segmented into three general categories, reflecting their educational levels, school success to date, learning abilities, and exposure to educational successes. Participants will remain in their designated groupings throughout the training and all groups will be exposed to the same training goals, materials, and lessons—but the time frames for and the intensity of the training will differ.

Group I will include youth (including college students) who are "highly likely to succeed." These males are currently performing well across a range of academic and social settings. Most of these youth will likely have been reared in two-parent households with some stability, educational preparation, direction, and support, or they may possess particular skills or abilities that will help facilitate their educational attainment and successful entry into the vocational marketplace.

Group II includes African American youth (early high school years) at the boundary between success and failure. These likely are young Black males who require more intense support, direction, encouragement, reinforcement, nurturing, love, and stability. They have the ability to "make it" but may lack (or do not perceive) the role models, the resources, the direction, and the opportunity to aid them in moving from "at-risk" to "at-promise" status. They may come from a variety of socioeconomic circumstances.

Group III includes those males for whom most programs are directed, but which tend to offer too little too late. These youth typically have poor academic records (either having dropped out, having stopped attending, or having been pushed out of school). They may reside in homes without viable, adult male role models, or in environments where the available models tend to be negative (e.g., street hustlers, pimps, etc.). As a result, many of Group III youth spend time "hanging with their friends," getting into trouble with the law, or engaging in socially inappropriate behaviors including premature parenting. (Some of them may have fathered one or more children for whom they are unable to care, and have no history of meaningful gainful employment.) Intervention for this group will commence during the middle school years and continue into their young adult years.

Because Group I will finish training before Group II, Group II will finish before Group III, and Group III will take the longest time to be trained and require more assets, it is expected that Group I graduates from the program will help Groups II and III and Group II will aid Group III. This intergroup awareness, support, and responsibilty is a desired outcome.

While there is no evidence that any African-descended male "has it made" in this society, it is also obvious that some have more opportunity, and thus relative success, than others (e.g., Group I). This group must be encouraged and reinforced to accept responsibility for and commitment to working for the improvements in the status of the other two groups. The training/indoctrination given to the three groups involves learning their cultural identity, mastering the topic areas presented, and reinforcing behaviors that commit them to others who have not been so blessed. Group I young men will be actively engaged in their educational pursuits (high school or college) and may be in fraternities, social clubs, athletic teams, vocational organizations, or church groups. A primary emphasis is that they must be encouraged to commit to and give back to the community in the way of time, energy, effort, and support. They possess skills, opportunities, and experiences that may be useful to their peers in the other two groups. (Thus, they are expected to participate in some aspects of the training of Groups II and III.)

The members of Group I will be followed through college. While attending the university, they will be asked to come home and make time to work with high school students (10th, 11th, and 12th graders) who are in the program. The first cohort of Group I college *graduates* will be asked to work with 9th graders (under the supervision of teachers/mentors) and remain with them until they attend (and hopefully complete) college degrees. The second cohort of Group I graduates will come home and work with 8th graders until they attend and earn college degrees. Subsequent alumni of the program will be asked to work with younger cohorts and remain involved with them until they graduate. Thus, educationally successful program graduates will shoulder some of the responsibility for helping the members of Groups II and III achieve academic success. In a similar manner, those who enter the trades, develop businesses, and otherwise develop marketable skills will be asked to come home and participate in the training and education of the community youth. In this manner, the Manhood Training program and its principles may eventually expand to reach youngsters in elementary and middle school and be able to follow them throughout their educations.

Whereas some of the Group II participants may benefit from short-term funded programs (3 to 4 years), the goal is to provide them with long-term support and guidance. It is critical that Group II participants not slide into Group III. They should be targeted during the first year of high school (9th or 10th grade) and followed through graduation from college, trade school, or some post–high school training. As with graduates from Group I, at the conclusion of their education, alumni from Group II will be encouraged to return to their community and participate in the training of the next generation of participants of the Manhood Training program (an "each one teach one" approach).

Group III are the youth most often labeled "at risk," and numerous short-term programs have been in place for them, with minimal success. They are left to raise themselves; they are in the streets; they tend to disengage from school; and they do not envision a meaningful/productive future. They may, unwittingly, represent the worst stereotypes of Black youth as portrayed in both mass media and professional literature discussing social problems in contemporary American society.

These youth must be targeted and engaged during middle school years, at the latest. Therefore, a major objective of the Manhood Training program is to work with schools, social service providers, and the legal system to have these males diverted into rehabilitative training rather than simply consigned to the juvenile "justice" system. To be an effective (i.e., successful) long-term intervention, contact between Group III youth and the Manhood Training program would need to be maintained 5 to 6 years *beyond* the high school years. During that time, these youth would be encouraged to find their genius by continuing their education/training and cultivating an ethic of lifelong learning and community responsibility.

Group training

The training for Group I is focused on consolidating their academic and social strengths, with the goal having them work with others. The projected time frame for their training is 8-10 weeks, 3 to 5 hours a week. Group I participants will be tested before and after the training to evaluate the level of awareness of program principles and to generally assess each participant's learning. Upon successful completion, a Rite of Passage ceremony will acknowledge their success and serve as a tangible sign of their transition to manhood.

After graduation from the program, Group I participants will be followed through their college years to support their continued growth and provide encouragement for using the skills they learned. As noted earlier, a major aspect of the training is to encourage successful youth to give back in the form of ongoing peer support and peer mentoring of younger cohorts.

It is likely that many Group II and Group III participants will require more time and attention if they are to be successfully indoctrinated in the Manhood Training goals and objectives. This process may also involve motivating some or all of them to examine their current value systems. As personal and systemic changes of this magnitude often require significant shifts in values, perceptions, and self-conversations, this process will by definition require a long-term commitment from the program staff as well as from other concerned stakeholders.

Group II and III training will be similar to Group I, except it will be administered on a more intense, involved, and longer level. Because some of these youth may not have had positive learning experiences, they may not have graduated from high school. Repositioning lifelong learning as an essential life skill will be a major objective of the Manhood Training program. Thus, obtaining a high school diploma (or GED), and some postsecondary education (e.g., college or vocational training) will be a standard part of each participant's customized program goals. These groups will meet weekly (or as needed) for 52 weeks and will be afforded individual and group counseling in addition to the training.

Again, successful participants will take part in a Rite of Passage graduation ceremony to honor their success. As noted, Group III participants may require both short- *and* long-term support from the program;

thus, follow-up services should be available to them over an extended period (e.g., 10 years).* Over time, the goal will be to reduce the absolute numbers in Group III while increasing the number of participants in Group I. That is, we want to move Group II youth to Group I rather than having them slide into Group III.

Parents

There is a direct relationship between student achievement and parental and familial involvement. Parents and parental figures who are directly, positively, and consistently involved have an impact on their children's academic and social development. These successful parents (or parental figures, including stepparents, grandparents, surrogate parents, foster parents, guardians, etc.) set and maintain age-appropriate boundaries for their children. They develop and enforce predictable consequences when the boundaries are violated, and they know the difference between discipline and punishment and have the willingness to administer *discipline* as appropriate. In general, they are able to articulate a clear sense of right and wrong that their children can use as a template for the social interactions with others in their lives.

Additionally, successful parents develop and maintain high standards for their children, combining them with clear expressions of love and support. This entails attentive, involved childrearing exemplified by a willingness to monitor the child's use of electronics (e.g., TV, computer, Internet, radios, cell phones, etc.) and getting to know the child's friends. It also means a willingness to visit the school and meet the child's teacher(s), to advocate for the child, and to provide consistent encouragement and monitoring of homework. Successful parents who communicate with their children provide support for children in the home and at school. They understand the child's strengths and weaknesses. Thus, the Manhood Training program involves the parents, surrogate parents, and family members.

Mentors/teachers

To succeed, youth need relationships with competent, confident, caring adults who believe in them. These adults will be the cornerstone of the Manhood Training program and must be willing and able to commit time, energy, and personal resources to guide and direct others. The success of

---

* This is the population with whom many of us work and for whom funding for so many soft money programs dries up before any significant positive results can be achieved.

the program is directly related to the extent of involvement of adult males from the community.

The adults may function as teachers, mentors, or teacher-mentors, depending on skills, experience, and level of their involvement. It is critical that a set of dependable African American adults take the lead in modeling behaviors to which Black youth require exposure (as the Web site of the 100 Black Men of America mentoring program says, "What they see is what they'll be"; http://www.100blackmen.org/mentoring.aspx). The teachers/mentors must commit to learning and supporting the curriculum and modeling appropriate behaviors for the youth. They must be dependable, willing to take on the extra work, knowledgeable about issues impacting contemporary Black American youth, able to communicate, willing to listen and to share, able to commit to the program over a substantial time frame, and equipped with an abundance of patience and energy. It will be their task to impart specific information (teach) and to assess the level of comprehension of that which they teach/share. They are expected to help develop the curriculum, teach it, model the corresponding behaviors, interact with parents and parent figures, and be available. As noted, it is important that they are comfortable and competent using interactive teaching approaches to ensure significant involvement of participating youth.

Most municipalities of any size across the United States have an African American community. Within these areas reside men and women who are working (or perhaps retired) and possess meaningful skill sets. Additionally, these communities are likely to have a cadre of Black community activists who are committed to the betterment of their communities and their neighbors. From these groups, 30 or so leaders should be sought to take the lead in providing services to the youth. These teachers/mentors will likely come from various backgrounds, such as teachers, social workers, doctors, attorneys, businessmen/women, electricians, or preachers. Many will simply be concerned citizens who want to give something back. They will be asked to participate in learning the training modules—first to review the curriculum, then to provide feedback as to how to improve it (customize it for their community), and then to teach it. They will also be asked to help with the recruitment, organization, and training.

It is important that a significant part of the teaching be conducted by local African American males who can model appropriate male role behaviors to the youth. These men must possess competence, experience, knowledge, desire, commitment, and motivation to provide consistent ongoing services. They should be men who have a history of community and personal involvement and who are committed to the future development of the community.

Some of the men will also function as mentors, sharing specific skills with the youth (pertaining to educational, social, and/or vocational attainment). Mentoring will take place beyond the teaching and the mentors will be encouraged to meet with the youth informally at mutually convenient times outside of program instruction. During these meetings, mentors might share their vocational (educational or social) experiences with the youth in an effort to motivate them to aspire to higher goals. Mentors will likely meet several hours a month with their protégés, maintain records of the meetings, and attend "staffings" wherein the youth are discussed. In short, adult mentors, along with the teachers, are the keys to the success of the program in that they interact with the youth, their families, and other important community stakeholders.

Training processes

The training will commence with a community discussion regarding the need to be a man before becoming a father. Early impregnation and the inability to care for one's offspring are essentially community problems and require community acknowledgment and ownership. Therefore, it is important to get "buy-in" with this concept. The issue of responsibility will inform the training. This will lead to conversations as to what being a man entails in the African tradition and a Rites of Passage program celebrating the movement from boys to men. The involvement of the broader community as stakeholders in the program is critical, and they should be informed of the program's existence, it goals, its presence, and its successes.

As noted, successful completion of the training would culminate in a culturally specific Rites of Passage program celebrating each participant's "crossing" from childhood to manhood. These celebrations would take place once or twice each year and involve participants' family, extended family, significant others, friends, teachers, mentors, and other important stakeholders. The ceremony would include African drumming, libations, presentation of the successful participants, and the acceptance of the youth by a community of elders who must confirm the entry into manhood. The author believes that it is important that the young men be honored and presented to the community in this "formal" manner. Young Black males receive a disproportionate amount of negative attention, and this would be an opportunity for them to receive attention for positive actions. Thus, planning for media attention, exposure, and community support would be critical elements in any effective Manhood Training celebration. As graduates of the Manhood Training program, the men will build an expanding cadre of young Black males who learn to be responsible for themselves, for their offspring, and for their communities.

Class organization

Training sessions will commence and end with an African-centered cultural ritual to convey unity, a sense of history, inclusion, pride, and togetherness. Behavioral guidelines for attendance, successful completion, and graduation from the program will be maintained. Participants will be expected to arrive on time and be prepared to fully participate in the activities. Participants will also be expected to listen respectfully to one another, add to the discussion as appropriate, and avoid creating or engaging with distractions (e.g., cell phones and pagers).

Long-term follow-up is critical to the success of the program, as it makes little sense to train the young people and then ignore them via nonreinforcement. Rather, they need to know that they count, they matter, and that the adults involved will remain with them as they mature. It is this long-term relationship that will ensure success and will provide the cadre of mentors who can make a difference.

Curriculum

Following are some examples of content areas that would be part of the Manhood Training curriculum.*

AFRICAN AND AFRICAN AMERICAN HISTORY

The training will commence with an overview of ancient Kemet, life in the Mother Country, the Middle Passage, survival during Enslavement, postenslavement, and contributions to U.S. culture and society.

PARENTING

The parenting curriculum covers awareness of children's needs, time management issues, the establishment of paternity, paternal rights and responsibilities, daily interactions with children, and learning to show respect for those who also care for your child.

---

* This is an overview of a curriculum and is not intended to be exhaustive. Enough is offered so that the reader should be able to glean an understanding of what would be presented and for what reason. The curriculum offerings should be tailored to the specific community needs for which it is targeted.

SOCIAL-PERSONAL DEVELOPMENT

These sessions focus on life skills development, including recognizing and managing anger, developing an awareness of the impact of domestic violence, learning to communicate (with focus on problem solving and negotiation), and understanding the toll and impact of drugs and alcohol. The session will also cover the impact of an African-centered personal orientation including inquiring of oneself,

"Who am I?"
"Am I who I say I am?"
"Am I all I ought to be?"

EDUCATIONAL TRAINING

The goal is to enhance the overall educational awareness in several interactive spheres, including completing high school, attending community college, the university, or vocational-training programs; learning about mental health issues that impact the community (including recognizing and reducing stress and strategies for nonviolent conflict resolution); developing an awareness of physical health issues, including reproductive health and an awareness of the diseases disproportionally impacting the Black community (diabetes, essential hypertension, obesity, HIV/AIDS, prostate cancer, colon cancer, etc.); financial awareness, money management, living within one's means; and the oppressive role of sports and athletics on Black youth (the program focus is on "using sport rather than allowing sport to use you").

VOCATIONAL TRAINING

The objectives include job readiness, getting and maintaining a job, moving from a job to a career, career advancement, learning to network and grow, and financial empowerment.

LEADERSHIP TRAINING AND COMMUNITY SERVICE

This training module focuses on learning to make a positive impact on your community by giving back. Mentor/teachers will model "giving back" via their involvement in the Manhood Training program, thereby setting the stage where youth can observe and appreciate the impact and value of community service.

Further research issues

There continues to be a need for meaningful, relevant, culturally sensitive research that focuses on gathering information about a wide variety of African American fathers in several situations. A reasonable starting point is to observe Black fathers in trying situations and in spite of these hurdles are able to "make it." Who are they? What are they doing? And what variables support their success? Studying, observing, and collecting data about men in the community who are legitimately "taking care of business" is clearly needed. The goal would be to duplicate the activities of these successful fathers as pertains to meeting their responsibilities, commitments, daily activities, and community interactions. As noted by several contributors to this book, these men hold the answers for the development of success models that can impact the community. Longitudinal observations can provide direction, training models, and actions for systemic change.

Additionally, there is the need to study and evaluate interventions such as the Manhood Training program. Will the success of the youth in this program also impact changes in their parents? What might be the most salient traits required of program staff (teachers and mentors)? What is needed to attract and maintain the participation of all parties involved? How long should it take to start seeing positive results? In general, program evaluators will need to understand which programs work, why they work, and who they are most likely to benefit. For example, are Afrikan-centered approaches to the systemic problems confronted by U.S. Black men working? What do they entail, who is attracted to them, and what are the results? If they work, can they be taught in a broader manner to more men?

There are additional areas for research that hold particular promise for understanding the motivation of effective, African American fathering. Much of the existent literature regarding African American males focuses on low-income individuals living in urban centers. What is happening in more affluent homes? How do these youth perceive their potential as partners and fathers? Do Black youth in rural areas face different challenges in their journey from childhood to manhood? Relevant data are needed across socioeconomic status variations, in different-sized communities, and from different geographic regions if we are to develop a comprehensive understanding of the challenges African American youth face and the resources they and their families can harness to meet those challenges.

Given demographic trends toward later marriage, nonmarriage, and persistently high levels of relationship disruption, we need to understand more about the lives of at least two distinct types of Black fathers parenting apart from their natal partners. First, what do we know about single, custodial African American fathers? What are their strategies for success and how do they avoid failure? Do their approaches to childrearing differ significantly from those of single moms? Are the resources they rely on different, and do they use their support systems the same way?

Many of these questions also apply to the second group: noncustodial, African American fathers who are maintaining contact with their children. What are the barriers these fathers face who are maintaining contact with their children? The literature suggests that relationships with the mothers can be a "gate" to access to children, but how much do we know about how to help these couples develop robust, co-parenting relationships? This is particularly critical when one or both parents are currently in a new relationship and/or household with additional children. How do we help fathers in these complex circumstances manage multiple, paternal obligations over time in ways that don't lead to fatigue, frustration, and, eventually, abandonment of one of more of the children?

A continuing interest of several of this book's authors is to expand our knowledge of the different roles men play in families and how they can successfully manage these roles over time. It stands to reason that many successful husbands and fathers were respectful boyfriends and, before that, good sons, but how do males connect these roles? (Or do they?) What is the role of generative fathering ? Who is preparing the next generation of fathers, and what are they doing to prepare them? Moreover, does the African American community have a clear set of expectations for males at each developmental level? If so, how are these communicated to youth and adults? If not, what are the risks to the entire community? A delicate balance must be struck between setting expectations too low (and enabling irresponsible male behavior) and setting them too high (driving males out of households in frustration).

At each developmental stage, Black males may also need to account for conflicts between and within various familial roles. For example, how do African American fathers interact with their sons and daughters over the years? What are the interactions that lead to children's success? Does the reciprocal reinforcement between fathers and daughters differ from that of fathers and sons? And later in life, how is the role of grandfather changing in Black families? How might grandfathers be more meaningfully involved with their children and grandchildren? More research is needed to understand how youth and adults resolve these potential conflicts.

How do we get more of our African American youth (and their parents) to see the educational system differently? Are educational strategies such as boys-only schools with a cultural specific curriculum doing better? In the past, the majority of the Black community understood the transformative potential of education and fought to gain access for its youth, often at great cost and sacrifice. Not quite a half-century later, a significant segment of the Black community perceives education as optional and the educational system as hostile territory. The authors of this book are living testaments to the power that education can bring to the lives of Black men and women and in service of their communities. Education can open the doors to careers that (in turn) provide the power to shape one's destiny. However, none of this is possible if African American youth avoid the very system that is part of their birthright, or if their parents are afraid to demand accountability from institutions that their tax dollars fund.

Dynamic economic and technological pressures are shaping changes in familial roles and responsibilities across all ethnic groups, including African American communities. There is little research comparing family process in African American households from divergent socioeconomic circumstances. Although there is a growing literature on African American, female-headed, single-parent households (mostly at or below the poverty level), there is relatively less study of economically stable, two-parent households. How equalitarian are two-parent, African American homes? How do the parents in these homes determine household (and "outside") responsibilities? (e.g. child care, finances, etc.?) How are these homes faring?

How do we break the cycle of youth making babies who, in turn, make babies? This question is at the heart of male contraceptive responsibility. Men must teach each other that the only way one can control when one becomes a father is by taking control of contraception. There are no "accidents"; if you are having unprotected sex, you are planning to conceive. Additionally, it is each male's responsibility to take care of his children. The most masculine thing a man can do is to raise his children.*

When young men become fathers, what tools and traits are needed for them to develop and maintain appropriate relationships with the mothers of their children and with her family? If there were clearer answers to these questions, service providers currently working with young African American males might be in a better position to help these youth acquire the interpersonal skills they need to meet their paternal aspirations (e.g., "I want to be there for my child"). However, this may also require a shift in service providers' belief systems about African American males and their suitability as fathers.

What is needed to encourage and support parents to consider and utilize nonpunitive disciplinary styles? How do we get parents to understand that hitting kids in an attempt to teach them lessons only reinforces the notion that they must hit to resolve conflict? Rather than increasing

---

* Even young males must take these words to heart.

the violence, we need models to increase the peace. We also need to re-educate folks (including some within the Black community) in African philosophy regarding the sacred nature of children and our obligations to their successful, competent, and healthy development. There is no evidence that hitting children is even remotely part of that philosophy, and yet somehow, some have advanced (and accepted) the myth that hitting children is a part of African American culture.

Conclusion

Clearly, the systemic family dysfunction facing the Black community is serious, long-standing, and pervasive. Thus, it is unlikely that specific, limited, brief, short-term interventions will be of much practical utility. Rather, a comprehensive, long-term commitment is required to reverse the single-parent, female-headed Black family trend imposed during slavery and ignored during Reconstruction and much of the 20th century. As Cunningham (2006) writes, "The situation cannot be addressed with quick fixes and no single initiative will do the job" and "without a critical mass of successful young men to serve as mentors and role models, the prospects for many young African American men will remain dismal. One goal of future efforts should be to create such a critical mass." (p. 230).

The Manhood Training program represents an effort to develop a future critical mass of trained, focused, and dedicated Black adults who can effect change in their environments. By providing comprehensive services to young, Black males over an extended period of time, it is hoped a cadre of young males will become the critical mass of successful men and fathers providing a transformational force in their community. It represents a structured program that will require focus and commitment from the Black community. A significant financial commitment will be required in this plan to train successive waves of participants. This sustained commitment would allow participants to help themselves while contributing to the improvement of their communities over time.

However, it remains to be seen whether or not the wider society is ready and willing to embrace and support such comprehensive programs, which are so sorely needed in the African descended community. Without long-term commitment, it is difficult to be optimistic about success. Certainly, some program participants will adapt to the current standards and "make it"—but too many will continue to be marginalized, minimized, or eliminated. The massive amounts of money used to incarcerate Black men and fathers suggests a societal predisposition to warehouse Black men. The question is *will society be willing to expend that same money to help them be productive, responsible citizens*? The good news is that this community can move ahead with this and other innovative approaches to solving the challenges it faces, with or without outside support, as long as it can find the will to do so.

Reference

Cunningham, G. (2006). A visible future: The African American Men Project and the restoration of community. In Connor, M. E., & White, J. (Eds.), *Black fathers: An invisible Presence in America* (pp. 221–242). Mahwah, NJ: Erlbaum.

Author Index

Subject Index